It's All
Thought!

The Science, Psychology, and Spirituality of Happiness

*Discovering, Enjoying, and Sharing
Life's Ultimate Expression*

TERRY L NEAL

Dedication

This work is dedicated to Cheri Anne McMahan, my wife and partner, and the pivotal person who served as catalyst for this text. It is uniquely to Cheri Anne that I owe the most heartfelt debt of gratitude. Her unwavering support has been beyond remarkable. Her resolute devotion to personal growth and development is a marvel. I stand in awe.

This book is dedicated to our mutual ascension on the scale of emotional maturity to that place we call happiness. Devotion to a state of happiness is our highest spiritual path.

Charitable Notice

---The proceeds from this publication are earmarked for direct contribution to a charitable organization designed to provide text and teaching materials covering similar information to inmates in prisons throughout the United States---.

Acknowledgments

A special thanks to the inmates and staff of the Sheridan Prison Camp for their constant validation while I served in the Education department, and for the profound support given as I developed the curriculum from which the enclosed materials evolved.

To my sister, Dr. Sherry L Meinberg, an author of several books herself, who was an incredible support throughout the prison experience. In three years she sent me 106 new books and wrote me exactly 1,000 letters! All of her letters were numbered, dated, and placed in envelopes that were also numbered and dated, so that when mail arrived out of order I would understand the sequence in which they were written. The essays that form the core of the chapters enclosed were originally written out in long hand and mailed to Sherry who keyed them.

To Cheri Anne McMahan-Neal who was always there, through thick and thin, the ups and downs, and who never backed away, or claimed the effort was too hard. Like my sister Sherry, Cheri Anne provided me with a constant flow of scientific publications and dozens of books. Her thoughts and ideas have been invaluable.

To Elizabeth Verburg, daughter, and another writer in a family of writers, I extend my thanks. Your stepping in to edit this copy was a special treat for me. Discussing the meaning and potential impact of the enclosed concepts was particularly valuable. What an immensely gratifying process.

As to the basic ideas for the book, they have come from personal reflection and daily meditation on the composite of hundreds of books and articles, coupled with hundreds of interviews and in depth discussions, which together centered specifically on the subjects raised herein. Notwithstanding, I think Dale Carnegie said it best:

> "The ideas I stand for are not mine. I borrowed them from Socrates. I swiped them from Chesterfield. I stole them from Jesus. And I put them in a book."

Introduction

This book is the direct result of a course of study I developed and taught while in federal custody at Sheridan Prison Camp. For ten quarters this class was over-subscribed, demonstrating something entirely unexpected to prison staff; given the opportunity, even inmates want to improve the quality of their lives. Originally the course of study on which this book is based, was entitled *Introduction to Deep Thinking and the Philosophy of Self Improvement.*

The period immediately leading up to my prison experience and the three years spent in the monastic setting of the prison camp, provided much time for study, introspection, and reflection. For the entire three years in prison I worked for the education department. By day I taught traditional high school course material. In the evenings I presented my own optional curriculum on *Astronomy, Ancient History & Archeology, Western Civilization, The World of the Patriarchs,* and my most popular course of study, the one you are about to embark upon.

Every quarter, inmates lined up in larger numbers to subscribe for this program. As each class began to unfold I was privileged to witness a dramatic and wonderful shift of consciousness in the lives of the men attending. Hardly anything could be more personally satisfying. The remarkable results experienced in the prison setting convinced me to make this work the focus and hallmark of the rest of my life.

There is much good news within the pages that follow, pointing to fascinating possibilities for the reader. Ideas will present themselves as we explore the history, science, psychology, philosophy, and the spiritual insights gathered herein to expand our understanding.

Chapters are presented in three distinct sections. The first section is entitled "Introduction to Deep Thinking." It is organized to set the stage for what follows. This segment contains preliminary discussions on astronomy, physics, biology, the brain, mind, and free will. It is designed to introduce thought-provoking samplings of leading-edge scientific discoveries as segues to the lessons that follow. Much of the information within is designed to challenge locked-in thinking patterns. As Arthur C. Clark once said,

"It is vital to remember that information - in the sense of raw data - is not knowledge; that knowledge is not wisdom, and that wisdom is not foresight. But information is the first essential step to all of these."

We begin our quest for happiness by reviewing information that can dramatically impact our understanding of the universe and our place in it. Some of this will be familiar; much of it may be new to the reader. Undoubtedly some portion of what follows will seem strange and wonderful. That is good. We need to open our minds and recognize how incredible the world truly is, and thence to consider just how remarkable we really are.

A word of caution: Chapter 2 is a brief primer on astronomy and quantum theory. If you are not a fan of science this may put you off a bit. Nevertheless, I encourage you to push on through, and glean what you can before moving into Chapter 3, which includes more science, but the kind that is bound to seriously **WOW** you, if you'll stick with it.

The second section is entitled "Expanding Understanding," and in many ways it is the core of this study. As this material is internalized it has the capacity to powerfully affect positive change in your life. However, in my experience its value is not appreciated unless one has dared to consider the science, thoughts, and conclusions provided in Section I.

Section III is entitled "Charting a New Course." In some ways it might be easier to simply ignore issues related to our purpose, religion, spirituality, or discussing aspects of the meaning of life, and who we might be. These are the areas wherein our most cherished concepts reside, and they can be literal minefields of discrimination. Frankly, I'd prefer not to step on the reader's triggers. However, to not at least review a few pertinent ideas regarding these sometimes touchy subjects would be tantamount to dishonesty. To a great degree, these elements of our thinking-ness are the foundation upon which our happiness is grounded. Nevertheless, to be very clear, I am not endorsing any particular spiritual path or religious affiliation.

Outside the prison setting, hundreds of thousands, perhaps multiple millions of men and women live lives of quiet desperation. These are those imprisoned in their minds. These are those who crave peace, harmony, and love. These are those who desire increased financial prosperity, improved relationships, and greater physical well being. These are those who seek lives of meaning and purpose, and those who simply "want to be happy." The primer that follows is designed to address all of these objectives, ranking happiness as the pinnacle of importance.

This book is meant to be both a teaching tool and a road map. It is designed to wake you up; to lead you out of the darkness of regret and into the marvelous light of a new day. Everyone has the right to a joyful life. Most simply do not know how to get there. If you read the enclosed and seriously apply its precepts, your life will improve. If you expand your study and underline or highlight things of particular meaning to you, and then incorporate these concepts and practices into your life, happiness, and greater enlightenment, will flow to you as surely as day follows night.

May Your Blessings Abound.....Terry Neal

It's All *Thought!*

Prologue

As my lifetime companion Maureen lay dying in my arms, I promised her two things. My first commitment was that when it was my turn to pass through the veil I would greet her as a better man than she left. My second promise was that I would make "service to others" the hallmark of the rest of my life.

Maureen and I were married 42 years. We were blessed with eight children, and before she passed, 24 grandchildren; the number now stands at 27. We were married as teenagers. Attraction and lust had long before matured into trust and a deep and powerful love. Due principally to my wife's tireless efforts we enjoyed a close and loving family. There is hardly a day in the lives of our children that they are not somehow involved with their siblings and their families.

Before Maureen left this mortal life she told the family that it was her wish that I be remarried within twelve months of the time she was gone. These words were hard to process, both for me and the rest of the family. Nevertheless, Maureen was insistent that I "not curl up in a corner, and suck my thumb, just because we were going to be separated." Dating and remarriage were the furthest things from my mind. And besides, I would be self-surrendering to federal prison soon, a result of the IRS decision to criminally prosecute me.

In several prior books, newsletters, and talk shows, I had accused the IRS and other federal agencies, namely the Department of Justice, and the Securities and Exchange Commission, of extensive abuse of power. The federal government's response to my allegations was to investigate me (read: unimaginable harassment). It continued for more than five years. Agencies of the government seized my bank and stock accounts, and virtually all of my material assets. Eventually I was arrested at gun point in our Oregon home, and held in jail awaiting indictment.

While I was being held in a county jail in Oregon, the IRS filed a civil penalty assessment against me for tens of millions of dollars, and purposely mailed it to our winter home in the Caribbean. When I did not receive it (because I was being held in Oregon), the prescribed timeline for response passed, and the penalty assessment became valid.

After an IRS special agent was caught lying on the witness stand during an appeals hearing to secure my release from jail prior to trial, I was permitted to return home. Here I was forced to stay the majority of the time for the next 3 ½ years. My focus on government's nefarious conduct had cost me dearly. I would lose my wife, my wealth, and my freedom. It also hurt my family and many of my friends, in more ways than one dare list. Towards the end of my pre-trial home confinement, eight months before I would report to prison, my wife Maureen succumbed to esophageal cancer. She passed in my arms.

In effect, I went to prison for my beliefs. Admittedly some of those beliefs were wrong. Over the period of my investigation, and throughout the 3 ½ years of pre-trial, federal agents terrified my family, friends, and business associates. Government personnel, intended to protect and serve, turned out to be highly skilled experts at twisting information and presenting outright lies as if it were truth. Eventually I would learn that some federal agencies even retain outside internet media hacks to distribute negative publicity on those they are attempting to discredit. Things within the federal hierarchy are frequently not as they seem. I was convinced that there was a deeply sinister reason that America has 730 percent more people in prison on a per capita basis, than the average of all the industrial nations. And, I had been bold in saying so.

Yes that's right, America has more than seven people in prison for each one in all of Europe, Canada, Australia, New Zealand,

Korea, Japan, and Taiwan, on a per capita basis. We have more people in prison than Russia, China, or just about anywhere else you can think of. These are not happy thoughts, but apparently they are true. So, how does one go from having information that is deeply unsettling to a place of health, happiness and freedom? That's what this book is about.

I now understand that my former obsession, with what appeared to be a profound lack of integrity in certain federal agencies, literally called into manifestation the very destruction I was warning others about. On over a hundred radio talk shows, I vented about specific cases of unchecked government abuse. In the end, I got almost exactly what I had written and thought about with such passionate intensity.

**I got almost exactly what I had
written and thought about
with such passionate intensity.**

This was a huge wake-up call. Somehow I had manifested the thing I most feared. I did not get what I believed I wanted; instead I got that about which I had expressed the most emotion. This was a conundrum that required much reflection.

One might legitimately ask how anyone living under the circumstances I've just outlined, could dare say they were happy. Yet, here I am saying exactly that! Life's stressors either encourage us to deeper inquiry or magnify our pain. One of the more fascinating aspects of human life is that we seem to be able to learn with greater efficacy when confronted with great trials. The choice to learn and grow, or succumb to self-pity and become a victim, is a critical one. The choice however, is uniquely ours.

In the end, we alone decide how everything will affect us. The real dilemma is that very few people understand the reality of this truth. The vast majority of us are instead struggling with the impact of our external world. In other words, we simply do not know a better way and therefore we find ourselves tossed about by the thousands of external circumstances to which we are exposed.

On a further personal note, a month before I reported to federal prison, I was to meet an amazing woman. Needing new glasses, I walked into her optical store in our rural town at the base of Mt. Hood in Oregon. It was an unusually quiet afternoon. I ordered the dreaded bifocals, and visited with the women working there. They seemed to be aware of my loss and showed sensitivity and compassion.

It became obvious quickly that Cheri Anne - the store's owner - shared my lifelong interest in ancient history, archeology, and world religions. And, to our mutual surprise, we were both aficionados of philosophy, astronomy, and quantum physics. This is a rare collection of studies for one person; for two it is downright strange. We agreed to exchange books. A couple of weeks later I lost my glasses. I returned to her store. Our friendship progressed.

Two years after the death of Maureen, Cheri and I were married in the visitor's center at the prison camp where I was interned. Although we had lunch together once before I reported to prison, we had not even enjoyed so much as a dinner out. For more than 30 months, Cheri would visit me at the prison camp each Saturday, Sunday, and holiday. We were privileged to sit together for 6 ½ hours at least twice weekly. These extensive visits provided us more time for uninterrupted in-depth discussions than the average married couple might have in a lifetime.

Cheri spent well over a thousand hours just driving to visit me. Our entire relationship evolved as a consequence of our internal synchronicity. No physicality was permitted. Layer by layer, the onion of our souls was explored. Layer by layer we became known to one another. As I was to learn, Cheri is an unusual woman. Introduced to the martial arts more than thirty years ago, she resonated strongly with the need for self inquiry. Cheri is devoted to her own spiritual quest. An extensive meditation practice is the hallmark of her spiritual endeavor, although she regularly attends a traditional Christian church. Cheri is unusually quiet about her spirituality, and she avoids religious labels because it causes so much confusion in people's understanding. But, I think it not unfair to describe her as a Christian-Buddhist-Hindu-Shamanist. She is also a Reiki Master. How curious is that?

Terry Neal

Author's Note

The reader is about to embark upon an exploration of self. It is likely therefore that you will encounter materials that challenge pre-conceived ideas and strongly held, emotionally-charged, points of view. Exposition related to subjects like, "Is There Meaning to Life?", and other topics of a similar nature, may encroach upon one's most cherished beliefs. These types of belief patterns are rife with subconscious judgment and as a consequence they can be literal minefields of predisposition. My intent is not to offend; nevertheless, I shall offer my thoughts and conclusions as I believe it adds value to the text. As a result, the reader's subliminal belief system may occasionally kick-in, causing an emotional response anywhere from a vague sense of unease, to skepticism, or perhaps even on to stronger reactions.

It will help if the reader will remain alert, practicing self-observation, and recognizing when one's buttons are being pushed. When that happens, and it will be clear by the way you feel about what you're reading, I recommend you consciously tell yourself to suspend judgment, so you may gain any further insight available to you by learning without prejudice. If you will simply ask yourself, out-loud if possible, how you feel about exploring certain subjects, you'll find yourself stepping up to a more understanding space. It's a healthier, happier place, as you recognize within yourself that you are rising above the embattled arenas of emotionally-charged opinions, and learning to listen, reflect, and observe, without succumbing to conflict.

A further caveat, the writing of this material has come in the form of "stream of consciousness," so the information is always related, but may not flow like something written in concert with a story-board outline, such as are textbooks. However, the presentation of the enclosed had a huge impact on numbers of those attending the course of study from whence this manuscript is derived, so it is presented in the same sequence.

The end results of every class where the enclosed materials were essentially the course outline; were dramatically positive. This remained so, even in those classes that included loudly outspoken inmates who felt compelled to rant on their points of view. I share this as preface to saying that were I to defer providing the reader with some of my own personal conclusions because they might not be "politically correct," or because I am overly concerned about giving offense to another's belief system, then I fall prey to the same basic problem one experiences by only giving credence to information currently deemed mainstream or socially-acceptable.

A large part of the personal growth each of us must make in order to gain a happier state is in learning to suspend judgment, and allowing ourselves the freedom to investigate life with an open-mind. How else can we learn things outside the box of our existing reality? How can we access new and better ideas to improve our lives if we pre-judge things on the outside of our current grasp of knowledge as unworthy, unacceptable, or worse? The walls of our prejudice are real. It is not easy to see the boundaries we've imposed upon ourselves, but they absolutely exist. And that's true for all of us.

The more evolved we become, the less frequently we will be offended by different points of view. It is only our ego that takes exception, gets insulted, or is irritated by conceptual positions that seem to be in conflict with our own. It is fine to have opinions, although if we suspended most of them we'd probably be better off. However, when we hold opinions, we should not allow them to be so etched in stone that we cannot neutrally reflect on other perspectives. This is especially important where contrary points of view are sincerely made and based on thoughtful consideration.

The material presented in this work is designed to provide fresh ideas on old paradigms. Some of this insight was gained by meditative states, what some may consider unorthodox methods. If some think I'm a quack because I've gained inspiration while engaged in a meditative trance, so be it. But, recognize that this very position is an obvious judgment based on pre-existing beliefs, not on thoughtful consideration of the quality of the insight.

No one needs to believe the way I do, that would probably be impossible anyway, because my beliefs are reasoned, but relatively fluid. Were this not so, I would likely be blocking out the continuing insights I hope to enjoy. Things do refine themselves as we look deeply within ourselves and mature in our own understanding, but, if we are too rigid about what we say we believe we become constrained. Yes, we may open our minds for new insight for awhile, but when we say to ourselves, in effect, "wow I'm glad I got that figured out" we have already begun to close down new sources of insight.

I am socially responsible, but my grasp of things does not necessarily fit within the norms of socially acceptable or politically correct conclusions. That, after all, is probably the most important point. We cannot truly evolve, we cannot get where we really need to be, by using the roadmap society unwittingly provides. If our cultural paradigms were really that effective almost everyone would already be happy. We must break out of our current models of thought and find a better way.

Terry Neal

It's All *Thought!*

The Science, Psychology, and Spirituality of Happiness

Table of Contents

It's All *Thought!*

"As a being of power, intelligence, and love, and the lord of your own thoughts, you hold the key to every situation, and contain within yourself that transforming and regenerative agency by which you may make yourself what you will."

James Allen

Chapter 1

THE PARADOX

"Happiness is the aim, the goal, and
the purpose of life."

Alexander Stoddard

The Desire for Happiness

For thousands of years, philosophers have reasoned that the pursuit of happiness, along with service to others, was the ultimate purpose in life. Many of the Greek schools of thought concluded that to achieve happiness was man's preeminent responsibility. In the middle 1600's, Blaise Pascal, a French philosopher and mathematician wrote:

"All men seek happiness. This
is without exception. Whatever
different means they employ, they
all tend to this end... The will
never takes the least step but to
this object. This is the motive
of every action of every man."

All of us, at our most fundamental level, are motivated to pursue happiness. And yet, there are numerous professional studies that tell us that our internal happiness index is registering a downward spiral. The situation is really quite serious. Here we are at the very apex of financial prosperity for all times (notwithstanding current aberrations), coupled with superb advances in health, medicine, technology and science. We collectively enjoy an expanding opportunity for leisure, and yet many people will own up to the fact they are deeply unsettled. They sense some kind of underlying unhappiness even in the best of circumstances.

Happiness Verses Depression

Harvard psychologist, Dr. Tal Ben Shahar reports that,

> "In the United States, rates of depression are ten times higher today than they were in the 1960's, and the average age for the onset of depression is fourteen and a half, compared to twenty-nine and a half in 1960. A study conducted in American colleges tells us that nearly 45 percent of students were so depressed that they had difficulty functioning."

Pretty scary stuff. On the other hand, you've likely heard of these kinds of studies before, and somehow, you suspect they really don't apply to you personally. Or maybe I'm wrong, and somewhere deep down you fear that the guys and gals in the white lab coats have it right, so you're flailing about unfulfilled and uneasy, trying to figure out how to cope with your anxiety-ridden, high stress world.

Are they right, all those philosophers and Pascal and Stoddard when they claim that everyone, everywhere, in every generation, seeks happiness? And, if so, what does that mean to you? Do you need convincing, that prophets and kings, philosophers and wise men, psychologists and all the Toms, Dicks, and Harrys, throughout time also observed essentially what Pascal so elegantly summarized? Can we agree to agree that we really can see that the motivation underlying our most basic actions is somehow connected with our search for happiness?

It's pretty clear that people want to be happy, or at least that's what most of us say. All the other things we seem to want are means to that end. If we're serious materialists, then the bangles and beads, the sport cars and trucks, the houses, yachts and airplanes, are all acquisitions we sincerely believe will advance us towards that hard-to-define feeling we call happiness.

The deeply intelligent, yet oddly disturbed Sigmund Freud cofounded the modern intellectual, pseudoscientific religion known as psychoanalysis. Of course, Freud never considered his form of psychology a religion, but the enthusiasm of its converts bore many of the same characteristics. Scores there have been who worshipped at the altar of psychoanalysis. Strange as it may seem, Freud and those that followed in lockstep after him, seemed more than a little suspicious that there was any such thing as happiness.

An exuberant sense of happiness was often considered by many psychiatrists and psychologists, as a form of over compensation for an 'as yet' unidentified emotional problem. These "experts" tended to be suspicious of anyone who believed in true joy, unfettered good humor, and pure objectives. From the outset, Psychology's mission was focused almost entirely on pathology; what was wrong, identifying the various emotional maladies, naming them, defining them, and endeavoring to understand them.

Positive Psychology

Things are changing in the intellectual world. It's now okay to revel in positive experiences, allow enthusiasm to expand, laugh for the pure fun of it, experience joy and deep affection. In fact, a whole new psychological discipline has recently evolved known as "positive psychology."

This new field of psychology is based on large cross-cultural surveys of groups of peoples. The results of these surveys and the analyses provided is delivering powerful insight regarding the effects of mindset on such things as physical fitness, life expectancy, and the quality of life. For example, Science Daily, August 2008, concluded from a group of 30 studies that a sense of happiness extends life by a significant amount.

A study by Yale University determined that being optimistic in middle age "increases life span by at least 7.5 years - even after accounting for age, gender, socioeconomic status, and physical health." The Yale report went on to say that "...having good long-term relationships provides as many physical benefits as being active or a nonsmoker." Did you catch that? A sense of personal self-worth, which flows from good long term relationships and feelings of happiness, is more important to your physical health than whether you smoke or not, or even exercise!

Numerous university studies conclude that when you become happier, your physical health improves. In fact, improving the level of happiness in your life appears to be the single most important thing you can do to improve your overall well-being; both physically and psychologically. This is impressive insight.

A recent twenty year study by Nicholas Christakis, M.D., Ph.D., Harvard University, and James Fowler, Associate Professor, CSU San Diego, published in the British Medical Journal, demonstrates that happiness is remarkably contagious. Say what? We didn't already know that? Perhaps we all realize this to some degree, but now we have a scientific study to confirm what many of us would naturally intuit.

In a Mayo Clinic study that spanned forty years, we learn that happy optimistic patients live 19 percent longer than their expected life span. This is after factoring in relative medical and environmental data. Wow! That's a really significant number.

Recent studies have also driven home the point that, notwithstanding everything we've been led to believe about our impressionable childhood struggles, they *do not* contribute significantly, one way or another, to our overall happiness as an adult. In the words of Dr. Martin Seligman, president of the American Psychological Association in 1998:

> "The major traumas of childhood
> may have some influence on
> adult personality, but only a
> barely detectable one. Bad
> childhood events, in short, do
> not mandate adult troubles."

He went on to say:

> "This means that the promissory
> note Freud and his followers wrote
> about childhood events determining
> the course of adult lives, is
> _worthless_." (Author emphasis)

So, did you get that? Childhood events determining the course of adult lives is _worthless_? How many of us are blaming childhood stressors for our current struggles in life? When we claim that the problems in our present are due to the seeming disasters from our past, it is only so because we believe it is so. It seems that if you tell a more supportive story about your past, things will actually begin to improve. Does that raise a question in your mind about honesty? We'll address this issue along with other vital elements for achieving greater happiness. Dr. Seligman sums up his reflections with a compelling comment:

> "Merely to know the surprising
> facts here - that early past events,
> in fact, exert little or no influence
> on adult lives - is liberating."

The up thrust of dozens of recent studies tell us that it really doesn't matter much who you are, where you come from, or who your parents are. It doesn't matter a great deal how your parents raised you, or whether they raised you at all. It doesn't matter how rich you are (or are not), nor ought you to be concerned with your birth order, or social status. The truth is (even if it feels funny and you want it to be some really cool altruistic thing), that you genuinely want to be a happy camper. This is true, even if you don't realize it, just yet. Perhaps the most important thing to recognize right up front about happiness is that unless you are happy with yourself you cannot be happy with: Where you are; Who you are; What you have, or Who you are with.

Unless you are happy with yourself you cannot be happy with:

> **Where you are;**
> **Who you are;**
> **What you have, or**
> **Who you are with.**

Pretty much sums things up, doesn't it? Everything we do, we do because it serves us in some way. This is as true of the late Mother Teresa as it is for a spoiled heiress seeking media attention. True enough, their conduct will surely be different, and the results of their activities will produce widely dissimilar payoffs, but the underlying motivation is to act in a way that they believe best serves them. Yes, Mother Teresa's life was all about helping others. She served the needs of thousands; and that served her.

Happy Camper

Perhaps a slight digression ought to be inserted here. The Freudian slip above, about being a Happy Camper, brings to mind an important little tidbit I should share with you as we embark upon our time together. When I wrote the essays that are the basis of this book, I was in a Camp. Not the sort of camp where you sing Kumbaya, roast marshmallows, and eat smores. I was in a federal prison camp. ...Pregnant pause...Yes, that's right, you're reading a book about happiness written by a guy who was in federal prison. Now, that may seem a little nuts, so I suppose you should know something more about the author. If you read the Prologue you will have picked up on some of the motivation for this book. What follows will aid in putting some of my background into perspective.

Lucky guy that I am, I decided to retire to the Caribbean in the early 1990's, and do some business and financial consulting. (Read: workaholic who just had to keep busy even though he was technically retired, and didn't have to work.) Previous to this time, I had been a corporate CEO, and founder of an international business. The company had grown to about 250 offices around the world, and I was feeling fairly worn out.

The Caribbean seemed like a nice place to go, at least for the colder half of each year, so my wife, Maureen, purchased a home right on the beach of one of those idyllic islands we frequently refer to as a tropical paradise. And amazingly, it was just that. Ah yes, the final goal of a lifetime of goal-setting and accomplishment. Hmmm. Actually, there were a couple of other life goals hanging out there, and one was to write a book.

Over the next few years, four of my books were published, and I recorded a fourteen hour lecture series, which was distributed along with a fifth manuscript. Together these eventually got me into deep yogurt with three agencies of the federal government. They did not like what I wrote. They did not like my talk show interviews. And, they did not like my latest business venture…working in the offshore financial services arena in conjunction with a couple hundred legal and accounting firms. The fact that I had secured 23 written legal opinions from various U.S. law firms for all aspects of this particular business project did not deter the government in the slightest. They simply ignored all legal and accounting counsel that conflicted with the position they had decided to take.

I admit that I threw the proverbial first stone, and clearly made significant errors in judgment. Ah well, so there you have it. From my perspective I felt like federal appointees were supposed to be reprimanded, and their nefarious deeds made public. Alas, that's not the way they saw it. Yep, I did the Don Quixote thing, jousting with windmills. My motivation was inspired by an oft-quoted phrase (at least I quoted it a lot), by Lord Actun:

> "Power corrupts and absolute
> power corrupts absolutely."

It wasn't just the books and my latest business venture that had made some ranking politicos angry. I fancied myself something of an outside whistle-blower, and so began to publish a newsletter directed to members of Congress and other influential people around the world. The newsletter was focused on federal abuse of power. By the time 9-11 hit, I was in full swing, telling anyone who would listen about the depth of deceit in Washington. The government went blitzkrieg on me, and oddly enough, the same three agencies I had been taking pot shots at for years, in my books, radio shows, and newsletters, slammed me, BIG TIME.

Now I probably need to stop the story for a moment, and tell you that I was a happily married man, and had been for many years. My lovely wife and I were blessed with eight children, and by this time they were grown and had made us grandparents more than twenty times over. To keep the story short, I'll simply say that agents of the federal government crushed me, and terrorized my entire family. While awaiting trial my wife's health failed. Maureen passed away in my arms eight months before I reported to prison. She died of esophageal cancer. We had been married 42 years. For the most part, we had had a magical life together.

To add insult to considerable injury, the IRS subsequently generated several special fines against me for what they referred to as "conspiracy to defraud the government," the same charge for which I was to be imprisoned. While the fines ran into the tens of millions, no detail was provided either to me or my legal counsel for a number of years. Meanwhile, I was stripped of all my material assets, including over $20 million in cash, plus property, securities, et cetera.

Lessons Learned

One might legitimately ask, "How can someone who has theoretically lost everything, including his lifetime companion and then his freedom, dare to write a book on discovering true happiness?" Well, I suggest that this little short story demonstrates my credentials for understanding some of the OBSTACLES to happiness. "What?" you might counter. But you had lost your wife! How could you possibly consider yourself happy, having her die in your arms? Admittedly, I was sad. Very sad. Even so, I realized that I was not unhappy, and there is an important distinction between the two.

I learned a great deal about love, honor, and service, during the nine months I administered Maureen's hospice care. I was ever so fortunate to provide this heartfelt, hour-by-hour, attention. She was sick, and frequently in pain, but always more concerned about others than her own difficult circumstances. What a wonderful lesson in love. I am happy to have learned this in such a poignant way.

I was relieved when Maureen was no longer in pain. Throughout those final months, we enjoyed particularly meaningful connections and deeply spiritual experiences. At the moment of her death I received a beautiful witness of the continuation of life beyond the grave. The potent insight gained as a consequence of the experiences leading up to, during, and after, the death of my lifetime companion have powerfully enriched my life. These were not unhappy events. They were sometimes incredibly sad and melancholy, but not wretched or miserable.

In the end, I learned with renewed significance, how important it is to be in touch with my own feelings. I began to gain in understanding and eventually in grasping the importance of sincere self-acceptance. I allowed myself to grieve and feel sad. I am human. These powerful emotions are a part of humanity. There is an uplifting richness of spirit as we permit ourselves to be what we are, rather than bottling up our emotions and presenting a tough exterior.

While confined at the Sheridan Prison Camp, which I am fond of calling the "Monastery in Sheridise," I was able to look deep within myself. And, before long I began to employ some incredibly powerful techniques that allowed me to release negative energy patterns buried deep within. The process of releasing and forgiving, coupled with an expanded mental paradigm driven by amazing new scientific and spiritual insights, made all the difference. A huge shift took place within me. Life took on new levels of meaning. Gratitude, love, and self-acceptance became my companion.

Over many years I've been a counselor to hundreds of the extremely wealthy on some of their most intimate matters, and I've seen people miserable at the top of their game. In thinking that through, I began to recognize that a happy person is not a person in a certain set of circumstances, but rather a person with a certain set of attitudes.

A happy person is not a person in a certain set of circumstances, but rather a person with a certain set of attitudes.

In the words of William James, philosopher and psychologist, and the man frequently referred to as one of the founding fathers of modern psychology:

"The greatest discovery of my generation is that a human being can alter his life by altering his attitude."

It is my sincere belief that what you will discover within this book has the power to dramatically change your life for the better! This is a bold statement. It is based upon the remarkable results I have personally witnessed after sharing the thinking, concepts, and techniques, presented in the following pages with men and women from all walks of life, as well as hundreds of men in county jails and federal prisons. It is with these last, the largely forgotten people where the misery index can be so very high, that the impact has been so powerfully beneficial.

As you might suspect, most prisoners are swamped with feelings of helplessness. They do not believe they can make major changes in their lives. They see themselves as victims of an unfeeling and unjust system, and to some extent they are right. That's not to say that there is not valid reason for most prisoners' incarceration. The point is that among these men, where happiness is only a fantastical theory and rarely a believable reality, incredible results have occurred.

Circumstances and situations do color life, but it is we, and we alone, who choose the hue, tint, and tone. And if we are lucky, ultimately we will come to realize that nothing real actually stands between us and happiness, only illusion and our own confusion.

Nothing real stands between us and happiness, only illusion and our own confusion.

Allow me another brief bit of background on how my obsession with happiness evolved. For the several months prior to my self-surrender to federal prison, (that's the legal term for turning yourself in), and just after Maureen had passed, I was deeply concerned for my family's well-being. Eight children - seven of them with children of their own - were suffering the loss of their mother. Maureen had been especially active with our household, and cared deeply about others. Family and close friends were in shock at Maureen's passing. Our matriarch was gone. At times, she had suffered miserably with esophageal cancer. I had somehow provided virtually all of her home care while dealing with aggressive federal agencies, facing criminal prosecution at the behest of the IRS, and undergoing two spinal surgeries. Now, only months after her passing, my family was to lose their patriarch, as I was trundled off to prison.

The circumstances of my life had all the ingredients of a sorrowful melodrama, which I suppose in many ways it was. For the eight months after Maureen's death, while I waited to report to prison, I set about determining how to best ease my family's loss. Many nights I lay awake, seeking support from a higher power. One memorable night, Maureen spoke to me in a dream. In her wisdom she told me that all the help I needed was right before me. I had but to refocus on the things I already knew were true, and be grateful for things as they were right now in the very present, and not only would our children's lives be improved, but so would mine and many others. I came straight up from my bed, a single snapshot of the future blazoned into my brain. In many ways this dream seemed much more real than the day-to-day activities of my waking life. The experience was so vivid, so powerful, and so incredibly intense, that it continues to shape my thoughts and choices to the present. That very night, just two months before going to prison, I got up and wrote a one-page paper to myself, endeavoring to sort out what I was thinking. I titled it, *My Reality*, and although I would write it somewhat differently today, it's included exactly as it was originally written to provide a frame of reference.

My Reality

I believe that each of us is capable of molding our realities to the degree permitted by the bounds of our creation. What those bounds are I am not entirely sure, but I suspect we are permitted much more maneuverability than we allow ourselves to believe. Life surely teaches us that form follows thought, i.e.: "What a man thinketh in his heart so is he." This philosophical model suggests that each of us are largely in charge of our affairs, or at least more so than most would concede. Believing this, I conclude that it is basically up to me to "conceive and believe" myself out of the box I currently view myself within. In other words, I accept that I am responsible for my series of tests in this world, regardless of whether or not I suppose that someone, or some institution, is being unfair in its dealings with me. If I am a victim, it is only because at some mysterious level, I allow, or perhaps even encourage, it to happen.

To escape my current reality, I must step up and see in my mind's eye, another improved reality. When I am able to vividly imagine a new reality, and believe fervently in its possibility, things will likely change for the better. This process is the essence of conceiving and believing.

Whereas "faith precedes the miracle," thought, conception, and a passionate desire for a new outcome must first pave the way, or belief will be unable to mature into faith, and generate sufficient power to advance a new reality.

Just the act of taking responsibility for my own reality helps improve things. I am not a cork bobbing on the waters of life. I can exert influence and call down power to steer a better course. Although I do not understand the *why* of everything that we may encounter in this life, I believe that in the end, everything will synthesize for our best interests. And, notwithstanding current circumstances, I feel better than one might expect. And I sincerely believe that things will work out in some marvelous way.

End

The mental and emotional act of taking full responsibility for my circumstances made a pivotal difference in my attitude. I was no longer a victim. It was not long thereafter that I came to realize that nothing is ever enough if we judge that we are not enough. It turns out that joy is centered in self acceptance; it is freedom from self-judgment.

> **Nothing is ever enough if we judge that we are not enough. Joy is self-acceptance; it is freedom from self-judgment.**

Working with this improved foundation, I set about changing the only person I could: me. I had two months to build a better me before reporting to prison. A powerful desire to transcend my current level of consciousness fueled much of my thoughts and actions thereafter. I wasn't sure how to best go about it, but I was certain that this was what I should be about.

Prison

Upon reporting to the Federal Detention Center at Sheridan, Oregon, the monstrously depressive environment struck me immediately. The Detention Center is one of three prisons at Sheridan. It serves as a holding facility for those awaiting trial in federal court (a process that can sometimes take years). It is also a transfer station for inmates of all security levels, waiting to be moved on to other locations. In my case, I was scheduled to be immediately shifted to the Sheridan Prison Camp, a minimum security facility just a quarter mile away. (Think of it as the male equivalent to Martha Stewart's "Camp Cupcake.")

At the detention center we were packed three men to a tiny two-man cell, and kept locked down 21 to 23 hours a day. On two occasions we were locked down all 24 hours. The first night I was fortunate to begin a close friendship with two young men in their mid - to late - twenties. One was "Jason," a hip black urbanite, suffering from extreme claustrophobia. The other was "Sean," an angry white tough guy, who had temporarily lost his faith in human kind. Both had already spent several years in prison, and other than prior drug use, this may have been the only thing they had in common.

Although I was supposed to be held in the detention center for one night only, before being transferred to the much more flexible camp, circumstances so combined as to keep the three of us locked together in the miniscule two-man cell for the next seven weeks. We endeavored to make the best of a bad situation.

On day two of lockdown, I suggested we somehow determine to make our small cell the happiest in the cellblock. Inasmuch as depression is the norm, and pervasive throughout jails and prisons generally, they agreed, probably out of simple respect for a guy more than twice their age. So, with that, we began to orally "write" prison comedy skits about the very things that were literally destroying others, due to unaddressed anger and hyper-anxiety. We learned to laugh at ourselves.

The initial jail-holding experience was indescribably difficult in many ways, but our practiced effort to find something humorous about even the most unsettling encounters set the stage for all that followed. Concrete and steel is the stuff of prisons and cellblocks, and it makes for amazing echo chambers. The noise is constant and the guards do little to help anyone sleep, and in fact, they often do quite the contrary. Nevertheless, we began to laugh so frequently and so hard that, during meals and our short releases to walk about the cellblock, a cluster of other inmates would approach us to find out what on earth could be happening in our "house."

Over time, all the inmates in cellblock J-1 at Sheridan Detention Center learned of our plan to be the happiest cell in the cellblock. Inmates that had been shuttled through a dozen or more prisons began calling us the "happiest cell in the entire prison system." We were able to laugh and inspire others, in spite of the gross ugliness of the prison environment.

By the third week, the whole cellblock had lightened up, and occasionally some of the guards were daring to be nice. In spite of policy to the contrary, one particular guard unlocked our cell seven Sundays in a row and allowed other inmates to cram in, or sit around the outside of the steel door, in order to take part in a civilized discussion about spirituality and the pursuit of happiness.

The 23 hours a day lockup eased off to 21 hours, and then 20 hours, providing time each day to meet with others at tables in the central eating area. The trustees over food preparation and serving were a dozen members of a notorious Hispanic gang known as the Nortenos. The gang's local lieutenant learned of my passion for Mesoamerican archaeology, and discovered that I had made several dozen trips to Mexico and Central America studying the history of the area. He decided that his contingent of Nortenos should learn about their heritage... from me. So, prior to my cell being unlocked for "walk" each day, there were tables set up for me to address the group. Anywhere else, this might have seemed surreal, but here under these odd circumstances, it was just a natural opportunity unfolding. And life improved.

Finally after seven weeks of maximum security, Sean and I were released to the Camp. The two of us simply walked out the front door of the Sheridan Detention Center. We walked out alone; no guards. It was so unnerving for Sean, who had already been in prison almost five years, he froze and refused to go any further for fear someone would claim we were trying to escape. We turned around and headed back into the maximum-security facility and reconfirmed we were being instructed to walk through an unguarded parking lot and down the road to Camp Cupcake. Now *that* was surreal! We were on the outside...at least for a few minutes. As it turned out, the camp didn't even have a fence around it. The men sent here were neither dangerous nor considered a flight risk.

A week later, Jason was transferred to the camp. He never got out of the orientation meeting. Due to a miscommunication with a prison staffer, an event to which both Sean and I were privy, Jason was set up to be an example to other inmates. In front of several men who had that same day been released from the Detention Center and walked to the camp, Jason was cuffed, chained, and taken to a higher security prison. The message was clear. You are not free. And, you are completely subject to the whims of those who are in charge. Deal with it.

The day I arrived at the camp, I was "hired" to work in the Education Department. This provided me with flexibility and the opportunity to interact with the majority of inmates. In addition to my daytime teaching assignments, I volunteered to provide Adult Continuing Education classes at night. This allowed me to develop my own course material over a whole range of subjects, from Astronomy I and II and Ancient World History, to my most popular courses: Introduction to Deep Thinking, and The Philosophy of Self-Improvement. For ten quarters, every optional nighttime class I taught was over-subscribed, requiring extra desks and chairs to be moved into my classroom. Other potential students were wait-listed for future classes.

Based upon literally hundreds of conversations with inmates, I began to realize that life gives us repeated opportunities to learn. When we don't, we tend to get stuck with a series of similar experiences until we "get" the lesson life is trying to teach us. I also learned that nothing has any real meaning outside of the meaning we alone give it.

Nothing has any meaning outside the meaning we alone give it.

Yes, I realize this may sound rather odd, but hold your judgment for a while. And, while you're at it, begin right now to neutralize all that drama that tends to pop up in your life by learning to laugh at yourself. Who was it that said, "Man is most comical when he takes himself too seriously"?

We tend to believe that so many things are vitally important. Maybe they are, but taking things so seriously that we forget to laugh, love, and be happy, is a serious mistake. In fact, when we find ourselves unhappy and unable to laugh, it's literally a life crisis.

> "When written in Chinese, the word "crisis' is composed of two characters. One represents danger, the other represents opportunity."
>
> John F. Kennedy

It's All *Thought!*

Section I

INTRODUCTION TO DEEP THINKING

Chapter 2

QUANTUM AND THE COSMOS

"The happiest person is the person who thinks the most interesting thoughts."

William Lyon Phelps

Introduction

This chapter is introductory. It provides a brief overview of some basic and not-so basic science. Future chapters will build on this understanding. The reason this material is included in a book about happiness is to encourage one to reconsider who they are in terms of what we have more recently learned. Scientists discover new and astonishing things continuously. Yet, most of us are so conditioned by our current affairs it is hard for us to be WOWED by new insight, ideas, information. Exposing yourself to important knowledge, which may well seem extraneous to your present state of existence, will move you outside the closet of your current reality.

As you consider the material presented within, you may find yourself flirting with questions that are either disquieting or larger than life. When we do this, our blinders tend to fall away as we grapple with larger concepts. It is when we allow ourselves to "think outside the box" of our day-to-day reality that we are able to draw on a more powerful and improved grasp of the majesty of the universe and our place in it. If we dare to step up and explore new ways of thinking we open our belief systems to new ways of understanding. It is only in this place that greater insight is available to us.

In my experience, those who refuse to learn new things and explore fresh ways of thinking are almost incapable of discovering and enjoying real happiness. They are stuck. To get unstuck requires opening one's mind to the wonders about us. In the words of Robert Louis Stevenson,

> "The world is so full of so many
> different things, I'm sure we
> should all be as happy as kings."

There is so much to learn, to enjoy, and to amaze us. But, if we fail to look around, and open our eyes to the many new and wonderful opportunities that truly surround us, we'll miss out on the richness of living. In order for us to move towards a more beautiful and fulfilling life, we must first awaken the explorer within, and shake off the tendency to lethargy. We must allow ourselves to be amazed, and knock ourselves loose from the narrow focus that inevitability foments ingratitude, loss of energy, depression, and general unhappiness. Can you remember back to the child you once were? Think back to that inquisitive, curious, interested, always learning person to whom everything was new and fascinating. Evoke that child, as we embark upon a world of discovery together.

Suspend your preconceived ideas for awhile. Determine to invest some of your time, right now at the outset, to rediscover the incredible wonder of creation. When we close ourselves off from being impressed by the new and the wondrous, we miss accessing the deeper joys of life, and may move right past them without ever knowing they are within our grasp. I encourage you to play around with the stuff that follows. Let go. See how long you can explore without judgment.

Science, philosophy, and spiritual inquiry, are humanity's grand approaches to discovering truth. Each searches for the truth about us, our world, and its place in the cosmos. Science is continually learning more of the laws that govern the operation of our physical universe. All of scientific inquiry is grounded on physics; it is the underlying foundation upon which all the sciences are based. The term physics is apparently derived from the Greek meaning nature. Physics is the study of energy and force and the study of matter and its motion through spacetime. In addition, it involves the study and analysis of nature and how the world and the universe behave. We begin by addressing some astronomy and astrophysics - the study of the very large, and then we shift to a brief overview of the quantum world – the study of the very tiny.

Special Note: It may have been a while since you were in school and what is outlined in this chapter may seem unnecessary to the topic of Happiness, but I encourage you to stick with it and forge through to the end. You'll be glad you did.

The Cosmos

Our earth is the third planet from the sun. Our sun is a typical star, in most cases very much like the majority of those you see in the night sky. Our sun's ancient and more traditional name is Sol. The sun and its planetary system we call the Solar System. Notwithstanding all of the planets, moons, and other celestial bodies moving around our star, the sun by itself amounts to more than 99 percent of the total mass in the solar system.

Our Solar system is located in the Milky Way galaxy. Thirty years ago scientists thought the Milky Way Galaxy might have as many as a 100 billion stars in it. Our sun is one of these stars. Ten years ago the general consensus of astronomers was that our galaxy might have up to 400 billion stars. The most recent astronomical information gathered by NASA probes in 2009 suggests there may be as many as three trillion stars in our home galaxy!

The most recent astronomical information suggests there may be as many as three trillion stars in our home galaxy!

Our sun is a fairly average star. Stars ranging from about half the size of our sun, to about four times its size, comprise the large majority of the stars that we know of. There are numerous smaller stars, and some so gigantic they are more than a 100 times larger than our own. Just like living things, stars have an identifiable life span. They begin as proto stars in stellar nurseries made up of huge clouds of hydrogen and helium gas. These gas clouds are speckled throughout with various complex molecules that have been fused together in the cores of earlier generations of stars, which subsequently exploded or dissipated out into space at the conclusion of their life cycle.

Stars are like giant factories, they forge hydrogen gas, the simplest of all atoms, into all the other atoms that make up everything we know. There are 94 basic elements beginning with hydrogen and ending with plutonium. The observable universe is still comprised of about 78 percent hydrogen gas, which is slowly being processed in to more complex elements by star factories. All matter, except hydrogen gas, began its physical existence after having been fused into its atomic and molecular parts within the nuclear furnace of stars.

Hydrogen is the first element of the periodic table. It is both the initial fuel of stars and the basic ingredient that is broken down and reconstructed into all the other elements of the periodic table. When hydrogen is cooked up at a high enough heat helium results, when helium ignites and becomes the fuel for stars, other elements like carbon and oxygen result. When stars die they seed the interstellar medium - the empty space between stars - with newly created atoms and molecules which eventually recombine through the dance and swirl of gravity into the worlds and everything in them.

A galaxy is a giant collection of gas and molecular dust along with billions of suns and their accompanying planetary systems all bound together by just one thing: gravity. Gravity is the most powerful force in the universe at our size and scale of things. Although science knows a lot about what gravity does and its mathematic predictability, no one knows how it came about, or just how it does what it does.

A galaxy is essentially an island universe spiraling in the immensity of space. These island universes are separated from one another by unbelievably large distances. But, even within the galaxies the amount of so-called empty space is enormous. The average distance between stars in our home galaxy is on the order of 22 million millions of miles, which in the U.S. would be the number 22 trillion.

For those not particularly familiar with astronomy, there seems to be some confusion as to what constitutes a light year. A light year is not a measurement of time, which the word "year" would infer. Rather, it is a measurement of distance. A light year is the distance that light will travel in one year moving at the constant rate of 186,242.397 miles per second. The speed of light is averaged to be 186,000 miles per second or in the metric system, 300,000 kilometers per second.

To ascertain how far light travels in a year you simply multiply the speed of light (186,000 miles per second), times 60 seconds, times 60 minutes, times 24 hours, times 365 days. A light year is about 5.88 trillion miles (usually rounded to 6 trillion), or about ten trillion kilometers in total distance. The distance measurement of a light year is the basic ruler with which astrophysicists measure the heavens outside the domain of our local solar system. That means the astronomer's primary ruler is roughly 6 trillion miles in length! Astronomers have a host of other distance measuring mechanisms, such as parsecs, mega parsecs, etc., but the light year is the most widely known.

The Milky Way is a great wheel of stars about 100,000 light years across. It is a spiral bar galaxy meaning that looking at it from the top down it would have the appearance of a giant electric fan, its blades slowly turning. At the center of our galaxy is a dense bar of stars that form a massive band across its nucleus.

Our sun system consists of eight primary planets and five dwarf planets. Other planet-like spheres will likely be discovered out beyond Pluto in the not too distant future. There is a constant flow of new discoveries about our local solar neighborhood every year. Many moons circle the thirteen planets in our home solar system, plus there are myriads of asteroids, meteoroids, and comets, in orbit around the sun. At its outer edge, the solar system is ringed by the Kuiper belt (pronounced "Kiper"), and then another large broad circle of debris called the ORT Cloud. Think of these giant outer rings like the outer rings on a large target where the bull's eye represents the sun. Recent space probes confirm that Saturn has 62 moons and Jupiter has another 63, totaling 125 moons orbiting these two planets alone. Alas, earth has but one; Mercury and Venus have none.

Our star's planetary system (the sun and its planets, moons, etc), is a relatively flat disk, like a dinner plate, with the sun in the middle. Perhaps a more appropriate analogy might be an old-fashioned record album, or "vinyl," with the sun in the middle hole with the circular bands around it representing the orbits of the planets. If you're too young to know much about record vinyls then consider the same illustration by looking at the flat side of a CD or DVD, and then at the very thin edge by comparison. Curiously enough, were we to view the solar system edge on, the thickness of an old record album, or the edge of a CD, is a good example of how flat the disk of our solar system really is. It's wide but very thin. The width of our planetary system, the diameter or measurement across the CD if you will, is believed to be about 19 trillion miles, or a bit more than three light years across.

Our sun system, is located about two-thirds of the way out from the super massive black hole that forms the nucleus, or galactic center, of the Milky Way. The Milky Way galaxy is also a relatively flat disk, just like our local solar system (or an old record album or a more modern CD), but our galaxy contains billions of other planetary systems. Every day there is new astronomical evidence coming forth to support the widely-held belief that there must be millions, perhaps billions, of planetary systems similar to our own, right here in our home galaxy we call the Milky Way.

Some of the moons in our solar system are essentially worlds in their own right, having active volcanoes and oceans under ice crusts that may harbor life. Moons are celestial bodies that orbit a planet, whereas planets are the major celestial bodies that are orbiting a star. All planets are shaped like giant basketballs, in other words they are round, whereas smaller moons are not necessarily so. Several moons in our solar system are quite large, about the size of the planet Mercury, and potentially more habitable.

Our local solar neighborhood is also home to numberless asteroids, at least dozens of which are about the size of one of the smaller U.S. states. The larger asteroids with which we are familiar, circle the sun in the asteroid belt between Mars and Jupiter, right along with about a million more rocky chunks of varying sizes. One of these, "Ceres", is large enough that it is now considered a dwarf planet. Without belaboring the definition, primary planets are those we recognize from our school days, except Pluto which has been demoted to a dwarf. Dwarf planets are smaller than primary planets but they still have enough mass, and therefore gravity, to pull their bulk into a sphere.

The current lineup of planets in orbit around our sun, counting out from closest to the sun to the furthest away is: Mercury, Venus, Earth, Mars, Jupiter, Saturn, Uranus, and Neptune. The current list of dwarf-planets in our planetary system is: Ceres, Pluto, Eris, Makemake, and Haumea (pronounced how-MAY-ah). It is now widely believed that many, or perhaps even most, stars have planetary systems of their own, meaning that our home galaxy may have tens of trillions of planets!

Our home galaxy may have tens of trillions of planets!

A galaxy is unimaginably huge, but there is an even larger structure than a galaxy: a super cluster or a metagalactic system. A super cluster is a group of galaxies circling one another in one area of the universe. Some of these groups comprise up to a thousand separate galaxies. Our Milky Way is part of a super cluster of galaxies, ironically called the "Local Group." One of our nearby neighbors in the Local Group is M-31 our sister galaxy, commonly known as Andromeda. We've always believed Andromeda was much larger than our own Milky Way but recently that has become an open question. In any event, our sister galaxy has well over a trillion stars of her own and probably trillions of planets. The enormity of the numbers boggles the brain!

Astronomy is more than the study of faraway stars, lifeless planets, and cold dark moons; it is the study of the universe in which we live. Ultimately, it includes the study of all things, living or not. Astronomy attempts to answer the question "What are we?" It approaches this question from a physical perspective without reference to spiritual implications, but this unfolding insight alone provides us with the knowledge that we are a part of something amazing and beautiful. We are planet-walkers living in a whirling complex universe filled with stars and galaxies.

We are a part of something amazing and beautiful. We are planet-walkers living in a whirling complex universe filled with stars and galaxies.

We can readily see that atoms and gravity work together to make stars, generate energy, light the universe, and produce all the chemical elements in our bodies. According to cosmologist Paul Davies:

"Through science, we human beings are able to grasp at least some of nature's secrets. We have cracked part of the cosmic code. Why this should be, just why *Homo sapiens* should carry the spark of rationality that provides the key to the universe, is a deep enigma. We, who are children of the universe - animated stardust - can nevertheless reflect on the nature of that same universe, even to the extent of glimpsing the rules on which it runs. How we have become linked into this cosmic dimension is a mystery. Yet the linkage cannot be denied. What does it mean? What is Man that we

might be party to such privilege? I
cannot believe that our existence
in this universe is a mere quirk
of fate, an accident of history, an
accidental blip in the great cosmic
drama. Our involvement is too
intimate... This can be no trivial
detail, no minor by product of
mindless, purposeless forces. We
are truly meant to be here."

The Quantum World

Above we have reviewed some information about the largest systems of the universe. Now, we shall overview a little
of the smallest systems in the universe. The quantum world is
the foundation upon which everything else is built. All that we
know of derives from the tiniest waves of sub-atomic energy,
which somehow manifests itself into particles of physical existence. Sub-atomic particles are the building blocks of the known
universe.

Ever since Einstein uttered his famous dictum $E=mc^2$, we've
understood that energy and mass are two sides of the same coin.
This elegant formula sets forth the oft proven assertion that
Energy equals Mass multiplied times the speed of light squared.
The "c", in the formula stands for constant, the only known universal constant is light speed. Light is always traveling at the same
speed no matter what the observation point. As we've reviewed,
light speed clocks in at 186,000 miles per second, or 670 million miles per hour. Light, and light speed, governs the known
universe.

The formula $E=mc^2$ multiplied out creates a huge number
which indicates that even a very small amount of matter contains a tremendous amount of energy. A fact demonstrated in
the 1940's with the creation of America's first atomic bomb. A
very small amount of matter generated a huge release of energy.
It takes immense energy to form the smallest amount of physical

mass. Greater energy means greater mass, and vice versa. All mass is a form of dense energy. In fact, everything of which we are aware is simply energy in one form or another.

All mass is a form of dense energy. Everything of which we are aware is simply energy in one form or another.

Numerous aspects of Einstein's theories of Special Relativity and General Relativity, along with Newton's classic physics, have been confirmed again and again, insofar as scientists are able to test and validate the far-reaching implications of these critically important explanations of the large. However, at the subatomic level the theory of relativity falls apart, and Quantum Mechanics, an equally important and central piece of physics, comes into play.

Both relativity and quantum work beautifully at their own levels, but appear exclusive to their worlds of size, and each fail miserably to explain anything outside their own realm. In the words of Brian Greene, a NOVA host astrophysicist, "The two theories underlying the tremendous progress of physics...are mutually incompatible."

Perhaps the largest problem with the reconciliation of General Relativity and Quantum Mechanics is that the former demands gravity and clockwork predictability, while the latter seems to ignore gravity and instead asserts the uncertainty principle. Oddly enough, both theories are demonstrably true, as something akin to organized chaos reigns at the subatomic level, the exact opposite of structures larger than atoms. Thus, the two most compelling bodies of work central to physics are indeed currently incompatible. This may soon change.

String Theory

There is a massive effort to articulate a unified Theory of Everything. This concept is generally referred to as the T.O.E., but some scientists refer to it as the Grand Unified Theory. In order to achieve the goal of unifying our two most powerful scientific theories into one elegant explanation, the theories of Quantum

Mechanics and General Relativity must somehow meld together. This is what String Theory attempts to do. String Theory is essentially a quantum theory that includes an explanation of the gravitational force.

String Theory is essentially a quantum theory that includes an explanation of the gravitational force.

String Theory ("ST") may provide the framework to explain the conflicts between relativity and quantum along with the WHY of the four forces of physics. During the past 100 years, physicists have accumulated strong evidence that all of the interactions between various objects and materials can be reduced to combinations of just four fundamental forces. These forces are (1) the gravitational force, (2) the electromagnetic force (this includes magnetism, visible light, radio waves, x-rays, gamma rays, etc.), (3) the weak force, and (4) the strong force. The latter two forces of physics come into play at the atomic and sub-atomic levels. Essentially, ST claims that the most elementary particles, of which all things in the universe are comprised, are infinitesimally tiny vibrating strings of energy.

String Theory claims that the most elementary particles, of which all things in the universe are comprised, are infinitesimally tiny vibrating strings of energy.

Atoms are made of protons, a positively charged particle, neutrons a particle of neutral or no charge, and electrons, a negatively charged particle. Both protons and neutrons are comprised of even smaller elements called quarks. String theory claims that the mass of elementary particles is determined by the energy of the vibrational pattern of each particle's internal string. If correct, there is only one basic building block of physical creation; infinitesimally small vibrating strings of energy.

Although there is a huge amount of scientific support for ST, it has yet to be proven. If it is correct then the heavier particles of our physical reality would evolve because their internal strings are vibrating less energetically. Differences between identical elementary particles would arise because their respective strings undergo different resonant vibrational patterns. Just like plucking the strings of a guitar, different tones are developed as the strings vibrate at different frequencies.

Another curiosity of ST is that the strings are believed to vibrate in higher-dimensional hyperspace, or in other words, in as yet undiscovered dimensions. According to Brian Greene, in his book *The Elegant Universe:*

> "What appear to be different elementary particles are actually different notes vibrating on a fundamental string. The universe is composed of an enormous number of these vibrating strings and therefore it is something akin to a cosmic symphony. Every particle of matter and every transmitter of force consists of a string whose pattern of vibration is a fingerprint."

Perhaps the most interesting part of the more popular rendition of ST is that it calls for eleven dimensions rather than the three physical dimensions with which we are so familiar, plus the fourth dimension we know as time. The basic three dimensions are width, length, and depth, or perhaps easier to grasp: left and right, forward and backward, and up and down. The extra dimensions of ST are believed to play out their roles at the tiniest possible subatomic levels, yet profoundly influence the basic physical properties of our universe. The math and the explanations for extra dimensions is complex, and beyond the purpose of this brief quantum overview. But, the mere fact that science has taken seriously that there are likely extra dimensions of which we are not yet aware is interesting in and of itself.

Until rather recently, the major problem with ST has been that there were at least five versions of the theory, and physicists were beavering away in different directions. Along came a fellow named Edward Witten, who observed that what appeared to be dissimilar theories were essentially different aspects of the same concept. Sort of like five different blind men describing an elephant by grasping different parts of it. Witten named his amalgamation of the five approaches to String Theory, "M-theory."

Another interesting aspect of ST is that it provides a rather sophisticated and theoretically sound connection between black holes (the stuff of relativity), and that of elementary particles; the quantum domain.

Summary

A black hole is a celestial object of such extremely intense gravity that it attracts everything around it towards itself, and in some instances prevents everything, including light, from escaping its gravitational pull. The primary way a black hole is thought to develop is when a very large star explodes, and then begins to collapse in upon itself, a consequence of runaway gravity. According to physicists, once the nuclear fire of a large sun begins to fade, meaning that heat expansion can no longer offset gravitational condensing, nothing remains to prevent the star from collapsing to an infinitely small size, a point called a "singularity."

At the point of singularity space becomes curved in the vicinity of matter, and time is thought to stop. We know that the greater the concentration of matter the greater the gravity, and thence the greater the curvature of space. Space and time are essentially different aspects of the same thing (so says relativity), and therefore in an astrophysics sense, science refers to space and time as simply "space-time."

A place beyond which gravity is so powerful that light cannot escape is called an event horizon. Because light and other forms of energy and matter are permanently trapped inside a black hole they cannot be observed directly. However, a black hole can be detected by the effect of its gravitational field on other celestial objects, and by the x-ray and radio frequency signals emitted by matter being pulled into the black hole.

Based on everything we've come to believe from our life experiences, the discoveries of quantum physics are bizarre and nonintuitive. Why? Because Quantum Mechanics tells us that matter is made up of nothing of substance. Everything that makes up our reality is composed of nothing more than energy vibrating at different frequencies.

Everything that makes up our reality is composed of nothing more than energy vibrating at different frequencies.

Both the cosmos and the subatomic world are much more fantastic than we dared think just a few years ago. Black holes are now a demonstrable reality and it appears that they form the center of most, and probably all, of the galaxies that fill the universe. Black holes may actually be galaxy causative, which has spawned a whole new scientific endeavor to investigate this possible correlation.

Another fairly recent revelation is that dark energy (whatever that is), apparently makes up 71.5 percent of the known universe, dark matter 24 percent, hydrogen and helium gas 4%, and all the things we can see and observe, such as planets, stars, and mass of every other form, constitute only .5 percent of the entire universe. Furthermore, dark matter is believed to account for 85 percent of the universe's actual mass, although scientists have yet to identify what it is made of. So...are we confused yet? Well, it gets even more interesting. According to an article entitled, "The Universe", in *Scientific American*, September 2009 issue:

(There are) "...deep and unexpected connections between the world of the very big and the very small...quantum fluctuations on the subatomic scale get blown up to astrophysical size by rapid expansion...In other words, the pattern seen on the CMB (Cosmic Microwave Background), sky is a giant image of the subatomic world."

Cosmologists (scientists that study the cosmos), tell us that the entire galactic process is one of stars and planetary systems being birthed in stellar nurseries, maturing through many phases, and eventually over unbelievably long periods of time, either exploding into space or shrinking into white dwarfs, neutron stars, or black holes. In either case, matter becomes chaotic and disorganized, and is eventually reprocessed into new stars, planets, or other celestial objects. The whole concept is one of inconceivable scope, summed up by the renowned biologist J.S. Haldane, when he said,

> "The universe is not only
> queerer than we suppose; it is
> queerer than we can suppose."

Other Considerations

Astronomer Frank Drake, the cofounder of SETI (Search for Extraterrestrial Intelligence), developed an equation in the 1960's to predict intelligent life in the universe. Projections suggested there was something on the order of tens of thousands of advanced civilizations in just our Milky Way galaxy alone. These numbers could be dramatically increased as Drake was estimating 100 billion stars in the Milky Way. Today the latest estimate is on the order of three trillion stars in our home galaxy, potentially multiplying Drakes original data many times over!

One must admit that it seems thoroughly reasonable that, with all these likely planets circling all of these billions upon billions of suns - in our galaxy alone - logic demands that there is life out there. This conclusion is mirrored by ancient prophecy:

> "And worlds without number have
> I created… But only an account
> of this earth and the inhabitants
> thereof, give I unto you. For
> behold, there are many worlds
> that have passed away by the
> word of my power. And there
> are many that now stand, and
> innumerable are they unto man…"
> Pearl of Great Price, Moses 1:33

Virtually all scientific publications report that the universe is about 13.7 billion years old. Recent calculations reported in Scientific American, now suggest that the universe is about 156 billion light years across. As unimaginably large as that is, the universe appears to be expanding at an ever accelerating rate.

Our local solar system, including the earth, is thought to be about 4.6 billion years of age. Whether the exact age is right or wrong is probably not as important as the concept that our earth and its sun is believed to be at least 10 billion years younger than other areas of the universe. If true, and assuming life has existed elsewhere for eons of time *before* the earth was formed, which is the assumption of most scientists, it should not take much of a leap of faith to believe there exists incredibly advanced societies somewhere out there amongst the stars.

Questions

Let's take a different perspective on the ages of things and consider for a moment how far mankind has come in just the past hundred years. Electronics did not exist a hundred years ago. In fact, a mere century ago, scientists did not even agree on the concept of the atom. The atom's theoretical model was then considered fairly controversial.

Consider what it might be like to go back in time with some of our gadgets to the period of the Crusades. This is only a thousand years ago, when 80 percent of the people died of simple tooth and gum decay. How might one explain a flashlight, a microwave oven, a cell phone, a portable computer, television, a digital camera, iPod, gun, or any other of a myriad of devices, to people so backward there was not one in ten thousand who could even read? Surely our technology would brand us as wizards of the highest order. In fact, the incredible power and knowledge we would possess on a comparative basis would certainly elicit a worshipful response from many, particularly if we used our knowledge and technological goodies to help others. (Then again, we might have a similar reaction if we just shot people).

By comparison, how would we view a civilization a thousand years ahead of us? Would we, or could we, even comprehend a society so advanced? If the last thousand years has made such an incredible difference in the development of mankind, what might a culture a billion years ahead of us look like? The point is that, assuming the sciences of astrophysics and paleoanthropology are correct, and the cosmological timeline is reasonably accurate, then the universe as we know it has been around about 10 billion years longer than that of our earth. And, apparently, the highest life form on the earth one billion years ago was a worm. I dare say none of us have much of a relationship with worms and by extension those a billion years in advance of us may have little interest in us. Or, would they?

So, why is all this Cosmos and Quantum stuff at the beginning of a course on happiness? Because as pointed out in the intro-duction, most of us are so conditioned by our current existence, it is hard for us to be WOWED by new ideas. By raising questions that are either disquieting or larger than life, we begin to let our blinders fall away, while we grapple with these bigger concepts. Remember, it is only when we allow ourselves to "think outside the box" of our day-to-day reality that we are able to draw on a more powerful and improved grasp of the majesty of the uni-verse, and our place in it. And yes it is true, that only when we dare to step up and explore new ways of thinking and open our belief systems to new ways of understanding, will greater insight become available to us.

Where do we go from here? Well, we've got some more sci-ence stuff to consider, the implications of which should be WAY MORE MIND EXPANDING THAN WHAT WE'VE COVERED. It will soon be very clear as to why we're tracking through all this seemingly unrelated material. So hang in there, this is all going to make a lot of sense shortly.

Before going to the next chapter take a moment and ask your-self two questions:

1   Are we fragile victims of events that are beyond our control?

2   Or, are we powerful creators with abilities we are just now beginning to understand?

> "You will hardly find one, among the
> profounder sort of scientific minds,

without a religious feeling of his own… His religious feeling takes the form of rapturous amazement at the harmony of natural law, which reveals an intelligence of such superiority that compared with it, all the scientific thinking and acting of human beings is an utterly insignificant reflection. This feeling… is beyond question, closely akin to that which has possessed the religious geniuses of all ages."

Albert Einstein

Chapter 3

WHAT IS REAL?

Alice: "One can't believe impossible things." Queen: "I dare say you haven't had much practice. When I was your age, I always did it for half an hour a day. Why, sometimes I've believed as many as six impossible things before breakfast."

Lewis Carroll,
Through the Looking Glass

Physics

The foundation of all the sciences rests on physics. Quantum Mechanics is the physics of the very small and it is downright weird. When we first come across the mind-blowing conclusions of quantum theory, it's like we stepped into a science-fiction fantasy novel. Nevertheless, sober scientists have proven again and again that everything we know of is simply energy vibrating at different frequencies. What seems so absolutely solid to us, things like the planets, our bodies, and the pavement, is simply energy at the basement level of creation. Michio Kaku, quantum physicist and frequent guest on the PBS NOVA series, summed up the situation thus:

> "It is often stated that of all the
> theories proposed in the past
> century, the silliest is quantum
> theory. Some say that the only
> thing that quantum theory has
> going for it, in fact, is that it
> is unquestionably correct."

Our universe is constantly in motion. Everything in it is vibrating at the submicroscopic plane - the foundation level of reality. Indeed, various scientific experiments indicate all living things seem to have their own unique energetic signature. And it is likely, that all things, living or not, emit an exclusive distinctive energy that can be recognized. At least that is true for everything scientists have so far examined for this particular characteristic. Furthermore, the stuff of our physical reality appears to arise from a single energetic source, a deeply mysterious place that science is just now beginning to grasp.

Another non-intuitive discovery is that there is no flow of time at the quantum level. All things quantum are in the constant state of an eternal "now." Time, as it turns out, begins only after matter is formed. No matter, no time. Physicist author Gerald Schroeder says it this way:

> "The discoveries of the past few
> decades in astronomy, high energy
> physics, and paleontology have
> revolutionized the understanding
> of our cosmic genesis. They have
> taken us to the threshold of time
> and the beginning of life. We
> have learned there was a time
> before which there was neither
> time nor space nor matter."

Some quantity of the energy of our universe coalesced into our physical reality in keeping with Einstein's famous E=mc² equation. Energy moved into form, sustains form, and can decompose or shift back out of form. The most elementary form of energy, electro-magnetic radiation or light, is described as a combination of waves and particles and, in fact, we've come to understand that the universe is just that: a constant dance of waves and particles. Waves of what? Waves of energy. Particles of what? Minute particles that make up physical existence at the subterranean level of reality. At the atomic level we call these protons, neutrons, and electrons. At the sub-atomic level there are a host of particles, such as quarks, leptons, etc. A light particle is called a photon.

The Field

Max Planck, the Nobel Prize winning physicist, widely referred to as the "father of quantum physics," agreed with Sir Isaac Newton, the "father of classic physics," about the essential substance of the universe. And they, along with such dignitaries as James C. Maxwell, who established electromagnetic theory, and Albert Einstein, who needs no introduction, were convinced that an invisible energy field permeated the entire universe and all of space and all of time. The energy field was once called "ether," but today it is better known as "Zero Point Energy," the "Zero Point Field," or simply the "Field."

The Field is that cosmic ocean of infinite possibilities found at the submicroscopic level of the universe known as the Planck scale, named after physicist Max Planck. So what exactly is this mysterious energy field? A number of physicists now argue that the field is synonymous with light energy, or what is technically known as electromagnetic radiation. Theoretical quantum physicist Amit Goswami, a prolific author and former professor of physics at the University of Oregon concludes:

"Light is the only reality."

According to Dr. T. Lee Bauman, "Light has been positioned as the cornerstone of modern physics and natural law." Notwithstanding, some physicists now conclude that the Field underlies even light, and that therefore, the Field is the foundation of light, life, mass, and the physical laws of the universe.

The Field is the foundation of light, life, mass, and the physical laws of the universe.

Richard Feynman, another Nobel Laureate in physics, estimated that the energy in one cubic meter of so-called empty space is so powerful that it could boil all the oceans of the earth. But by the turn of the millennium, Dr. William Tiller, Professor Emeritus at Stanford, and author of some 250 scientific papers and books, had projected that there was more $E=mc^2$ energy in a thimble-full of the Field than in all the known particles in the observable universe! Say WHAT?!

The Field is apparently everywhere present, or in other words, omnipresent. From a scientific point of view we might want to call it the source of everything. This new understanding has given rise to the expanding belief by some that the Field is conscious, and therefore is itself the Source, the Spirit or Power of God, Infinite Intelligence, the Light of Christ, or whatever name one chooses to represent the Creator. This thought was first set forth by Max Planck himself, when he said:

"All matter originates and exists only by virtue of a force…We must assume behind this force the existence of a conscious and intelligent MIND. This mind is the matrix of all matter."

Materiality of Thought

Many scientists, philosophers, and research theorists, have arrived at another remarkable conclusion. Strangely enough, it is a conclusion taught by mystics and prophetic writers of the ancient world. It could be summed up by saying: The Universe rearranges itself around conditions of thought.

The Universe rearranges itself around conditions of thought.

This seems an incredible claim! But thought underlies all emotion and actions, whether felt, spoken, or performed. And, we see the basis of this concept presented in much of the world's great wisdom literature including the Bible and a host of other ancient religious texts. Three brief examples from the Bible might make the point:

> Genesis 1:3: "And God said, Let there be light and there was light."

> Matthew 17:20:"If ye have faith as a grain of mustard seed, ye shall say unto this mountain, Remove hence to yonder place; and it shall remove; and nothing shall be impossible unto you."

> Luke 17:6: "And the Lord said, If ye had faith as a grain of mustard seed, ye might say unto this sycamore tree, Be thou plucked up by the root, and be thou planted in the sea; and it should obey you."

The lessons taught in the above citations are multiple, but particularly relative to the concept of faith. The take home message seems to be that assuming one believes something strongly - belief being the essence of faith - and then is able to concentrate the power of such thought, then reality can be changed. Strange as it may seem, quantum experiments have repeatedly provided validation for this very same concept.

When I went to school, we learned that atoms were the building blocks of nature. For most of us, this is still the concept we accept to be correct. Atoms, we were taught, had a solid nucleus with one or more orbiting electrons. Atoms collect together to comprise things, sort of like piling together large quantities of blocks or billiard balls. But, quantum research has now shown that atoms consist almost entirely of empty space. In fact, atoms are believed to be 99.99999999 percent empty space! There's basically nothing solid about the building blocks of so-called solid matter. Stuart Hameroff, MD, author, and renowned quantum researcher, gives us perspective on this situation:

> "If we use a basketball to represent
> the nucleus of a hydrogen atom,
> an electron circling it would be
> about the size of a marble orbiting
> 20 miles away - and everything
> in between would be empty."

Mass

As you look about, consider that everything in your physical reality is comprised of infinitesimally tiny points of matter, which at their most elementary level is merely energy surrounded by what we think of as absolutely nothing. Incredible, isn't it? All mass, the total of everything material we can see, touch, taste, or smell, is made up of nothing of substance - or at least nothing that we recognize as something of substance.

Science teaches us that cells, the basic component of all forms of life, are constructed of molecules, which in turn are made up of atoms that are assembled from protons, neutrons, and electrons. These subatomic particles are comprised of even smaller elements called quarks. There are top quarks and bottom quarks, charm quarks (isn't that charming?), and - believe it or not - strange quarks. They come in three varieties, branded as red, white, and blue. And, to make it even weirder, quarks are thought to use gluons, a mass-less force particle, to "glue" them together into various combinations. This is all very strange to us at our level of existence. Maybe that's why one of the quarks is called a strange quark? But really then, can you imagine a mass-less particle? How can a particle, which is mass by its very definition, not in fact have mass? It just keeps getting more bizarre.

The elusive Higgs particle, predicted by the standard theory of physics, but as yet undiscovered, is generally considered the main reason for the construction of the $10 billion dollar Large Hadron Collider ("LHC") by CERN, in Switzerland. The LHC is the latest and most complex in a series of high-energy particle accelerators, built by physicists to investigate the subatomic world. According to a number of magazine and newspaper articles, the LHC is very likely the most complicated thing humans have ever built.

The physics laboratories of CERN represent the combined efforts of over sixty countries. The scientists at CERN are working at the leading edge of quantum understanding. As a point of fact, it was scientists working at CERN on particle physics experiments that came up with the World Wide Web. What a curious evolution of events. Surely the Web is the most transforming technological development of modern times!

The discovery of the Higgs particle may provide insight as to how energetic vibrations take on bulk and are transformed into the physical universe of which we are familiar. A major problem with the standard model of physics, taught in colleges and universities around the world, is that no one can figure out where mass (physical stuff) actually comes from. Everything observed at the subatomic level derives from wave lengths, or as we covered earlier, energy oscillating at different frequencies. Yet, quarks and electrons are generally thought to be the real primary constituents of all matter.

As one looks more deeply into the matrix of matter it is hard to escape experiencing an almost mystical sensation. Why? Because scientists have decided that atoms themselves are just momentary condensations of the Field. Everything seems to be nothing more than a temporary energy signature or vibration that simply pops into, and out of, existence. Yes, that's right; things appear to be pulsing into and out of existence about every ten thousandth of a second. If you feel lost about now, don't be overly concerned, so is just about everyone else trying to understand how to interpret some of the results of high-energy physics experiments.

So if everything is comprised of energy vibration, from whence comes the sense of mass? You know the stuff that seems so solid and somehow triggers the predictability of gravity? Well, it's theorized that the Higgs particle (if it really exists), acts something like warm honey when you draw a knife through it. It creates a drag in space and time giving rise to substance as we know it. Now that's a pretty strange thought.

Double Slits

The most famous experiment of quantum physics, the absolutely replicatable double-slit experiment, demonstrates with a high degree of redundancy that matter is not what we intuitively want to believe it is. You see, it is well known to scientists that unobserved (unmeasured) electrons behave as waves of potential. In other words, there is nothing there unless someone watches it. Now, of course, that sounds completely crazy! But, wacky or not, quantum physics is telling us that nothing physical exists until something watches, measures, or thinks about it.

Wacky or not, quantum physics is telling us that nothing physical exists until something watches, measures, or thinks about it.

The science that underlies the conclusions immediately above has been around since 1801 when Thomas Young conducted the first double-slit experiment with light. The results were so completely non-intuitive that for some time scientists kept the outcome largely to themselves for fear of losing creditability with the public. Things have changed. Numerous studies and hundreds of books, magazines, and newspapers, are continually reporting on the amazing implications derived from the bizarre functioning of things at the quantum level of existence. As an example, Wikipedia reports that "In September 2002, the double-slit experiment of Claus Jönsson was voted 'the most beautiful experiment' by readers of Physics World."

From my perspective, one of the best media depictions of the double slit phenomena is presented in cartoon form in the upgraded, second release of the movie "What the Bleep Do We Know," retitled, "Down the Rabbit Hole." I recommend this upgraded film wholeheartedly. If you decide to get it, I recommend you purchase the Quantum Edition, because it includes one-on-one interviews with a number of scientists on the very subject being addressed here.

When subatomic energy acts as a wave of potential, it is said that matter is in a state of superposition. That's when its particle identity does not yet actually exist, and it is in multiple places simultaneously. Believe it or not, experiment after experiment has proven this superposition state to be absolutely true. By analogy, think of a plate of unset Jell-O. No form is yet in place. But all kinds of different forms can be easily made from the unset Jell-O the moment it cools. Put differently, atoms are not miniature billiard balls, as they are frequently portrayed, but instead, microscopic clouds of possibilities. In fact, there appears to be no such thing as a solid, stable subatomic particle. These things exist only as a potential of any of its future selves; the sum of all its probabilities. Okay, hang on a bit longer. I know this is sounding really weird.

As soon as something like an electron is observed in an experiment, it stops acting like an energy wave, or potential possibility, and collapses into a particle that can be located. Put another way, endless potentiality collapses into a single particle and pops into our reality as a something.

> **Endless potentiality collapses into a single particle and pops into our reality as a something.**

Bang! Just like that! It's all very weird and wonderful.

The Observer

The conclusion to which we are ultimately led is that in quantum physics the observer influences the object under observation. Thus, consciousness has a direct impact on the basic building blocks of our physical world.

> **Consciousness has a direct impact on the basic building blocks of our physical world.**

At its underlying elemental level, physical matter is not yet anything. Reality at the subatomic threshold is only the prospect of some future thing. It cannot be divided or adequately described. It has no meaning in isolation. The act resolving a probability cloud (energy at the wave state or "superposition") into something solid or what we might call "real" is the involvement of an observer. Therefore, we can say with some certainty that, thought affects matter! Yes, that's right.

Thought affects matter.

This relatively recent understanding suggests that the fundamental ingredient in creating our universe is the living consciousness that observes it. It would seem that consciousness is critical to the process of converting the quantum universe into our common reality.

Let's review. Many of the strange conclusions that high energy physicists arrive at come out sounding absolutely nutty. For example, elementary particles are actually just a wave of probabilities that coalesce into existence only when observed. This event is frequently referred to as the "quantum collapse." So yes, quantum physics is telling us that the things we think of as real (the stuff that matter is made up of, i.e.: atoms and their subatomic particles) are actually only a fuzzy cloud of probabilities jumping in and out of existence. In essence, there is really nothing physical about physical matter!

**In essence, there is really
nothing physical about
physical matter.**

Tell that to your car when it runs into a tree. But seriously, the bottom line is that we now know that matter (the objects we have always seen as most solid and firm), is virtually nothing more than a wisp of charged energy in mostly empty space. And, we've learned that all substance, at its basic subatomic structure, has more in common with the energy equivalent of a thought. As a result, some physicists are suggesting that all of reality is actually projected thought, which curiously enough, has led many of them back to contemplate the meaning of Deity, inasmuch as the entire concept literally begs us to consider there is deep intelligence at work.

Nobel Laureates Werner Heisenberg and Niels Bohr are widely reported to have observed:

> "Atoms are not things, they
> are only possibilities."

To these two famous quantum physicists, and numerous others, the universe exists as an infinite number of possibilities until something happens to lock one of these myriad potentials into place. And yes, experiments actually prove that a person's awareness (observation or measurement, if you prefer), seems to be the only thing required to turn possibilities into reality. Heisenberg concluded in his pivotal paper known widely as the "Copenhagen Interpretation," that the universe is thought and observation in action. Niels Bohr concurred.

The universe is thought and observation in action.

So, do you believe this? It is amazingly easy to discount mentally. After all, nothing presented in this chapter is intuitively confirmed by your common sense. Are you able to integrate new information like this, or will you likely discount this kind of revelatory insight? For the most part, those that will discount this information will do so because it is either threatening to their preconceived belief system, or it simply does not fit into their daily habits of thinking.

Inasmuch as everything is built upon atoms and their constituent parts, and because we now know that human consciousness can directly affect these very things, questions naturally arise as to what affect we can have on our reality. And, because there is no apparent space and time considerations at the subatomic level, could an outcome of our focused awareness actually change our own history? --- Now that's a disturbing question. Everything we know and believe tells us this would be absolutely impossible. Yet, in an article in the May 2007 issue of Scientific American, entitled "A Do-IT Yourself Quantum Eraser," the subtitle claims:

"Using readily available equipment,
you can carry out a home
experiment that illustrates
one of the weirdest effects in
quantum mechanics. By removing
information about things that
have happened, a quantum eraser
seemingly influences past events."

Tree in the Forest

We've learned there are all kinds of things that are completely non-intuitive, things that violate our common sense, which once our mind has been opened we discover are absolutely possible. Against this backdrop let me share a personal story that may help illustrate the point:

I was just thirteen when first confronted with the classic science question "If a tree falls in the forest and no one is there to hear it, is there sound?" Like every other kid when they first hear this question, I was absolutely certain there would be a crashing noise in the forest whether anyone was there to hear it or not. To be told there would actually be no sound at all was more than disturbing, it was downright ridiculous. Every ounce of my common sense said otherwise.

Once I began to learn something about radio, television, and other transmitter-transceiver devices, it became clear that unless there was someone or something tuned in to certain audible frequencies there is no sound. Instead, there is only energy waves imbedded with information radiating outward from a given source.

Right now as you read this, your personal space is being penetrated by volumes of wave length information. These frequency radiations might be AM and FM radio, satellite television signaling, marine radio, single-side band, Ham broadcasts, multiple emergency frequencies, innumerable cell phone signaling, and so forth. Yet, unless your radio is on, or your phone is individually being paged, you are simply unaware of these waves of information passing right through your space. All the frequency radiations mentioned directly above are actually waves of light energy imbedded with information, but the same principal is true of sound waves. One only hears sound or perceives noise, when a sound wave is broadcast on a frequency one's brain is able to receive and convert into audible information.

We know that sperm whales are able to signal other sperm whales up to 1,000 miles distant through bass notes propagated through water. These notes are broadcast at a frequency below the hearing level of humans. Most of us are reasonably familiar with dog whistles that can bring canines at a run, but the sound of which is too high a frequency for humans to register. So, is it sound the whale or the dog is hearing? Of course it is. But it is not sound to a human ear; it is only sound waves propagating through a medium, in this case water or air. There is only sound to humans when the frequencies being broadcast falls within the range of human hearing, and there is someone there to hear it.

Common Sense

We are able to translate sound either through exposure to certain frequencies audible directly to us, or indirectly through conversion of waves of information by a transceiver of some sort into the range of human hearing. Okay, we know all of this. But, is it naturally intuitive? Or, did we first have to open our minds to new insight that our prior common sense would have had us believe was near insanity? After all, we can't see anything actually happening, we've just learned it is so.

Consider your common sense experience in another vein. You and I are residents of a spherical earth that is spinning in space at about 1,000 miles per hour. This is easy to calculate inasmuch as the earth is over 24,000 miles in circumference and it makes a complete revolution every 24 hours. Simply divide 24,000 miles by 24 hours and bingo you get 1,000 mph. We know this is true, but can you tell this by anything that's going on in your daily routine? Where's the immediate evidence of our world spinning about at high speed?

Once you know the earth is round, and if you know the measurement of the earth at the equator, you can figure out the spin pretty simply, but until you have gathered these facts you will likely deny the truth of your rapid movement in space, because you do not see evidence of it in your daily activities. That pretty much explains why notwithstanding a Greek philosopher had correctly calculated the circumference of the earth in 300 BC, it took another 1,800 years before people would even begin to accept the truth of the matter.

The earth makes one complete orbit of the sun in slightly less than 365.25 days. To make this trip the earth is speeding around its orbital track at the rate of about 70,000 mph. Do you feel this? Why isn't your hair blowing back? At the same time you and I are spinning around the earth's axis at a 1,000 mph we're speeding around the sun at 70,000 mph. Furthermore, the sun along with you and I, and all its planets, moons, and other celestial captives, are traveling at break neck speed around the core of our galaxy at just shy of 500,000 mph! Do you see any evidence of this reality? Not likely. It is true enough and not disputed in scientific circles, yet there is no intuitive or common sense support for its validity, even though it can be scientifically demonstrated and cross-confirmed in a host of different ways. So, how much faith should you put in your internal belief system? Wouldn't you say it is immensely important that we open our minds to new information? Do you do this? Will you do this?

Time

Time, gravity and light are all connected in mysterious ways. There's lots of speculation about what causes the dimension we call time, and how light and gravity, the two known forces of physics at our size and scale, create the effect known as "time's arrow." It's rather obvious to virtually everyone that we only move forward in time however, the laws of physics suggest we should be able to move both forward and backwards in time. Aside from the ethical questions, if it's possible to move backwards in time, why doesn't anyone know how to do it? It's all very much a mystery.

The truth is we don't know the whole truth about gravity, time, or light. We can measure their effects quite accurately, and describe them mathematically, but we are trapped within the kingdom outlined by their boundaries. Perhaps because we live within time we cannot really get a good grasp of what it is. We have produced timing mechanisms to measure our journey through life here on earth, but time is a relative thing. And, as it turns out, gravity is also a relative thing. We know for example that gravity affects the weight of mass, yet most people are not aware that gravity also affects the flow of time.

I am a 200 pound male. My weight, like yours, varies a bit over the course of a day, week or month, but basically I weigh in around 200 pounds year after year. Were I lucky enough to have NASA send me to the moon, while in space I might weigh absolutely nothing. On the moon I would weigh in at slightly more than 34 pounds. So what happened? I am the same guy, the same height, the same mass, but now I'm only 34 pounds. As it turns out, everything on the moon weighs one-sixth of what it does on earth. That's because the force of gravity on the moon is one-sixth of what it is on earth. The change in the gravitational force causes a parallel change in the weight of mass. In other words, weight is RELATIVE to the gravitational force where we reside.

Time is also affected by gravity. The greater the gravitational field the slower the forward movement of time. If I was to be beamed to a hugely dense planet in another system, and assuming I could handle the other affects of such a transit, time would slow way down. Well, that's not entirely true…time would seem normal for me, but watching people on planet earth would be like hitting the fast forward button on a DVD player. When I returned you would be older than I would, and if I was gone long enough, and the weight differential was large enough, I might hardly age at all while you had grown much older. This is not just conjecture; numerous tests have proven this is actually the case. The gravitational field of a black hole is so powerful it stops time altogether. Time is RELATIVE. It seems that if you don't mind being really heavy, you can be infinitely old. Ha! (Tongue held firmly in cheek.)

The same type of scenario plays out with light. We know that the faster one travels in relationship to the speed of light the slower the clock ticks. Were one able to move at light speed, time as we know it would stop all together. We would have moved beyond time; strange but true. Surely, nothing in our day-to-day world reveals these known realities of relativity, nevertheless the affects are known by science, and they have been proven again and again.

John Gribbin, Cambridge astrophysicist and science writer, has pointed out that all forms of electromagnetic radiation (light), is timeless. He goes on to say:

> "...you can say that distance does
> not exist for an electromagnetic
> wave...everything in the universe,
> past, present, and future, is
> connected to everything else by a
> web of electromagnetic radiation
> that 'sees' everything at once."

Summary

According to Einstein's theories of relativity, nothing in this world can ever move faster than the speed of light. To do so infers we would then be moving back in time. It appears that light forms the outside boundaries of our physical universe. Or, at least we think it does. On the other hand, we know scientifically that the quantum level of our existence operates beyond time and space. So whether you are at the quantum level, infinitely heavy, or moving at light speed, time stops completely. Pretty darn bizarre; but that doesn't stop it from being true.

> **Whether you are at the**
> **quantum level, infinitely heavy,**
> **or moving at light speed,**
> **time stops completely.**

Light is believed to be the source of all known energy at our size and scale. So, what is light really? Science can describe it, we know a lot about what it can do. On the other hand, it is for absolute certain that we do not really know what light is. In addition to its being the source of all things, it also seems to set the boundaries of the kingdom of our reality. Here's an interesting bit of insight culled from the Doctrine and Covenants:

"And the light which shineth
which giveth you light, is through
him who enlighteneth your eyes,
which is the same light that
quickeneth your understandings;
Which light proceedeth forth
from the presence of God to
fill the immensity of space - The
light which is in all things, which
giveth life to all things, which
is the law by which all things
are governed..." DC 88:11-13

New evidence from a host of scientific disciplines, including astronomy, quantum physics, biology, and paleoanthropology, have scientists all over the world daring to face the conundrum that the universe is clearly tuned for life, and it has been since its inception. Hundreds, perhaps thousands, of recent discoveries have tipped those working at the leading edge of scientific exploration upside-down.

Science is supposed to represent a secular approach to the pursuit of truth, unfettered by religious predispositions. This is surely a good thing. But, more and more results incoming from the forefront of scientific endeavor sound virtually mystical, and sometimes downright spiritual. Some of our greatest and brightest minds are now admitting openly that there must be PURPOSE in the universe, as its formation cannot have been an accident. The old saw "evolution did it" no longer holds up. An evolutionary process is clearly a part of the laws of the physical universe, but as Max Planck, the father of quantum theory, put it: there is "mind behind the matrix."

Based on everything we would normally believe from our personal life experiences, the recent discoveries of quantum physics are bizarre and nonintuitive. Nevertheless, it may just be that life is a sophisticated program designed to educate and enlighten, or to be some form of process that allows us perceived encounters in a holographic environment. If we are indeed experiencing a kind of temporal holodeck life within some form of projected quantum matrix, it leads directly to the question: Who is running the program? This question is for you to ponder.

We've learned that consciousness and energy seem to be the creative source of everything in our collective reality. And let's remember, the physical universe is essentially nonphysical. It arises from a field more subtle than any known energy. It looks more like intelligence or consciousness than like matter. And yes, these are the conclusions arrived at by scientists around the globe.

Lest one think there is no basis in quantum theory, it is sobering to know that this is the science that all of our recent technological goodies - everything from computers and cell phones, to DVD's and iPods - have come. It is estimated that thirty percent of the world's total GNP is now based on the technological application of quantum theory. Whew! Guess we have no option to throw these conclusions out by suggesting the scientists are all smoking something. Ha!

It would seem that our role in the universe is pivotal to why the quantum world works as it does. What does this mean to us? How do we use this information? What is going on? Truly, what do you think? Does the universe rearrange itself around conditions of thought? And, what is REAL anyway? Leo Tolstoy once said;

> "Happiness does not depend
> on outward things, but on
> the way we see them."

Maybe that is a truer statement than we have heretofore dared think? At the close of the last chapter two questions were posed for you to consider as you read through this material:

1 Are we fragile victims of events that are beyond our control?

2 Or, are we powerful creators with abilities we are just now beginning to understand?

So, what do you think?

> "When we understand us, our consciousness, we also understand the universe and the separation disappears."

Amit Goswami,
Author and Physicist

It's All *Thought!*

Chapter 4

QUANTUM, LIFE, AND LIGHT

"I am determined to be cheerful and happy in whatever situation I may find myself. For I have learned that the greater part of our misery or unhappiness is determined not by our circumstance but by our disposition."

Martha Washington
First, First Lady

Introduction

One of the most amazing things learned from scientific research is that all things seem to be connected in some way. The scientific name for this connectedness   is "phase entanglement." It is the theoretical model arrived at by many quantum physicists to explain the otherwise unexplainable connection that things at the quantum level have with each other. There are numerous and compelling laboratory experiments that demonstrate the accuracy of this widely tested aspect of the quantum world, notwithstanding that the results seem to fly in the face of common experience. The very concept of entanglement sounds more like a spiritual or religious explanation of quantum events rather than hard science. It is a widely-held scientific model, nonetheless. Entanglement is presented in greater detail later in this chapter.

In Chapter 2, we reviewed the supposition that scientific endeavor and spiritual inquiry represent humanity's grand approaches to discovering truth. Each of these disciplines is searching for the truth about us and our universe. In earlier epochs, some religious institutions claimed direct knowledge to knowing the path to happiness. Some still do. Today, science has much to tell us about that seemingly elusive, almost unexplainable sensation we call happiness.

The purpose of this chapter is to introduce additional insight garnered from recent scientific work, and pull this together with material already reviewed. You may find the information in this chapter stunning in its potential application. I encourage you to keep an open mind. Dare to imagine. Dare to consider new alternatives to what you think you know. Prepare yourself for dramatic insights that point to clear and specific thought processes each of us would be wise to pursue.

All matter is made up of elements. An element is a substance that cannot be broken down into less complex substances by chemical means. Hydrogen, Helium, Carbon, Oxygen, Iron, and Gold, are examples of elements. The smallest component of an element is an atom. An atom has a small nucleus made of positively charged protons and an equal number of neutrons that have no charge. Moving in orbit around the nucleus is an equal amount of negatively-charged electrons.

A proton and a neutron have about the same mass. Their massiveness is calculated to be 1,837 times greater than that of an electron. The number of protons in an atom of an element is referred to as its atomic number. Atoms arranged in order of their atomic number constitute the elements of the periodic table.

Cells

All living things, be they plant or animal, are made up of microscopic units called cells.

All living things, be they plant or animal, are made up of microscopic units called cells.

Cells are alive. They are able to perform numerous functions, perhaps as many as 100,000 different duties in one form or another. (Some cellular biologists claim that number exceeds a million.) Cells stay in constant communication with one another, making adjustments and changes in routine as needed for themselves, and the greater need of the complex communities of which they are typically a part. We know that the human body is a remarkably complex structure. Biologists are now telling us that each of us is comprised of about 100 trillion cells!

To put that 100 trillion number in perspective the human body has about a hundred times more cells than the estimated stars in our massive sister galaxy, M-31, the Andromeda Nebula. But, cells are very small, and at least by comparison, stars are very large. It's all a matter of scale. Approximately 10,000 human cells will fit on the head of a pin, and that is small, but compared to an atom a cell is massive. It would take about two billion atoms to cover the head of a pin. In at least some sense, we could say that our body is a galaxy of cells working closely together to keep us alive. That same appearance of interconnectedness can be observed at various magnitudes of scale. A discussion we shall save for another time.

The cellular level is what many scientists think of as the threshold of consciousness. Speaking to this conclusion, Dr. Candace Pert, an internationally recognized scientist and research professor at Georgetown University in Washington, DC, has stated succinctly that the cellular level is the threshold of consciousness adding:

> "After all, there is always the
> perspective of the cell."

Dr. Pert goes on to share another remarkable conclusion:

> "...you are biologically hardwired
> for bliss - all you need to do is
> tap your own body's unlimited
> natural capacity for living in joy
> and connecting to the divine."

At the biological level consciousness seems to begin at the level of our cells. Interestingly, it is within the nucleus of the cell that our DNA code is stored. Each of us has a unique DNA sequence; this is the recipe for the cellular community that constitutes our physical make-up. All 100 trillion of your cells maintain this recipe book for the reconstruction of you. Perhaps it would be more correct to say "recipe books," inasmuch as the typewritten pages of a person's DNA sequence would fill 600 books of 1000 pages each.

Cells are comprised of large numbers of molecules. In turn, molecules are formed from a complex of atoms. The cellular level appears to be the interfacing threshold between ordinary matter, the stuff of our world, and the extraordinary universe of quantum events.

The cellular level is the interfacing threshold between ordinary matter and quantum events.

Just as the huge spaces between stars contain vast amounts of subtle energy, the empty space that makes up over 99.99999999 percent of each atom, is abundant with energy thousands of times more powerful than any other force of which science is aware. At least this is true as far as we know, and at our scales of time and size. So, not only have scientists learned that atoms are mostly empty space, but that actually the empty space is not really empty, it is teeming with unbelievably powerful energy.

The parts of the atom that actually have something we think of as mass to them, are comprised of subatomic particles that themselves are made up of nothing more than temporary energy signatures. We have already concluded that everything derives from the energy configuration at the foundational base of our reality. It seems reasonable that we might also conclude that it is at the atomic scale, where atoms bind together to form molecules, that new creation is constantly being manifested.

It is at the atomic scale where atoms bind together to form

molecules that new creation is constantly being manifested.

Dr. Joyce Hawkes, a preeminent, award winning, biophysicist, put it this way:

> "In the micro world of the inner composition of your cells, energy and matter interface in ultra fast blips of times: nano - or pico - seconds. When an event occurs in these swift pulses ... the cells enter a type of quantum reality - no longer linear and no longer predictable. ... Possibilities exist here that we have barely begun to understand or develop. ... _Yet, we can influence them with our consciousness._" (My emphasis)

New scientific efforts have demonstrated that within a living cell, molecules communicate not just by chemicals, as we've been taught, but by light (electromagnetic signaling), at low frequencies. Further, it appears that even individual molecules have their own unique frequency signatures.

Focus

Recall that light is energy, traveling as a wave through space. It is technically referred to as electromagnetic radiation. Visible light is that part of the electromagnetic spectrum that humans can see. Visible light represents only a tiny sliver of the information available in the full bandwidth of light's radiation. Light is described as a combination of waves and particles. That's because depending on how we look at it, light will behave like a wave of probabilities or a particle; a single bit of reality.

Depending on how we look at it, light will behave like

a wave of probabilities or a
particle; a single bit of reality.

Light is a wave of energy until we observe it closely, and then it jumps into being particles, or tiny packets of light called photons. Energy waves are not solid, but spread out like waves on the ocean or like sound waves. Only when a "probability" wave collapses into a particle of reality can it be located in a specific time and place. This event is called the "collapse of the wave function." It is all very bizarre and amazing, even to the scientists that pronounce the results. Nobel Laureate physicist Richard Feynman is famously reported to have said:

> "Anyone who thinks he
> understands quantum physics
> does not understand it enough
> to understand that he did not
> actually understand it!"

Scientists from universities and laboratories around the globe have continually reconfirmed that photons and electrons - tiny bits of matter - are influenced by being watched. Nobel Laureate physicist Richard Feynman, in his summary of the famous and oft-repeated double slit experiment, quotes prior physics Nobel Laureate Werner Heisenberg as saying:

> "The path [of the electron]
> comes into existence ONLY
> when we observe it."

Further, it has been widely reported that the more intense the watching, the greater the observer's influence on how particles behave. Subsequently further experiments demonstrated the same was true of atoms, a significant increase in the magnitude of scale. There is little escaping the conclusion that thought impacts things. Once again it would seem that our thoughts are much more powerful than we dare think.

**It would seem that our
thoughts are much more
powerful than we dare think.**

In Lynn McTaggert's book, *The Intention Experiment*, which followed directly on the heels of her scientific reporting in *The Field*, she shares these thoughts on light:

> "If you could get all the photons
> of one small light bulb to
> become coherent and resonate
> in harmony with each other,
> the energy density of a single
> light bulb would be thousands
> to millions of times higher than
> that of the surface of the sun."

Stop and consider what you've just read for a moment. By aligning, or focusing, the photons of a single household light bulb you could create a surface considerably hotter (thousands to millions of times greater), than the surface of the sun. Say what? The energy of a single light bulb could somehow become hotter than the sun? Is that not truly amazing? Now consider that an observer (you or me), is actually the formative cause of things moving from their probability state into physical reality. We don't know how or why an observer influences the outcomes of sub-atomic events; we only know that they do. Let's consider what the take home message might be to all of this. The answer is: "Focus." Focused intention; focused attention. Focus changes outcomes. This is a fact!

What are you focused most upon? The answer to that question is relatively easy to conclude; it's whatever you are getting the most of over time. To put it somewhat differently, you are experiencing what your emotions and thoughts are most powerfully and frequently focused upon. One triggers the other. Stop and think a moment. What are you experiencing right now? How are you experiencing it? How do you see things? Are you making mental assessments regarding what you are experiencing? Is that judgment? Why are you judging? Dare to focus on that thought for a while!

McTaggert went on to report in the *Intention Experiment* that, "British physicist Roger Penrose and his partner, Stuart Hameroff, from the University of Arizona, were in the vanguard of frontier scientists who proposed that the microtubules in cells..." (Microtubules form the skeletal framework or basic structure of cells) "...are actually 'light pipes' through which disordered wave signals were transformed into highly coherent photons and pulsed through the rest of the body." Most of us are aware that wave signals can carry information, that's the basis of radio and television, but let's also remember that ordered light can do other things as well.

Consider again the illustration above where ordered light from a single light bulb could be so focused as to be effectively hotter than the surface of the sun. It is a pretty wild thought; yes? Yet, doesn't this sound a lot like how we can technologically re-order light to become more highly organized, or FOCUSED, into something immensely powerful, like a laser beam? Highly focused light can be used to cut through steel. We know this, but it's still pretty darn amazing. Okay, so let's now relate that to another form of light wave. As it turns out, thoughts appear to be generated as ordered frequencies. So, what might thoughts cut through when highly focused?

Thought

Studies demonstrate living things radiate photons. We do this at a frequency just out of range of the visual spectrum. Some apparently gifted people claim to see human radiation in the form of a halo or aura. Whether or not you believe there are persons capable of observing human radiation is not the point. Scientific research has confirmed that each of us does have our own individual energy field. And, the human energy field, or one's aura if you prefer, can now be actually monitored at a distance; more about this in a later chapter.

In the early 1970's, I was privileged to work in an experimental program with a newly discovered technique developed in Russia for revealing human energy radiation on film. Although only involved with Kirlian photography for a three month period, the results were astounding. Even with rather primitive technology we could literally see that humans are surrounded with an energy field basically in the shape of the human body. Many refer to this radiation field as our energy body. We also learned early on that with clear intention and focused attention, humans are able to boost their radiation levels and shift the color of those emanations in concert with the emotional content they are then focused upon.

Today there is considerably more sensitive equipment providing new insights on the earlier discoveries of Kirlian photography. This research has been expanded to all kinds of living things, demonstrating that all life forms both receive and emanate light photons. There is no real debate on this issue. We do have an energy body and it does show up on film. However, the point in introducing this information is as it relates to our thinking.

One series of experiments that I participated in were run in a darkened room with a number of subjects. We were separated from one another and not allowed to observe each other's procedure. This was to protect against our influencing another subject's test results. At one point, I quit becoming the lab rat, and moved on to becoming the lab assistant administering a number of these experiments. The essence of these tests required that we focus on emotionally charged words, such as love, arousal, anger, healing, faith, disappointment, and so forth. As the subject concentrated on a given emotion, their hand or fingers would be photographed to see what difference holding a given emotion in mind had on their energy field.

Lab tests using Kirlian photography were executed sequentially and performed as follows: Before placing a hand on a glass exposure table, the film equivalent of a copier platen, the subject was instructed to concentrate for 30 seconds on one of the words provided by the lab technician performing the experiment. After a five minute quiet time, subjects were given a new word to focus on for an entire minute before placing his or her hand on the glass to be photographed. The cycle continued once more, with the focus time raised to two minutes. The photography was performed by time-lapse under dark fabric in a dark room. Once the film for each set of experiments was developed, I was able to compare each sequential exposure to the different emotionally-packed words previously focused upon.

The results were simply amazing. For the first time, we were seeing the human energy body. Some of the participants believed we were observing the human spirit. Whether that is accurate or not I cannot say, but what was dramatically clear was that each of us project energy at varying levels of intensity, and much of the time within a color spectrum we can easily identify. We learned that the colors and the intensity vary between people, but the similarities are much more common than the differences. What caused the changes in the strength of the radiation, the shift of the colors, and the overall brilliance of each exposure? It was obvious enough that the changes were wrought solely by the varying thoughts that we had been instructed to focus upon.

Thought is affecting you right now. Thought is driving the energy of the broadcast you are projecting right now. If you were able to see your own energy emanations this very minute what do you think they might tell you? You can easily know what you are projecting...it will be the result of what you are feeling. So, what are you feeling right now? Is it wonder? Is it excitement? Is it skepticism? What? Whatever it is, that will be what you're sending out into the world.

The composite of what you are feeling, including your level of physical, emotional, and spiritual health, coupled with whatever it is you are focused upon, comprises that which you are at any given moment. Although you may be thinking this is not particularly new news, the really powerful message here is that you can change your feelings almost immediately, simply by changing the focus of your thoughts.

As we were to discover during our Kirlian testing, most people, after only a short training session, can change their focus from one emotional response to another within five minutes. It takes concentration and a certain mental discipline, but with effort virtually anyone can do it. The exception seemed to be that if you had pulled up some particularly harsh feelings from a past experience in order to generate the emotion of anger, victimhood, desperation, or some similar fearful sensation, it could take a much longer time to rid yourself of these negative overtones. This leads to a couple of conclusions: Negative thoughts are pollution to your entire system. And, anyone can be happy whenever they choose by simply focusing on uplifting thoughts.

> **Anyone can be happy whenever they choose by simply focusing on uplifting thoughts.**

Just as light radiates forth affecting to some degree everything in its path, and then continues on throughout space and time, every thought you have ever thought is still out there radiating forth through space-time. Thoughts, like light, are both energy emanations that can now be measured. Energy is eternal; you cannot destroy or stop it. When one thinks about thought, and begins to recognize that our thoughts are the sum of what we actually experience, we are led to conclude that each of us is living the sum total of every thought we have ever thought in our life. This philosophy was taught by the Yogas of old, the Buddha 500 years before the Christian era, and by Jesus the Christ in the meridian of time.

So then, do our thoughts matter? You bet they do!! They matter in more ways than we could ever have previously imagined. The gifted Esther Hicks, of Abraham-Hicks Publications, sums up thought and matter, this way:

> "Matter is the evolution of energy. First there is thought, then there is thought form, and then there is matter. Matter is only thought that has been thought upon by more."

"Curiouser and curiouser," said Alice in Wonderland. Think on that thought for a while. Improved technology now allows for more refined studies of quasi-related subjects, such as eastern energy healing by Chinese Qigong masters and the healing art from Japan known as Reiki. There is also a Tibetan version of Reiki based on ancient Sanskrit writings.

Scientists, performing laboratory research on a number of Qigong and Reiki master healers, reported that they were able to so focus their minds that the photons emanating from the hands of the healer to their patients appeared as the most highly organized light emissions found in nature. Scientist Dr. Gary Swartz, Harvard PhD in psychology, along with Dr. Melinda Connor, concluded that certain master healers could so direct their intention that it could be measured as electrostatic and magnetic energy, both elements of the light field. We can surmise then that an ordered and disciplined mind can indeed order light energy.

For what it's worth, at a younger age, I would probably have considered all this pure Voodoo. However, after my wife Maureen passed away from esophageal cancer, I met and eventually married a woman who is a Reiki Master. I have personally experienced her remarkable ability to channel energy. Strange? Yes. Thought-provoking? Indeed. Valuable? Absolutely.

DNA

Another interesting phenomenon that suggests that we may be more than we've been led to believe, are the results of a series of experiments on human blood. In Gregg Braden's book, *The Divine Matrix*, he reports on this subject. In one particular study, scientists working with precise instrumentation, measured light photons within a contained environment demonstrating that they were disordered and appeared to be located randomly. When introducing human DNA into the container the light particles rearranged themselves into regular patterns. In other words, DNA, the basic blueprint of all life forms, has an impact on light particles. Light photons organize themselves in the presence of human DNA.

> **Light photons organize themselves in the presence of human DNA.**

What does it mean? No one is really sure, but it opens up a whole new arena of conjecture. In another vein, it seems that human blood can be taken from a donor, and separated into an external testing device, and still be reactive to the emotions of the donor. In a groundbreaking accidental discovery, a lab technician gazing at a playboy centerfold somehow caused his blood cells (previously removed and separated into a laboratory dish), to react wildly. Yes, that's right, the blood cells were no longer resident in the donor, yet they were still responsive to the thoughts and emotional reactions of the donor. Definitely something weird was going on.

Braden went on to report that the U.S. Army "performed experiments to determine precisely whether the emotion/DNA connection continues, following a separation, and if so, at what distances?" Braden cites the journal *Advances*, regarding the Army's continued research on this curious phenomenon, quoting Dr. Cleve Backster as saying that at one point the donor was separated from his blood cells by 350 miles for the experiment. The cell's responses to the donor's emotional surges were then cross-checked against our nation's official atomic clock located in Colorado. The time interval measured between the emotional surge and the cell's response was zero. The effect was simultaneous. *But, how can this be?* Isn't it a basic tenet of Special Relativity that nothing can travel faster than the speed of light? And, wouldn't the emotions of the donor have to travel the 350 mile distance and therefore take time? Yes, one would think so, but in the quantum world there is this thing called entanglement.

Entanglement

Entanglement is the quantum event that tells us that, on some level, subatomic particles are intimately linked BEYOND space and time. Wikipedia reports this observation regarding entanglement:

> "...quantum mechanics has been highly successful in producing correct experimental predictions, and the strong correlations predicted by the theory of quantum entanglement have now in fact been observed."

Somehow everything and everyone is intimately linked. How do we know this? Our cells and their atoms are all constructed of quantum particles. Therefore, if quantum particles have linkage, so must we. The implications of this discovery are simply mind-boggling. We are all connected, and in some intimate way, we remain unified with our source.

Albert Einstein was initially upset by the implications of quantum physics, particularly as it related to entanglement. He was also frustrated with the lack of perfect predictability of things at the quantum level. Einstein is famously quoted to have said, "God does not play dice with the universe." To which the Danish quantum physicist, Niels Bohr, a Nobel Laureate himself, replied, "Stop telling God what to do!"

In an early attempt to discredit quantum theory, Einstein, along with physicists Boris Podolsky and Nathan Rose, developed a thought problem demonstrating that subatomic particles existing in superposition (the wave state), could be separated by infinite distances and still be entangled such that whatever was done to one would instantly impact the other. In other words, not only are things connected, but information could be exchanged faster than the speed of light.

In Einstein's thinking, entanglement would be a violation of relativity, because one thing could affect another beyond time, or in a place of no elapsed time, which would be faster than light speed. As reviewed in chapter 2, faster than light speed is a definite no-no of relativity. He called this predicted outcome of quantum theory "spooky action at a distance." Einstein observed that were Quantum Mechanics to be true it would infer that reality is observer-created.

Einstein observed that were Quantum Mechanics to be true it would infer that reality is observer created.

Albert Einstein did not live to see the proof of his so-called "spooky action at a distance." Multiple experiments, beginning with John Bell's mathematical work published in 1964 (today called

Bell's Theorem), followed up by research at Columbia University, Berkeley, the University of Paris, and today dozens of other published and peer-reviewed studies, all confirm both the concepts of entanglement and the observer effect. The quantum level is beyond our understanding of space and time, and there IS linkage between quantum particles.

Multiple experiments have proven that the quantum level is beyond our understanding of space and time.

At the quantum threshold, messages are executed simultaneously, regardless of the distance involved. *So what does all this have to do with us?* Well, we're just beginning to sort out the incredible possibilities, but to begin with, it should be clear that there is some kind of hierarchy in the universe. It begins with energy, progresses to subatomic particles, and then these particles bind into atoms. Atoms collect and compound themselves into molecules. Molecules combine to become the basic elements, or they sometimes become living cells. It is right here that energy either lives, in the classic sense, or is formed as inert mass. Truly fascinating!

When energy becomes cellular, there are two essential options that we know of: either the cell converts sunlight – in some cases heat energy - into chemical energy and oxygen through the process of photosynthesis, or, it becomes part of the animal kingdom, which consumes the chemical energy made by plants or is stored in the cells of animals that had eaten plants. In her book, *Cell-Level Healing*, biophysicist Dr. Joyce Hawkes, says:

> "Inside the cell membrane an entire cosmos of complexity and beauty lives in the watery medium of the cell sap, the cytoplasm. More than 90 percent of the cytoplasm is water, and one can only speculate how our thoughts might affect this cell-water and thereby affect the critical functions of the

other sub-cellular components.
Masaru Emoto's provocative
work certainly challenges us
to consider the messages we
give our watery milieu."

Water

Dr. Masaru Emoto's six books, beginning with *Messages from Water*, have made a big splash (ha, ha), around the globe. Dr. Emoto reminds us that the human body is 75 to 90 percent comprised of H20; simple water molecules. In fact, all living things on planet earth are made principally of water. In 2006, Emoto published a peer-reviewed paper with Professor Dean Radin of Princeton University and a number of others. The Journal of Science and Healing described a double blind study of approximately 2000 people in Tokyo where they had increased the aesthetic appeal of water stored in a room in California, compared to water in another room at the same location. They had accomplished this solely through their positive intentions.

Emoto's continuing research points directly to the conclusion that water reflects human emotional energy at the microscopic level, just as water reflects physical images in the visible light spectrum.

Research points directly to the conclusion that water reflects human emotional energy at the microscopic level.

Emotional energy imprinted in water can be observed at its freezing or crystallizing threshold. Thousands of photographs have been taken through dark-field microscopes of crystallizing water that first had emotional energy imprinted upon it. These photos are not just impressive to look at, their images are haunting to consider in terms of what they tell us about ourselves.

It seems that whenever expressions of consciousness are directed to water it generates a cascade of changes in the water itself. All of us know that calm surface water reflects our physical image through the refraction of light off its surface, but few of us have understood that water may also reflect our emotional energy at the microscopic level.

Due primarily to Masaru Emoto's work, we have learned that feelings of gratitude and love generate bright, white, and beautiful, crystals in water, whereas negative and mean-spirited emotions reflect dark, ugly, and polluted images. This is pretty remarkable stuff. Inasmuch as we are primarily made of water, it clearly begs the question: If thoughts can do this to water, what can thoughts do to us?

> **Inasmuch as we are primarily made of water, it clearly begs the question: "If thoughts can do this to water, what can thoughts do to us?"**

The one structure that all life has in common is the cell. All cells are comprised primarily of water. Water is THE element all living things have in common. How interesting it is that water is also the element that has now been shown to reflect the intensity and emotional content of our thinking.

Review

So, what have we learned from the chapters *"Quantum and the Cosmos," "What Is Real?" and "Quantum, Life, and Light"*? Let's reconsider a few of these things. We know that we are thinking, conscious beings. We are planet-walkers in an immense swirling galaxy of incredible wonders. We are informed that our Milky Way Galaxy easily has the potential of supporting tens of thousands, perhaps millions upon millions of planets infused with life. And, we may yet discover some forms of life off-planet but within our own local solar system. Admittedly, it is unlikely that mind and consciousness as we currently understand them, exists on the planets and moons of our local system, but it's really too early to even be certain of this. At least lower forms of life could easily exist in the vast water oceans recently discovered on two of the moons in our solar system.

Astronomy and astrophysics are telling us that our atoms are star stuff; elements cooked in the cores of stars. Everything that we know of within our physical reality is comprised of atoms. Atoms in turn, are a construct of subatomic particles and these arise from energy. Matter and energy are the different sides of the coin of our existence.

Whereas life likely exists throughout the universe at this point, we are only certain it exists on earth. Yet, we know that the basic elements of life are common, both on earth and off-planet. The larger question about life on other worlds would seem to be the issue of consciousness. In the words of astronomer-cosmologist Paul Davies:

> "… The existence of mind in
> some organism on some planet
> in the universe is surely a fact
> of fundamental significance. …
> This can be no trivial detail, no
> minor byproduct of mindless,
> purposeless forces.   We are
> truly meant to be here."

In "*What is Real?*" we reviewed the Zero Point Field, which may have sounded a great deal like "the Force" in the *Star Wars* movies. Yet, science is telling us that everything that makes up our reality turns out to be composed of nothing more than energy vibrating at different oscillation levels, wave lengths, or frequencies. And because energy is the ultimate force, so it would also be correct to call the Field, the Force.

The Field is often referred to as the cosmic ocean of endless possibilities. And although this metaphor sounds suspiciously like a religious tenet, especially one of Eastern origin, according to that pragmatic German Nobel Laureate, Max Planck,

> "We must assume behind this
> force the existence of a conscious
> and intelligent MIND. This mind
> is the matrix of all matter."

We've also learned that the Field is nothing less than the foundation of all light, life, mass, and the physical laws of the universe. We observed in *Quantum and the Cosmos* that mankind is evolving at a rapid rate. Just a thousand years ago, over 80 percent of Europeans died of simple tooth decay and associated gum disease, and only one person in ten thousand could even read. (That era is often called the Dark Ages for a good reason.)

It is important to note that notwithstanding the remarkable progress of humankind, we tend to resist new information, especially if it threatens our preconceived belief system. And so it is, and strange as it may seem, that most people would rather live comfortably with a lie than face having to integrate new emotionally-threatening information. Therefore, it is doubly important to realize that, unless we are prepared to ask big questions and legitimately seek more truthful answers, we condemn ourselves to limited ways of thinking and stunt our personal growth and development.

We've reviewed the incredible claim that an amazing aspect of the universe is that it may well arrange itself around conditions of thought. Whether this is absolutely true or not, we do know that thought impacts matter. Several times we've stressed that there is really nothing physical about physical matter, at least this is true at the basement level of creation. And, we've concluded that our role in the universe seems somehow pivotal to why the quantum world works as it does.

We've considered that all living things are comprised of cells. Cells appear to be the threshold of life. We also understand that the human body is comprised of a huge metropolis of cells networking together to keep us alive in our physical form.

It has been demonstrated that each of us have our own energy body and project our own energy field. We've learned that the thoughts we focus upon change the color, projection, and brilliance of our energy. Put another way, thoughts matter. They matter a great deal. It seems our thoughts matter considerably more than we have ever dared believe.

Normally our ability to see is considered critical to understanding our reality, and yet, we view the universe through an incredibly small sliver of the light bandwidth. It's as if we barely have a keyhole view of our world. As it turns out, the visual spectrum allows us access to only a minuscule amount of the information carried in light. Therefore, we can say with considerable certainty, we simply don't know what we don't know.

Recent scientific research tells us that light self-organizes in the presence of living DNA. DNA is stored within the core of each of our individual cells. All life is composed of cells, which are themselves comprised of about 90 percent water. Our recent awareness that the water within us is directly responsive to human emotions is surely of great importance. Water can be radically affected by both positive and negative thinking, which precipitated the question: "If thoughts can impact water, what can thoughts do to us?" Considering we are mostly water, this is a compelling question.

Finally, we have learned that all of us are somehow connected. Not only are we connected, but our messages at the quantum level are communicated instantaneously, irrespective of the speed of light. We also know that time does not actually exist in the quantum world, and neither does time exist in any energy wave or light particle inasmuch as these things move at light speed. Physicist author Gerald Schroeder put it this way:

> "Einstein showed us, in the flow of
> light, the corollary of the Eternal
> Now: I was, I am, I will be."

That should give us pause. What is it we are predominantly thinking? What is it we are beaming out into the world? What emotions are being carried out from us in the light of our radiation, eternally moving throughout space-time?

Perhaps it is fair to conclude what the Nobel playwright George Bernard Shaw so famously summarized:

> "Life is not about finding yourself.
> Life is about creating yourself."

Chapter 5

LIGHT, THOUGHT, AND HAPPINESS

"So I declare what I found in my research of the atoms: There is in fact no matter."

Max Planck
Nobel Prize, Physics

Light

At the basic level of our creation we are energy. Energy is constantly in motion. This is not conjecture; it is a well known aspect of Quantum Mechanics. We are indeed vibrational beings. In fact, all things both living and not, at the atomic threshold are constructed of the same stuff: quantum subatomic particles. These, in turn are simply energy oscillating at different frequencies. Light is the ultimate energy, it invigorates everything, and may well be the source of everything. Light is vibrating even in the darkest regions of space. Packets of light energy – photons – are radiating below the visual spectrum even in the blackest of blacks. Einstein proved that light is timeless. The photon's timepiece is stopped at zero. Light is pulsing throughout our universe and is everywhere present, it is therefore omnipresent.

Humans come equipped with vibrational frequency translators that work in conjunction with our brains to allow us to interpret the physical world around us. These vibrational translators are our eyes, nose, ears, and our sense of touch, taste, and emotions. Interestingly, our eyes allow us to interpret considerably less than even one percent of the information carried in light, yet the vast majority of us are highly visually oriented. Most of us think of light as only that narrow segment of the electromagnetic force that we can actually see; the visual spectrum.

Except for wavelength, all forms of light, whether visible to our eyes or emanating in a frequency we cannot see, such as radio waves, microwaves, infrared, ultraviolet, x-ray, or gamma ray, are identical. The electromagnetic spectrum includes all light energy from the slowest oscillations (long wave lengths), to the highest oscillations (short wave lengths). With current technology we can now detect light with wavelengths spanning thousands of kilometers to ones shorter than the width of an atomic nucleus.

With our natural unaided eyes we are only able to distinguish an infinitesimally small portion of the total light field. We see only the prism color band from red to violet. Higher vibrations than violet are known as ultra violet. Lower frequency vibrations than red are known as infrared. Our eyes allow us to observe frequency oscillations within that narrow field of light vibrating between 400 and 700 nanometers. (A nanometer is one billionth of a meter) Everything above and below the 400 to 700 nanometer oscillation spread is invisible to the naked eye.

To put the above information in some sense of scale, were the total light bandwidth laid out on a football field - stretching from goal post to goal post - the portion we could see with our natural eyes would represent less than the width of a grain of salt located somewhere in the middle of the field. All the vibrational frequencies we cannot see in the electromagnetic spectrum would be represented by the entire width of the football field from end zone to end zone, EXCEPT for that narrow slice the width of which is represented by a single speck of salt. Think on that for a moment. The implications are staggering.

There are two important points to the above illustration. First, we are generally most aware of those things we observe visually, and that's a very small percentage of what's going on around us. And secondly, the things we think of as solid and substantial are merely our brain's interpretation of an energy signature vibrating at a frequency we are able to sense.

So, the physical world is information inlaid within energy vibrating at different frequencies. The reason we do not see our surround as a giant matrix of energy patterns is that this energy is oscillating at light speed. In other words, things are moving way too fast for us to see. This can be a hard notion to wrap your mind around. But, consider for a moment what happens each time we go to the theatre. A film is merely a series of photographic still shots. There are literally gaps between each of the photographic frames, but the film is projected at a speed where our senses see only a continuous stream of information. Our physical world is like that. Everything is flickering in and out of existence at light speed. Our individual sense of continuity exists because of memory.

Literally, we perceive things by resonating with them. So, it follows that to know things of the world around us is to be "in synch," or in harmony with these things, or to be on the "same wave length." The human brain is a highly discriminating frequency analyzer. The brain, like our visual acuity, only perceives things within certain wave lengths; otherwise we would be swamped with masses of wave-frequency information. It has been demonstrated that wave-frequency patterns can hold incredible amounts of information. For example, I recently read in a scientific periodical that all the books in the U.S. Library of Congress (almost every book ever published in English), could fit within something about the size of a sugar cube were it constructed of simple wave-frequency patterns. Pretty amazing!

Energy and Bio-Photons

Dr. Fritz-Albert Popp, founder of the International Institute of Biophysics in Germany, began his original research by confirming the existence of biophotons. His research demonstrated that living things emit a unique energy signature. In other words, all of us are continually giving off light photons in a range not directly visible by the human eye. Of course we know that light is the carrier wave of all kinds of information, i.e.: radio waves, television signals, etc. So, as it turns out, we seem to be radiating information about ourselves at all times and under all conditions. In the case of humans and perhaps to some degree all other life forms, the vibrational frequency we radiate vacillates with the thoughts we are focused upon. And, the strength of our individual broadcast appears to be powered by the emotions we are feeling.

> **The vibrational frequency**
> **we radiate vacillates with the**
> **thoughts we are focused upon.**

The quotation at the head of this chapter, by Dr. Max Planck, the "father of quantum physics," continues:

> "All matter originates and exists
> only by a force, which the nucleus
> parts bring to vibrate and holds
> together the atoms as a tiny sun
> system. *Matter itself doesn't exist.*
> There exists only the invigorating
> invisible and immortal spirit
> as the source of material."

The message here, as repeatedly reviewed, is that matter is simply a form of dense energy. Energy has become form, sustains form, and can shift back out of form. Taking this one step further, it seems that energy that does not vibrate at a resonant frequency will not harmonize. Remember, thoughts are also energy vibrations. Thoughts are broadcast on a frequency that equates to the scale of their emotional set-point. Therefore, consistent with the quantum understanding that "like attracts like," we draw unto ourselves things that are synchronized or harmonious with the patterns of our thinking. Once again, from a slightly different point of view, we come to the conclusion that what we are and what we shall become depends upon the quality of our thoughts. We do not get what we say we want. We get what our mind is focused upon.

**What we are and what we
shall become depends upon
the quality of our thoughts.
We do not get what we say
we want. We get what our
mind is focused upon.**

Biology and Thought

Dr. Bruce Lipton, a cellular biologist who produced break-through studies on the cell membrane, develops in his book and subsequent DVD the "Biology of Belief," that only about 5 percent of our makeup is actually gene specific. This means that blaming our gene pool for our pet problems is largely a cop-out. Lipton provides solid evidence to demonstrate that it is our thought patterns (our beliefs), that switch the rest of the genes within our individual recipe sequence either on or off. Just because a given gene is resident in our DNA does not mean it will get turned on. In effect, Bruce Lipton says that from a biologist's perspective, virtually all that we are is encompassed by the medium of our habits of thinking. Seems like we've heard this before…

At this very moment each of us is the sum total of all the thoughts we have ever thought, said, and felt. In the words of James Allen, in his book, *As a Man Thinketh*, written in 1904:

> "What we are was designed and
> built by our own thoughts in our
> minds. If we nurture ignorant
> or evil thoughts, pain will soon
> follow. If our thoughts are healthy
> and beneficial, joy will follow
> us as surely as our shadows
> follow us on a sunny day."

Like Attracts Like

Thought always attracts what is like unto itself. We simply gravitate towards those things we mentally image that are powered with emotional content. The things we visualize with feeling are drawn unto us irrespective of our wants. That's because like attracts like.

Our words reveal the frequency of our thinkingness. Thus, to be wise requires we choose our words carefully. Whereas it may be true that visual imaging is more powerful than language, words definitely matter. They matter a great deal. Our words reinforce and generate continued thought chains. These, in turn, resonate and are responded to by things of like vibration. So it is that people who are alike attract each other. People who are not alike do not harmonize, because there is only a weak attraction going on, or none at all.

Perhaps you may be remembering about now, that you've heard it said, that when it comes to love relationships, opposites attract. And, of course all of us know situations where that seems to be true. There are times when a person is attracted to something that is not a part of their own character. This is usually representative of a personality not fully rounded, and that is perhaps a bit extreme in one area. For example, a very shy person might be attracted to an outspoken extrovert. One seeks the other because their individual extremes need balance. However, in broader terms, an understanding that like-attracts-like is a pervasive rule present throughout the universe. From a relationship point of view, the old adage, "birds of a feather flock together," is significantly more potent than the meme "opposites attract." (A meme – rhymes with "dream", is a rather new word meaning "a repeated unit of cultural transmission.") Therefore, if you want to know the vibrational set-point of the average of your thought patterns look at the people and the things you attract into your life.

If you want to know the vibrational set-point of the average of your thought patterns look at the people and the things you attract into your life.

Some of us are happy to understand this connection. Most are "put-off" by such an in-the-face explanation. Why? Because so many of us are not really satisfied with where we are in life, what we are doing, the quality of our relationships, the obsessions and possessions of our current reality. Yet, would it be honest of us to deny that we are continuously affecting those around us with the energy field we emanate? And, are we not able to see that we attract or repulse based upon the harmony or lack thereof, of the vibrational patterns we unknowingly emit? All living things appear to be attracted through the harmony of their vibrations. Even nonliving things may have this remarkable characteristic.

Entrained

I have a friend of over forty years, named Andrew, who is a well-known collector of antique clocks. Almost thirty years ago he insisted on buying a house from me that I had not even considered selling. He encouraged my wife and I to build a new home on a particularly scenic 40-acre piece of land we then owned. His underlying motive was to get our historic house with its 10-foot ceilings throughout, so he could hang his antique clocks, many of which were over 8-feet high. Eventually Andrew put around forty antique clocks in the house. It was an amazing experience to be there on the hour and hear the chimes, cuckoos, bells, and so forth. But the more amazing thing was the ticking of many of these mechanical masterpieces. They were synchronized! How on earth was this possible?

Andy wasn't sure why it happened, it just happened. That seemed truly bizarre at the time, but later I was to learn that mechanically ticking objects, operating at the same beat, will entrain, or harmonize, within a few days of their being left close to one another. Entrainment is a term in physics, which refers to oscillating systems that fall into a synchronous pattern. How does it work? No one knows for sure, but the process is everywhere about us, and it is common throughout the world.

Dr. Rupert Sheldrake, author, biochemist, and Fellow of the Royal Society at Cambridge, and a Fellow at Harvard, has expanded upon a theory of former Harvard psychologist William McDougall regarding morpho-genetic fields, called M-fields for short. Sheldrake believes that the theory of M-fields will explain the entrainment phenomenon. In his books and papers on the subject of morphic resonance he speaks to M-fields being invisible organizing structures that have a modifying effect on plants, animals, and human behavior. He suggests that these M-fields tune in, resonate, and regulate things of similar structure, in accordance with the harmonics emanating from an archetype or alpha dominant.

Sheldrake predicts that M-fields are the unexplained occurrence whereby learning something becomes easier once it's been learned before by someone else. This might also explain strange chemical behavior where some substances seem to actually "learn" to perform a task much more rapidly once the task has already been performed. This almost philosophical approach to chemistry and biology has a growing number of supporters, and sounds a lot like the earlier writings and concepts of the famous Swiss psychiatrist Carl Jung, who wrote extensively on psychological archetypes and the collective unconscious. Jung suggested that there existed some kind of field outside time and space that reverberated betwixt things of a similar nature. In a similar vein, during the 1950's and 1960's it was widely reported that monkey's learning things on one island somehow transferred that information to another population of monkeys on another island through a form of entrainment. This curious event resulted in the Hundredth Monkey Theory, a much debated theoretical concept.

Speaking of strange entrainment, Andrew, of the clocks above, shared with me quite recently that when he was suffering from a relatively serious illness. He would sit in his study for hours on end, listening to the various antique clocks ticking throughout the house. Eventually he would tune in to just one of the two dozen that are stationed throughout his new home. By allowing himself to be quietly entrained with one individual clock he dropped into an almost hypnotic, meditative state, which resulted in his becoming much more centered. Eventually he would arouse himself feeling refreshed and improved.

When Maureen passed away of cancer, we had been married 42 years. We had eight children together. Over the years we hosted twelve foreign-exchange students in our home. In addition we took in some "honorary" children for extended periods of time; friends of our children needing some assistance for one reason or another. An interesting phenomenon evolved as our five daughters' physiology matured. All five girls harmonized their menstrual cycles with Maureen's. Likewise, the same happened when other young women were living with us. No one tried to do this, as heaven knows it made things a little crazy around our home. Yet, the women of the household had clearly become entrained.

Maureen had three sisters, all close in age. I'm told that the same situation evolved in their household when she was a young woman. Many households have noted this curious phenomenon. It is not unique. Things harmonize, whether we're aware of it or not. All of us are routinely synching up with those around us. Marcus Aurelius, emperor of the Roman Empire a hundred and sixty years after Christ, summed up harmony this way:

> "He, who lives in harmony
> with himself, lives in harmony
> with the universe."

Quite powerful insight, made more so by its pure simplicity. In my experience there are relatively few people quite ready to grasp its greater significance. Consider for example, how easy it is to pick up the energy pattern of others. It is actually rather hard not to synchronize with someone you know. If they're down and complaining, it will only take a few minutes for you to be viewing things from a darker perspective. Thankfully, the opposite is also true. Take a moment and consider your own inner harmony. Are you easily caught up in the stressors of life? Are you aware of the impact something simple like the daily news has upon you? When a co-worker or family member is upset, have you looked within to observe how long it is before you are also feeling stressed?

Words Have Power

We express ourselves through words. The words we use often reveal what we're feeling; and what kind of balance, or lack of same, we're sensing about ourselves. Words may evoke new sensations. They can add to the stressors of our life, or spread a soothing balm. Words have power. Words affect us all. Here's a big clue about what's going on inside of you related to the words you choose. The words one uses to describe others, is a clear reflection of the way one feels about him or herself.

The words one uses to describe others, is a clear reflection of the way one feels about him or herself.

When our words are negative our thoughts are too. When our thoughts are negative, and charged with emotion, we are broadcasting that negativity out into the world. Thoughts broadcast with power begin the manifestation process. We are continually invoking the essence of our emotionally powered thoughts to manifest in our future experience. Think on that! Consider standing outside yourself and watching your words. Remember, your words reflect your thoughts!

Much of your thinkingness is simply a reflection on unfiltered input. Take the time to watch what's flowing into your brain. Pay attention. Awareness is the first step. Once you're aware, you can begin to make reasoned choices. Step outside of yourself, and observe your actions neutrally; you'll discover you're operating on auto-pilot almost all the time. Reflect on what emotions you routinely allow to become associated with various types of thought. Awake from your robotic responses. This is the way to happiness.

The take home message here is: Be aware. Observe neutrally. Recognize that when we're around others who are complaining, we'll shortly find ourselves thinking negative thoughts and complaining more. The low vibrational set-point of complainers is not where we want to be. Move yourself away from that environment. If you can't get away, start reframing the negative discourse of others into something more positive. People tend to stop their whining (or get mad and leave), when a listener presents a more upbeat, philosophical, point of view.

It is amazingly true that each of us is literally creating our life, moment-by-moment; through the thoughts we permit ourselves to dwell upon. It's important that we not forget that it is always the thoughts receiving our greatest attention that are well on their way to manifesting in our experience. Dr. Norman Vincent Peale once said:

> "Change your thoughts and
> you change your world."

Truer words are rarely spoken. Change your thoughts and your world will indeed change. It cannot be any other way. All of our lives are full of choices. Every moment of every day we are choosing. Each choice moves us up or down in vibrational resonance. When we avoid choosing, and default to others' decisions, positions, and conditions, we begin to lose our individuality and are even more susceptible to the mindset of others.

Each of us has the right to choose the life we want to live. If we avoid choosing, we diminish our options. Of course, not choosing is a choice too. One cannot reside in a happy state without marshalling mental resources, and paying close attention to the thoughts circulating in one's own mind. It is vital then that we become decisively proactive in order to lift our vibrational setpoint and be happy and at peace within.

Emotions

Most people ignore their own internal state, tending to blame the way they think and feel on others, circumstances, or on society at large. However, none of us can really afford to be indifferent to the energy level we emit. It will always have a corresponding effect on us personally and a gradient impact on those around us. This is absolutely true, whether you understand it or not, or even whether you believe it, or not.

Perhaps I can equate this elementary principal another way. For over 36 years I have been a private pilot and much of the time fairly active in flying my own aircraft. Of necessity, I understand something about the physics of flight, i.e. the basic forces of Weight, Lift, Drag, and Thrust. But, whether I understand the principals of flight or not, they are still true and they still matter. Consciously or not, I depend upon these principals, because they are what allow me to stay in the air. In my ignorance, I could assume that one flies because an engine turns a propeller that makes a plane go forward, after all it won't go without it. But there is a whole lot more to flying than a propeller; just as important is the shape of the wing, the weight and balance of the aircraft, the drag caused by the design of the entire structure.

Tens of thousands of commercial flights each day depend upon the application of the principals of flight, but the multiple millions of people on board rarely have a clue as to why things happen the way they do. On the other hand, without the paying customers the flights would be grounded. So, my point is that whether or not you understand that you are personally responsible for the vibe you put out, you are! You can learn about it, and benefit greatly by it, or you can deny it and lose the value that could be gained. But, even if you choose to deny it, who are you really kidding? Who will incur the greatest loss by your denial of the truth? ...That's right... you will.

Emotional Index

A number of psychologists, psychiatrists, and philosophical authors, have produced charts outlining a hierarchy of emotions. Overall, I prefer the one developed by the clinical psychiatrist and author, David Hawkins, M.D., Ph.D. He has performed exhaustive research in this area, and compiled some fascinating interpretations. The first few times I read his books, I only glanced at his *Map of the Scale of Consciousness*. It took me some time, but once I began to think deeply about what he was presenting, it was a real eye-opener.

Reflecting on his approach to consciousness, and comparing it with similar work done by others in his field, I began to outline my thoughts on a gradient scale of emotions. It struck me with great power that any one of us can quickly measure our personal evolution by simply giving thought to the scale of our feelings.

Any one of us can quickly measure our personal evolution by simply

**giving thought to the
scale of our feelings.**

After reflection, comparison, and consideration, I have fashioned a hierarchy of emotions entitled the "Emotional Index", which I believe is easy to follow and quickly illustrative of where a person's thoughts and feelings reside.

Beginning at the bottom of the column "Feelings in Play," work your way up and consider what tier best describes the thoughts that tend to predominate in your life. Look across the chart horizontally to discover the descriptive level of your present vibration. The Emotional Level reveals your vibrational set-point.

Reference the Emotional Index often, this gradient understanding allows you to more easily recognize the way your subconscious mind is coloring new incoming data. The emotional tier you are now experiencing reflects your subconscious self-view. These are the lens through which you view the world and the lens through which you view yourself.

Emotional Index

Feelings in Play	Emotional Level
Serene Happiness, Transcendence, Pure Love	Enlightenment
Harmony, Tranquility, Serenity	Peace
Deep Gratitude, Unconditional Love, Pure Kindness	Compassion
Worship, Reverence, Beauty all around, Love	Love
Elation, Ecstasy, Profound Pleasure	Joy
Forgiving, Merciful, Caring, Absolving	Forgiveness
Cheerful, Hopeful, Confident, Buoyant	Optimism
Believing, Reliant, Faith, Confident Dependence	Trust
Excitement, Enthusiastic, Infatuation, Obsession	Passion
Satisfied, Gratified, Ease, Pleasured	Content
Affirmed, Audacious, Validated, Daring	Courage
Self-important, Impatient, Arrogant, Scornful	Pride

Weary, Dull, Tedious, Monotony	Boredom
Distrustful, Doubting, Negative, Cynicism	Pessimism
Aggressive, Irritated, Frustrated, Hateful	Anger
Besieged, Inundated, Weighed down, Beleaguered	Overwhelmed
Fearful, Withdrawing, Jealous, Worry, Nervous, Angst	Anxiety
Depression, Misery, Gloom, Anguish	Despair
Shame, Blaming, Remorse, Humiliation	Guilt
Hopelessness, Weak, Wretched, Useless, Helpless	Powerless

When one devotes themselves to the process of thinking higher vibrational thoughts, each upward shift is accompanied by a significant increase in personal power and a corresponding rise in happiness.

Each upward shift is accompanied by a significant increase in personal power, and a corresponding rise in happiness.

According to Hawkins lifetime clinical research, living at the vibrational level of Love, indicates one will live in a happy state 89 percent of the time. Living in a state of Unconditional Love, will keep one in a state of happiness 96 percent of the time! (*Transcending Levels of Consciousness*, pg 30)

The vibrational level of Love indicates one will be in a happy state 89 percent of the time. Living in a state of Unconditional Love, will keep one in a state of happiness 96 percent of the time!

Ultimately everything we feel is driven by how we think about a given situation. Change the way you think about something - this most often means suspending judgment - and you change the way you feel. Sounds simple, but as we all know it takes serious intention, and careful attention to change any habit, particularly those we think of as addictions. Let's remember that mental habits are usually considered attitudes, but strongly held attitudes can also be full-on addictions. (More about this in later chapters) It takes great awareness, focused intention, and continued attention; before we can make the breakthrough from our more addictive thought processes to making the changes needed in our lives.

Goals

To become a more evolved individual we must design our lives with care. Written goals are particularly valuable because the process of writing requires we crystallize our thinking and choose our words carefully. To be happy we must become masters of our thinking. Writing out what we want in life allows us to be clear and to be positive.

> **To be a happy person we must become masters of our thinking. Writing out what we want in life allows us to be clear and to be positive.**

When writing out goals it is NOT a good idea to frame objectives in terms of what we don't want. Doing so sets our vibrational thought pattern at the wrong frequency. Yet, that is exactly what most of us do. For example, setting a goal to get out of debt actually attracts the very thing you do not want; debt. Still, the average person will tell you that their primary financial goal is to what? "Get out of debt!" No wonder it is rarely accomplished. And why is that? Because when our goal is to get out of debt we are still focused on debt rather than being centered on prosperity. We are vibrating in resonance with debt, not prosperity. Financial goals should be set forth in such a way that one is inviting abundance and wealth. Remember, we want to vibrate and resonate with what we DO want, not with the lack of what we want.

When thinking of goal-setting, a great many of us immediately think in terms of financial issues. Why? Generally it's because we secretly believe that with greater power to do things, we'll have the funds to fix what needs fixing and the resources to do what we really want. That's what we used to call the "Rockefeller Approach"...got a problem...throw money at it. The real quandary is we don't really know what we really want. Yet, we secretly believe that money will fix whatever it is that needs fixing, thus we fixate on money. It becomes our primary ambition.

Depressive States

When one takes the time to deeply reflect on life's objectives, one will usually wake up to the realization that the most important thing for each one of us is to live with a positive energetic sense of joy and happiness. And yet, we can have those feelings this very minute. If we will enthusiastically engage in choosing higher vibrating thoughts, life improves. When we are happy we are automatically charged with positive energy. When we are despondent, nothing seems quite worth doing. Depression is largely a habitual pattern of thinking. It's real enough, but we are capable of climbing out of this emotional abyss. What we rarely recognize about our depressive states of mind is that we are broadcasting the very thoughts that evoke the dark emotional experience we are having.

Depression is a vibrational frequency that attracts the very opposite of what we really want. Anti-depressives will never get us where we want to be. They are simply a mechanism to cover up the symptoms of the underlying problem. Yes, sometimes the symptoms are so powerful we need a break just to get our heads around a different way of being, but taking that break comes at a cost. Drugs, particularly those that are effective, are highly addictive. Real progress only comes as we reach for higher thoughts.

Thoughts create the reality we will be experiencing. When we take control of the words to which we give voice, and we are specific with our INTENTIONS and careful about that to which we give our ATTENTION, we will automatically draw to ourselves the essence of the words we have chosen. This is vibrational harmony. Can you see why it is so important that we be positive and optimistic? We would be wise to keep reminding ourselves that our thoughts equal our point of attraction.

> **We would be wise to keep reminding ourselves that our thoughts equal our point of attraction.**

Listen to your words. They do indeed reveal your thoughts. It is usually quite a wake-up call when first we focus on listening to our own chatter. Once we really get it, we're likely to become embarrassed at many of the things we've retched up and broadcast without thinking in the past. The message here is to work on your words and consider them carefully, as they make a real difference in our state of mind. It would be intelligent of us to become wordsmiths of happy expressions whilst we perform surgery on our former vocabulary.

One other point we might want to consider at this point: In my world view nothing is purely one thing or another. The happenings around us may actually reveal more to us, about us, than what is obvious at first blush. By this I mean, that the experiences of our world have multiple dimensions, and everything about you has multiple aspects. In other words, everything has physical, mental, emotional, and spiritual implications. Everything. This is a deep concept which we will not pursue at this point, but it may be something you'd benefit by considering.

> **Everything has physical, mental, emotional, and spiritual implications. Everything.**

It's All Thought

Appreciation, gratitude, and thankfulness, are all essentially the same emotion. It seems that this feeling of positive reception is the highest vibrational match to creation. In Chapter 4, we reviewed Masaru Emoto's research on water, learning that the most beautiful microscopic reflections in water came in response to the energy imprints of gratitude and love. Expressions of thankfulness, appreciation, and gratitude produce powerful energy. This is the energy you want to permeate your space. It is the source of a new life paradigm where life is wonderful and happiness is able to grow and mature. This particular emotional vibration is the ground floor for all the good stuff we want to have, experience, and become a part of. Unless we groom and evolve an attitude of thankfulness we cannot rise to a place of lasting happiness. Learn to focus on gratitude. Being thankful for everything, as it is and as it may become, is life changing. Make time for gratitude, it will make all the difference. Gratitude reigns supreme. Love is the power that flows out of gratitude.

> **Gratitude reigns supreme.**
> **Love is the power that**
> **flows out of gratitude.**

As we develop new habits of thought, keep in mind that what we predominantly feel will ultimately manifest in our experience. So once again, watch your thoughts. It truly is all about thought! Thought undergirds emotion. Together they accelerate manifestation.

If we're frequently tired and rarely enthused about things, life is no fun. If we're excited, enthusiastic, and filled with love and happiness, what could be better? We are literally designed to enjoy life; the ups and the downs, the predictable and the unpredictable. Life is a bit like a roller coaster; it's the thrill of the ride not the end of the ride that you are wanting. Wouldn't it be boring if life was always a flat, uneventful ride? Enjoy the journey regardless of the ups and downs. The ups are the fun; the downs are our opportunity for personal growth and development. Be open to life. Be excited about life. Be eager to learn and grow. Optimism promotes a vibration of fervor and enthusiasm. What we eventually come to realize is that what we really want from life is great energy, joy, and an abundance of love. That's real happiness.

> **What we really want from**
> **life is great energy, joy,**
> **and an abundance of love.**
> **That's real happiness.**

Happiness is the whole end and aim of life. Happiness breeds more happiness as it builds inner strength. When we are gently at peace and in a happy state, we are vibrating at a high frequency. Good feelings reinforce us. When we're happy, we can hardly fail. Negative feelings are expressed through lower vibration and low energy. Good feelings are of a higher vibration, which in turn promotes higher energy for life.

Repressing negative feelings, or covering them up and denying they exist, is not the same as consciously deciding to not act on negative feelings. Usually repressed emotions will end up being expressed in some form. When we are feeling burned out and bummed out, insecure, angry, vulnerable, or jealous (all expressions of fear), we need to recognize these sensations for what they are. It starts with awareness; if we're not awake to what is going on we simply cannot address the needs of the moment. Once we're in a place where we are observing our own programming we'll be able to catch ourselves before we react. As we learn to do this we are free to choose a response from a place of higher vibration.

In my experience, the best response to inappropriate action or poor behavior on the part of another is limited external reaction. Those engaged in negative behavior subconsciously push for an emotional reaction. They rarely understand this, and would probably deny it, but that's the way it is. When someone is highly agitated, he or she may subconsciously be seeking an overreaction, or at least an equally bad response to their own current emotional set-point. The ego believes an overreaction by the other party will justify one's own inappropriate actions and keep the anger and victimhood game in play. In Chapter 10 we review the ego, our best friend and worse enemy. For now, let's just say that without sincere and legitimate humility we are unable to rise above ego demands, and find a space of grace, where peace, beauty, and happiness reside.

When a person is being emotionally, psychologically, or mentally abused, but rises above their own ego's desire to respond with anger, they hold on to a higher vibrational level, thereby protecting themselves from spiraling down to the negative mindset it requires to "get even." The negative energy put in play by the offending person will dissipate much more quickly this way. Many people, when they feel they've been attacked or abused in some way, will give back anger for anger; when this happens conflicts escalate.

Recognize that anger, fear, and all their associated emotions are horribly destructive. To respond to negativity with negativity will almost always hurt us personally. Emotionally destructive feelings generate a cascade of negative low vibrations, which in turn attract more negativity. General mindset negativity, coupled with emotionally destructive feelings, if sustained over time, will spawn a myriad of emotional and psychological problems. If these are not dealt with satisfactorily, they will in turn progress to manifesting themselves in our bodies. Thoughts matter!

Quit Complaining

For quite some time a certain field of psychology taught that conflicted individuals should openly express negative emotions. Many were encouraged to find someplace safe to yell and scream in order to get their negative feelings out. Perhaps for someone so out-of-touch with their emotions that they can no longer feel anything, this process might represent a step up, but for the vast majority of us, this is an extremely poor solution to dealing with negative influence.

Much research has been compiled to empirically demonstrate what enlightened sources have taught all along. Blasting negativity out into the world makes things worse. Spewing out negative vibrations attracts more of the same right back to us. What's worse, these kinds of low vibration exercises begin to express themselves in our character as habit patterns. Mental habit patterns such as these are not life sustaining. They are instead, literally life threatening. Yelling and screaming might work in the short term to help someone break out of apathy, but to incorporate this kind of habit pattern in one's life is to flirt with real self-destruction. What we really want is the higher vibrations of increased energy, love, and happiness.

Another observation: When we spend much time defining what we like and don't like, we are quietly imposing limits on our happiness. On the surface this seems wrong, however we are best served when we learn to let go and become more flexible. It helps to look at old experiences in new ways. It's valuable to explore negative experiences and look for something good about them. Leave the stuff you don't like behind, and focus on the things for which you are grateful. Challenge yourself to discover good. Something good is always there.

Perhaps the most important single action that most people would immediately benefit from would be to quit complaining.

> **Perhaps the most important single action that most people would immediately benefit from would be to quit complaining.**

To do this requires we reduce our focus on what is wrong, and pay closer heed to what is going well. To move towards greater happiness, we need to chart a better course. We need to take the high road. We commit ourselves to leaving the negative, nasty, hurtful, thoughts behind, and rise up to a place of gratitude. Find something to be thankful for and focus on that. Work at being more courteous and kind even when you don't want to. Learn to check yourself, most especially when you don't want to. Learn to enjoy experiences and quit branding them. Live! Love! Be renewed! It's all up to you. Decide to be different. Dare to be happy! It's your choice.

Choose Your Feelings

Can you remember a time when you felt confident and strong? Do you remember a single event? Yes? Then focus on that. Focus on feeling good about yourself. Concentrate on feelings of self-worth. Only a few minutes of flowing focused energy on this single idea can make a world of difference. Be open. Learn to forgive; it is the first and most important step before you can know peace. Relax, laugh, and move forward. By being open to new ways of viewing life's struggles, by forgiving and just letting go, we are sending a signal to our emotional control center to reset our happiness index. We are also literally sending a signal (our immediate vibrational signature), out and into the universe that says, in effect; we want new results.

To move on and rise to higher places of being, each of us must eventually face our stored emotionally-conflicted memories. To heal suppressed emotions and step up to a higher way of being, we must call them up and face them down. Ultimately we need to give those ugly, difficult, memories, a new vibrational frequency. We can do this. Of course, it's uncomfortable the first few times we reflect on old injuries. So what? It's absolutely worth it. Can you see why we need to proactively set ourselves free of their lower vibrational harmonics? All of us are stuck somewhere, the key is to identify these energy-sucking negative feelings and get them to a place of higher vibration.

Changing the way we view old experiences, or changing the lenses through which we view our world, is not the same as being naively optimistic. We are not trying to generate some kind of artificially pleasant spin to offset prior hurtful situations. We simply need to address those mental poisons that are interfering with our energy and purge ourselves of their negative influence. The hurtful, miserable, thoughts and feelings that hide out just below our conscious mind need to be addressed and put in perspective.

Set time aside in a safe place and begin to allow damaging feelings of the past to float up to the surface. Experience them once more from your newly elevated place of being, and recognize that they only have the power to hurt and make you afraid, IF you continue to allow them to do so. What our old thinking has done, our new thinking can undo. Lifelong habits of poor - lower vibrational - thought can be changed. We can deliberately rework prior wrong thinking and neutralize its emotional impact.

To continue to think and feel in the same old negative ways will not facilitate positive change. Instead, we must specifically and actively pursue a new course of right thought. Remember the old adage credited to Einstein? "The definition of insanity is doing things the same way over and over again and expecting different results." Well, we want better results! Don't we? Yes of course we do. Therefore we must rise to doing things from a new perspective of thought.

Luckily, all of us can pursue our own mental and emotional reconstruction project right in the privacy of our own sanctuary - inside our head. Once we realize how empowered we can really feel as we rise above the myriad stored vibrations of fear, insecurity, and loathing, we'll want to go through this purification process again and again. Anyone can become more open, forgiving, relaxed, and genuinely happy. The only question is will you do the work? Or, will your old habit patterns kick in allowing you to enjoy learning new things but putting the work off for some future time? The latter choice usually results in our forgetting our intention to change, and then settling back into our old familiar comfort zone. But wait a minute: Is it really all that comfortable there? If so, why read about how to enhance your happiness?

Interrupt your soap opera. It may help to remember that the drama is really about what is going on inside your head. Change your reaction, or perhaps better yet, don't react at all. Let life flow without getting hooked into an emotional jag. Let your issues go. Let them move right through you. Do not allow the negative stuff to stick. Rise above it. Love will eventually trump hate. After all, hate is simply fear, and love can neutralize fear. So, begin right now to cleanse yourself of long-held fears. Dare to love. Most of all, dare to love even you!

The process goes like this: Release (let go of harmful thoughts), Cleanse (clean up old habits of thinking), invest the quiet time to examine your conflicted memories, and put a better spin on the stored frequency patterns of old hurts. Stay centered and let the old negative vibrations go. Blow the dams of your locked-in emotions. Let your joy rise, and feel the energy surge. Free your soul.

1 Release, let go of harmful thoughts;
2 Cleanse, clean up old habits of thinking;
3 Invest time to examine your conflicted memories;
4 Find a higher vibration for the stored patterns of old hurts;
5 Stay centered and allow lower vibrations to dissipate; and
6 Let joy rise and feel the energy surge.

Take the time right this minute to increase your freedom, and allow yourself more of that delicious enthusiasm to bubble up and flow outward. Low energy equals low enjoyment. Change it. Reach for a higher frequency. Reach for a stronger, more loving vibration. Free yourself from old self-defeating thought patterns. Yes, that's right: Just do it! Do it now!

Deliberately choose thoughts so you'll feel better right this moment. Keep in mind that your focus causes you to vibrate, which in turn represents your point of attraction. Choose the words you think and say wisely. Consider where your words might resonate on the Emotional Index. Reach for a higher vibration.

Practice smiling. If that's not easy, it should speak loudly to you. Yes, it is important. Don't ignore it. Practice smiling. Do it every chance you get. Do it in the mirror until you change your look. Focus on being playful, on laughing, on having fun. Make others happy along the way. Remember, emotions are vibrational, behind and underlying your feelings, "It's All Thought!"

The quotation, "As a man thinketh in his heart, so is he," is a clear statement that includes every aspect of our lives. It is so encompassing as to include every element and condition, every feeling and circumstance. With this in mind, we should remember that every thought produces a vibration, and every vibration attracts those things in harmony with it.

Every thought produces a vibration, and every vibration attracts those things in harmony with it.

Take the time right now to cast new light on the darkness of old hurts. Inject a higher vibration into the uncomfortable memories that are stored in you; those that have locked-in low energy patterns. Decide to live in a place of joy - right now. Take steps this very moment to make your world a happier place. Smile. Smile bigger. Grin. Laugh. Happiness is your choice. It always has been. It's time to take action. Do it now.

It's All *Thought!*

Section II
EXPANDING UNDERSTANDING

Chapter 6

OUR CULTURAL LENS

Happiness does not depend on
outward things, but on the way we
see them.

Leo Tolstoy

What Lenses?

Our cultural lenses form the unconscious belief system through which we view our reality. All of us are wearing these lenses, whether we know it or not. Every experience, every sensory input, and all incoming information, is first filtered and compared through the lenses of our prejudice. These are the assumptions through which we know our world. The entire process is virtually unconscious, yet we live and breathe these embedded beliefs, and all of our thinking and interaction is a reflection of them.

Symbolism is a construct of cultural lens. All of us attach emotional meaning to symbols. We rarely know we're doing it, but we frequently respond to symbols, making decisions based almost entirely on the emotional imprint we have previously infused into a given sign, symbol, or icon. Symbolism is prevalent in Biblical text, and in the earliest known records of all civilizations and societies. At first blush, it seems that the inference of one thing through the presentation of another is counter-intuitive to modern western thought. Or is it?

When Disney studios used the "Circle of Life" motif in *The Lion King* they did so by using a theme we could all recognize and with which we could individually identify. The circular image of birth, youth, maturity, and death is a pattern that all of humanity comes to understand. Closely connected is the ancient theme of innocence to experience. This is the story of the life-path from a lack of knowledge and sophistication up to a position of insight and wisdom. The archetype (an ideal example of a type) of this repeated thesis is the chronicle of Adam and Eve in the Garden of Eden. It is interesting to note that the presentation of these two themes, Innocence to Experience, and the Circle of Life, are invariably linked in the most important of mankind's history, legends, and mythologies. For many of us, these two concepts were first introduced in the biblical story found in the Book of Genesis.

Pre-existing Beliefs

It is certain that all of us view the world through our own cultural lens. It's as if all of us are wearing tinted glasses that shade and color what we see through the knowledge we've gained thus far. Our mind constructs everything we observe through any and all of our senses by first reflecting it through the mirror of our memory. It then filters and amends all of our thoughts, feelings, and experiences in conjunction with our pre-existing political, social, scientific, and religious predispositions.

> **Our mind views everything through the mirror of our memory. It then filters and shades all of our thoughts, feelings, and experiences, through our pre-existing political, social, scientific, and religious predispositions.**

Things are never quite as they seem, but generally speaking, our understanding of events and things tend to work for us in our particular cultural setting. We usually think of our immediate response to new things as "logical" or "common sense." But common sense can, and frequently does, elicit a much different reaction depending on one's cultural bias. In the study of almost anything, it is important to step outside our cultural bias and attempt to view things from a neutral point of view. Our thinking is so colored by our prior experiences, and our subconscious belief system, that it makes dropping our data filters quite difficult.

As a general rule, people are unfamiliar with the nature and creative power of their own thoughts. Yet, it is within our own subconscious mind that we develop the thought programs which determine our levels of happiness.

> **It is within our subconscious mind that we develop the thought programs which determine our levels of happiness.**

We are only conscious of a small amount of the new incoming information captured by our brain. As a result, our subconscious generally decides how we react to new circumstances, situations, opportunities, and threats. The truth about truth is that we rarely know what the truth of any given situation really is. It can come as quite a shock when we first grasp how far we are removed from the greater reality of our existence. Of course, most people don't bother to pursue truth to any great degree, because they would rather stay in what they believe is the safe zone...that place of denial...that place where we say in effect: "Don't tell me because I don't want to know," or perhaps for some of us, "Don't tell me because I already know."

The Human Brain

How we routinely respond to new information is the result of our habits of thought. So, if we aren't really considering what is going on, or in other words, if we are really not very aware, we automatically relegate our life choices via our preexisting habits of thought. As a result, "We'll always get what we've always got."

According to Dr. Joe Dispenza, author of *Evolve Your Brain: The Science of Changing Your Mind*:

> "The human brain processes about
> 400 billion bits of information
> per second, but only integrates
> 2,000 bits per second."

Just stop and think about this for a moment: 400,000,000,000 versus 2,000. It's an incredible divergence! What might we be able to do by using a larger amount of the information we are already processing? The thought boggles the mind. But some will say, what about our physical capacity? Are we able to use, or even comprehend, the vast amount of information to which we are exposed? Good question.

The late astrophysicist Carl Sagan once observed that man was incapable of comprehending something relatively simple, like the atoms in a single grain of salt. He was operating on the information and scientific belief system of his day; something more than thirty years ago. However, recent discoveries have shown that the brain is considerably more robust, and has dramatically greater computational power, than had been previously believed.

The human brain fires continually through some 100 billion neurons (brain cells), and 60 trillion synapses. Synapses are the connections where messages are correlated to other thoughts, memories, or feelings. These connections group to form neural networks of associated thought. Any time we respond to outside stimuli, or experience emotion, call up a memory, or think a new thought, new synapses are developed and strengthened. But, the fact that there are more neurons and synapses than previously believed is trumped by new evidence concerning glial cells. Glial cells are non-neuronical cells that provide nourishment to neurons and assist in signaling transmission.

There are more glial cells than neurons within our brain, and in other places throughout the body, where neurons have been discovered. Scientists just now are recognizing the importance of glial cells in the overall thinking process. In the past these cells were considered essentially useless, extra material that served primarily as insulation to neurons. The number of possible mental connections is so incredibly large that neuroscientists now suggest that the human brain is capable of more information transfer, and neural network interactions, than the total number of subatomic particles in the known universe!

The human brain is so potentially advanced that it is capable of more information transfer, and neural network interactions, than the total number of subatomic particles in the known universe.

Awake and Aware

We literally have a universe of thought potential within our minds. The latest scientific data confirms the brain's incredible capacity to hold and process information; nonetheless we have extremely aggressive mental filters in place. If Dr. Dispenza is right, then it appears that we are screening out almost all of the new information coming to us. So what can we do to change the programs running in our brains in order to allow us to utilize more of the information to which we are continually exposed? The simple answer is that we must first recognize the extent of our conditioning. We need to wake up. We need to be aware. We need to grasp what's really going on. Clear awareness requires we become a neutral observer.

Few people are aware of their cultural conditioning, and therefore are oblivious to the need for change. To begin with, it is important to recognize that everything we perceive in the world of our reality has been processed through the filter of our consciousness, or perhaps more correctly, our subconscious. How this takes place is determined primarily by the mind's own structure.

The mind's structure is largely an effect of our previous experiences, including all the input from well-meaning family and friends, most of which arrived well before we were old enough to challenge or consider it. Childhood experiences are critical to the emotional and intellectual development of a child. During the first six years of a child's life at least 75 percent of their brain growth is completed. (That's a widely reported number at the websites of several universities.) So, how much deep thought were you giving to your subconscious programming at age six?

It appears we have good reason to suppose that by about six years old each of us have evolved a working paradigm, or ideal model, of how we view the world. Therefore, our internal auto-pilot (our subliminal operating instructions), is based upon assumptions and conclusions formed early on and without the benefit of critical thinking. These mental assumptions, which are essentially the programs that govern the vast majority of thinking, emotional responses, and physical and mental health, are rarely examined by us.

Subliminal operating instructions steer us through virtually all of our life choices without our ever knowing these underlying programs exist. It seems we're operating on autopilot about 99 percent of the time. Well-meaning "Auto" is filtering out virtually everything that does not agree with its currently understood directives. No matter our huge potential for processing information, our subconscious is screening out the new input – information that could possibly be used to improve us and the world around us. This is why we have such a shortfall of new information integration.

If the only things we allow in are things that do not threaten us or disagree with our pre-existing programs how can we truly learn new stuff? How can we take big steps up? How can we really grow? The answer is to change. Really? Well, yes, but change isn't easy, especially if it's about the way we think. So, how do we learn to think differently if we're processing that very thinking through the programs that we wish to improve? It's a bit of a conundrum. Yet, change is the answer. But, we've really got to want it. We've got to pony up the horsepower and focus, focus, focus. We must dedicate ourselves to be honest and clear with ourselves and our own subliminal instructions. We must truly desire to change. We must intend it. Then we must give it constant attention.

Symbols

As pointed out earlier, we tend to store concentrated bits of information in the form of symbols. The process of conveying packets of information via a single symbol is very much alive in the world. Reflect for a moment on a few icons like Coca-Cola, UPS, Nike, BMW, Fed Ex, and the like. Each of these companies' logos means something specific to us. There are thousands of symbols like these with which we are familiar. Each time we are confronted with one, our minds' eye is stimulated with some mix of factual information and emotional response.

Think for a moment about your emotional reaction to the Nazi Swastika. How about the Christian Cross, the Star of David, the Hammer and Sickle of the old Soviet Union, or the Crescent Moon of Islam? What is your logical reaction, and emotional response to the American flag? The longer you reflect on any of these symbols, the more information flows into your mind.

The same symbol may evoke a very different response depending on its setting. For instance, a small rendering of a polo pony on a garment a century ago would have carried a very different significance that it does today. The American eagle was formerly a symbol of the conquering Roman Legions. Later Nazi Germany flew the eagle flag. I suspect that your response to the American eagle was likely modified when you considered its Roman influence. And, if you are old enough to have been deeply moved by World War II, your visceral response to the German eagle notation would surely have sobered your initial feelings regarding eagle symbology.

A person's response to any given symbol tends to modify over time. Therefore, the interpretation of a given symbol's meaning is a time-sensitive issue. Winston Churchill's famous dictum, that "If you aren't a Liberal in your twenties, you haven't got a heart, and if you're not a Conservative by your forties, you haven't got a brain," is a catchy phrase that may not be true for many, but it quickly makes the point that people tend to shift their philosophical positions over time. The stylized donkey that represents the Democratic Party versus the elephant of the Republican Party are symbols easily recognized by any American of voting age, but they surely elicit different responses from different people.

Let's consider a cultural lens you probably were not aware you were wearing. In our age and our culture, the Satan-Serpent association is strong because of our pervasive familiarity with the Garden of Eden story. This is generally true whether or not you consider yourself religious. Viewed through our cultural eyes the serpent is generally bad; its association negative. This was not the cultural linkage of the ancient world.

There is a different, yet legitimate, way of viewing serpent symbology even within the context of one's own religious pre-disposition. Now, STOP reading for a moment and consider: If you had a strange or slightly uncomfortable feeling reading the statement "...within the context of one's own religious predispo-sition," it is a clear validation that your mental filters are firmly in place and you really don't want new input on this subject. Your brain will now tell you it's really not important for you to learn about something like this, and it has nothing to do with the sub-ject of this book.

Be truthful with yourself. Are you mentally and emotionally willing to consider other possibilities with your preconceived no-tions? For example, will you explore something that might come up against your religious filters? Can you handle information that may ruffle your feathers, so to speak? Are you able to assume a mental posture of neutrality and allow yourself to consider new points of view? Will you reconsider your mental paradigm around something like serpent symbology?

Taboos

Generally speaking, most of us are so entrenched in our cultural taboos that we are largely incapable of approaching subjects where we have some form of deep-seated emotionally attached belief. So, what are beliefs anyway? Beliefs arise from thought. Beliefs are thoughts that we have thought upon long enough, or were embedded early on enough, that we accept them as truth.

Beliefs arise from thought.
Beliefs are thoughts that
we have thought upon long
enough, or were embedded

**early on enough, that we
accept them as truth.**

That's something to consider carefully because it is only through new knowledge and the attention we pay to it, that our cultural lenses may be adjusted. There is no need to be cynical about currently accepted truth. We only need to tell ourselves that we are interested and willing to observe new information. Tell ourselves we love gaining new insight and exploring new ways of thinking. Affirm to ourselves that we like to learn.

Serpent Symbology

The story that follows is a historical download of information with which you are likely, unfamiliar. It is included in order to dramatize that you are unconsciously wearing a specific cultural lens. **IF THIS DIGRESSION IS UNINTERESTING skip to the end of this chapter and read the Conclusion before moving on.** To learn how the ancients approached the serpent subject, and WHY, you'll need to set your "common sense" aside as it is so thoroughly shaped by cultural bias. Now, let's explore this idea.

Mesopotamia is the place archeologists refer to as the "Cradle of Civilization." It is here that the serpent motif was first recognized as representative of the Creator; the god of life. Throughout the ancient world, in cultures around the globe, another name for the creator-god was the rain god. All things require water to live and this was well understood from the earliest times. Rain was the ultimate source of water. The serpent was associated with rain for reasons set forth below, but the serpent was even more widely associated with healing, resurrection, and eternal life. The serpent was cross-culturally understood as the primary icon of godly power, and it also represented the concepts of wisdom and salvation.

As long as humanity has kept records, serpents were used as emblems of the power of God. In ancient times, and as widespread and diverse as Australia, China, Japan, Mexico, Australia, New Zealand, Babylonia, Sumeria, Egypt, India, and Central America, serpents were viewed as symbolic of god, and particularly associated with both healing and resurrection. To this day, serpents, and flying serpents (dragons), signify divine heritage and royalty in many Asian countries, while in the west serpent symbology continues to represent wisdom, knowledge, and the healing arts. As a point of fact, the symbol of the American Medical Association, the Caduceus, shows twin serpents coiled around a physician's staff.

The serpent's association with healing and resurrection is widely believed to be a consequence of the snake's "apparent" ability to regenerate itself and come back to life. Snakes occasionally become dormant, looking very much dead. They lay dull and immobile for a period of time and then are able to slough off their dry old skin and emerge looking like an entirely new snake. This ability to periodically replace its entire body at a single setting without bleeding or infection is remarkable. When it accomplishes this miraculous feat the serpent frees itself from ticks, scars, and blemishes of all kinds. Such ability is beyond the power of humanity. This early connection between the serpent and healing and the concepts of resurrection and rebirth became a permanent facet of serpent worship.

Archaeologists refer to the area of Mexico, Belize, Guatemala, El Salvador, and Honduras as Mesoamerica. The moniker Mesoamerica also refers to a time frame prior to the arrival of Europeans to the Americas. Mesoamerica is the geographical area where the oldest and most advanced civilizations in the western hemisphere developed. It is here that serpent typology represented Quetzalcoatl, the Aztec name for the Mayan Kukulcan, the creator god (god of rain), and giver of resurrection. The latter half of the title-name Quetzalcoatl, or "coatl," is the Aztec word for serpent.

The great civilizations of Mesoamerica include the Olmeca, Mayan, Zapotec, Toltec, Teotihuacanos, Mixtec, Totonacs, Otomis, Huastecs, and the Aztec. All of these high civilizations were literate and quite advanced in mathematics, astronomy, medicine, etc. All revered the serpent as a symbol of god, or as a representation of the power of god.

On opposite sides of the world the apparent process by which these societies arrived at their common symbolism with the Creator was apparently the same. Water is the source of all life. Clean fresh water was an everyday concern of the Ancients everywhere. Seeds would not sprout and life could not be sustained without clean life-giving water. The undulating body of a snake is symbolic of a riverbed. A riverbed is never straight. It always undulates, usually in a long slow curving fashion. A mirror image of the curving riverbed, or the body of a snake, is seen in the Milky Way, and the constellation of Draco, found in the Northern night sky. (The word Draco is Greek for serpent.) The heavens are symbolic of the residence of God. It is from the sky that water comes, which is the source of all life, and from which the rivers fill. Thus, serpent symbology signified the god of rain, the creator god, and the giver of life.

The Greek word *geras* (the root of geriatrics), denotes the cast-off skin as in the example of a serpent's rejuvenation. Since the snake's old skin is sloughed off in one piece it is reflective of casting off the old body and taking on a new one. This remarkable phenomenon was seen as evidence of the possibility for the rebirth of humankind. There are additional serpent symbologies with curious links to the mesmerizing stare of the snake, its forked tongue, the chevrons frequently displayed on its scales, the healing value of potions made from the venom, and more. But, ultimately the serpent represented the creation of life, healing, resurrection and eternal life. These three concepts are perhaps the most powerful godly associations there could possibly be.

In Egypt, the main feature of the Pharaoh's crown was a serpent's head. The historic scepter of Pharaohic authority for all of ancient Egypt was a bronze serpent staff. It was in ancient Egypt that the biblical Moses threw down his rod, which then became a serpent. The symbology of this act could not have been lost on the Pharaoh or his court, and in fact, the Bible records that the King's counselors replicated this mysterious feat. Due to the power believed to be represented by the serpent on the crown of Pharaoh, the transformation of a rod into a serpent was a direct assault on Egyptian beliefs.

We learn from several biblical passages that Moses had a remarkable serpent staff. This serpent staff was so imbued with power that at least 500 years after the Exodus, the people of Judah were still burning incense to it! (II Kings 3-4). Hezekiah, a famous and powerful king of Judah, living many hundreds of years after Moses, referred to the staff as Nehushtan. Nehushtan means brass or bronze serpent. The Egyptian correlation surely provides insight as to why Moses carried a bronze staff fashioned as a serpent. Not only was it the symbol of power for the Egyptians, but it also held that same reverence with the ancient Jews.

It should be remembered that Moses was born in Egypt, and grew up in the royal household of Pharaoh. In the New Testament of the Bible, Acts 7:22 states, "And Moses was educated in all the learning of the Egyptians." The Israelites, who escaped Egypt with Moses in the exodus, had been reared in Egyptian culture. Although the "children of Israel" may have lived as a unique people within Egypt, the family lineage had been there for at least 200 years. Traditional dating claims 430 years, but for several reasons, Biblical scholars tend to put the actual time spent in Egypt as something over 200 years. Either way, the families who were descended through the Old Testament patriarch Jacob (whose title-name was Israel), were in Egypt a very long time, and must have become, in all practical ways, Egyptians themselves. Therefore the Israelites had to be intimately familiar with serpent symbology, just as a number of biblical verses demonstrate.

It is in the first five books of the Old Testament, known by the Hebrews as "Torah," or in Greek as the "Pentateuch," where the most ancient of biblical writings refer to serpents. Significant passages include the serpent in the Garden of Eden tempting Eve (Genesis, Chapter 3); Jacob's blessing on his son, Dan, where he says that Dan would be a "serpent by the way" (Genesis 49:17); the miraculous sign given to Moses and Aaron when their rods are turned into serpents (Exodus, Chapters 4 and 7); the fiery serpents who bite the children of Israel, and the bronze serpent, held on high, that brings them healing (Numbers 21).

When Aaron threw his rod down before Pharaoh, it became a snake. When Moses set the plagues upon Egypt, he did so my stretching forth his serpent-rod. When Moses parted the sea for the passage of his people, he raised this powerful serpent scepter, his icon of power. In the wilderness Moses struck a rock with the same rod to bring forth water so that the children of Israel might live. The serpent-scepter was considered so sacred that it was stored in the Ark of the Covenant, the most prized possession of the Israelites. As previously noted, the serpent rod of Moses became so revered that a full five hundred years after his death, the Jews at Jerusalem were burning incense to it. (II Kings 3-4)

Possibly the most powerful use of serpent imagery in the Scriptures reads: "As Moses lifted up the serpent in the wilderness, even so must the Son of Man be lifted up, so that whoever believes in Him will have eternal life." (John 3:14-15) Here we see serpent symbology associated directly with Christ and eternal life.

In Exodus 32:19-23, Moses condemned Aaron for making a golden image of the Egyptian goddess Hathor, or perhaps the image was intended to represent the Canaanite Baal. Yet, Moses himself produced a brass image of the most ancient religious icon, the serpent, and then held it before the people as an agent of healing and a foreshadowing, or type, and symbol of the resurrection. (See also John 3:14-15). Notwithstanding, the Garden of Eden story and our western interpretation, in the earliest of the Hebrew Scriptures, the snake commanded reverence and loyalty.

In ancient Egypt, all the great crowns worn by the divine Pharaoh included the serpent's head. No matter which crown was being worn - the blue crown, the informal crown, the great double red, or the white crown - we find the snake icon mounted in front, directly over the forehead. The serpent was always there, a reflection of the Pharaoh's linkage to God.

Imhotep, meaning the "Serpent Holder," was the world's first named architect. Imhotep designed and oversaw the building of Egypt's first pyramid. He is also revered as the world's first official doctor. Imhotep was a priest, scribe, sage, poet, and astronomer-astrologer. He served under Pharaoh Djoser, who is thought to have lived from 2630-2611 BC. Almost 3,000 years after his death, during the early Christian era, the memory of Imhotep the Serpent Holder was still so revered it bordered on worship. In the earliest Christian writings, we see that Imhotep the Serpent Holder was believed to be an early foreshadowing, or type, who represented the coming of Christ. Once again we see a favorable and powerful connection between the serpent and early Christianity.

In Egypt, the serpent was the symbol of Isis, the consort of the son-of-god, known as Osiris. The serpent was also a symbol of their son Horus, who was supposed to be incarnate in Pharaoh. The serpent was connected to the great father god Ra, later replaced by Atum, the personal god of Pharaoh, and through which Pharaoh claimed direct lineage. Curiously, the Egyptian Atum in English is Adam.

It is not an accident of history that the legendary Cleopatra chose to be joined to the Egyptian cobra in her death. She was identifying with Isis whom she represented as the high priestess. The sacred serpent was her symbol under whose protection she would be led into eternal life. December 25th, the celebrated day for the birth of Jesus, was also the annual festival of Isis from the most ancient of times. Again the serpent and the Christ are associated.

Philo of Alexandria, a revered early Christian scholar, was so impressed with the serpent's ability to rejuvenate itself, and its other unique abilities, that he wrote in some of the earliest Christian writings that the serpent is "the most spiritual of all animals."

German coins of the renaissance period reflect a serpent-resurrection theme. The German "Thaler," from which the U.S. dollar got its name (it's pronounced dollar), showed Jesus on the obverse side of the dollar coin and a serpent on the reverse side, both on a cross or tree. The serpent's role alluded directly to the resurrection.

The existence of a serpent resurrection tradition was widespread. It was common amongst the ancient seafaring Phoenicians, the tribes of Africa, South America, and various islands of the South Pacific. It was understood throughout the high cultures of the entire ancient world. As presented earlier, the idea most intimately associated with the serpent was resurrection and eternal life. Thus, the snake Bai was configured as guardian of the doorways of the chambers of Egyptian tombs. These represented the mansions of heaven.

We find representations of the serpent everywhere in the ancient world, including the spiral, sky bands, chevrons, and the stepped fret. These symbols appear on pottery, clothing, and in temples new and old. Ancient vases show gigantic snakes winding over the sun, moon, and stars, representing Sky Serpent symbology. Elsewhere the snake appears below a growing plant, or coiled above the belly of a pregnant woman. The snake was the symbol of creative energy, resurrection, and immortality. In India, the serpent represented the Kundalini, source energy and creation.

Summary

The serpent symbology evoked when Moses raised the brazen serpent onto a pole in order to heal the Israelites was such powerful imagery that eventually it evolved into the Caduceus, the universal symbol of the healing arts, and it is still the icon of physicians worldwide. Perhaps the bronze serpent of Moses has further symbolic elements in addition to those outlined in the Gospel of John. The instrument of judgment had become the means of deliverance, and the symbol of pain and death was to become a symbol of healing. The Christian cross would evoke these same sentiments some 1500 years later.

The serpent symbology of the Judaic, Christian, and Islamic scriptures does not seem to have a static meaning. This is precisely because it does not always represent the same thing. From a Biblical point of view, it may be that as Satan used the serpent for his purposes in the Garden, so did God use the serpent to reproach Pharaoh and for the healing of Israel in the wilderness. One can observe a progression in serpent symbology in passages of the Bible. The progression appears to go from evil in the Garden to mildly good in the blessing of Dan to a compelling tool of God's power in Pharaoh's court, to becoming a symbol or instrument of healing in the wilderness. Ultimately the image of the serpent is used by Christ to illustrate His saving power over death. Does that challenge your preconceived ideas?

Conclusion

The point to this historical review is for you to consider your own mental reactions to new information. Do you sense a shift in your thinking? Are you surprised? Did this new slant on serpent symbology challenge your embedded paradigm in some way? Mostly we believe what we believe without giving it much thought. Why is that? It's because so much of what we believe was programmed when we were too small to realize it. To expand our understanding of things, as we automatically view them into something more balanced and truthful, we must observe neutrally and suspend judgment.

> **To expand our understanding of things, as we automatically view them into something more balanced and truthful, we must observe neutrally and suspend judgment.**

Our cultural lenses are so seductive we rarely realize they're on. They represent our unconscious belief system, our paradigms; those thoughts we have granted the power to rule us. We live and are governed by these beliefs. All of our subconscious and most of our conscious responses are triggered only after having been filtered through our belief system. Our belief system constitutes our cultural lens.

> **All of our subconscious and most of our conscious responses are triggered only after having been filtered through our belief system. Our belief system constitutes our cultural lens.**

Our paradigms force us to view everything through the lenses formed by that very same belief system. Much of this system is a response to instant judgment. We automatically discard what we subconsciously believe we are not going to agree with, usually well before we've given any consideration to new data. When we suspend our immediate tendency to judge, and allow more unfiltered information to flow into our minds, we are in a much better place from whence to progress and evolve. If we do not learn to suspend our powerful tendency to judge through the lenses of old paradigms, we are destined to always view everything through the mirror of memory. If we never perceive anything new, how will we change and grow?

Science is now telling us that our beliefs are important to who we are, how we live, and what we may become. From the hormones that regulate, build, balance, and repair our bodies, to our basic immune response, human belief is a major factor in quantum biology. We live our lives based on our beliefs. These are the paradigms through which we experience our world. Our beliefs define our relationship with ourselves. They define our relationship with God. Thus it is, that the great question at the core of your life is, what do you believe?

What do you believe?

Not what do you think you believe, or what you would like to believe, but what do you truly believe about yourself and the world about you? These vital beliefs are in firm control of your entire life.

These vital beliefs are in firm control of your entire life.

Are you where you want to be? Does your current belief system encourage you to be grateful, centered, calm, joyful, loving, harmonious, wise, and kind? Can you honestly say that life is good? Life is lovely? Life is wonderfully abundant? That you love life? Do you have a childlike wonder and curiosity at the beauty and complexity of the universe? Do you want these things? If you do want them, but they're not nearly as much a part of your life as you wish, then you must re-work your belief system. You must change your cultural lens. Consider the Emotional Index again with these thoughts in mind.

Emotional Index

Feelings in Play	Emotional Level
Serene Happiness, Transcendence, Pure Love	Enlightenment
Harmony, Tranquility, Serenity	Peace
Deep Gratitude, Unconditional Love, Pure Kindness	Compassion
Worship, Reverence, Beauty all around, Love	Love
Elation, Ecstasy, Profound Pleasure	Joy
Forgiving, Merciful, Caring, Absolving	Forgiveness
Cheerful, Hopeful, Confident, Buoyant	Optimism
Believing, Reliant, Faith, Confident Dependence	Trust
Excitement, Enthusiastic, Infatuation, Obsession	Passion
Satisfied, Gratified, Ease, Pleasured	Content
Affirmed, Audacious, Validated, Daring	Courage
Self-important, Impatient, Arrogant, Scornful	Pride
Weary, Dull, Tedious, Monotony	Boredom
Distrustful, Doubting, Negative, Cynicism	Pessimism
Aggressive, Irritated, Frustrated, Hateful	Anger
Besieged, Inundated, Weighed down, Beleaguered	Overwhelmed
Fearful, Withdrawing, Jealous, Worry, Nervous, Angst	Anxiety
Depression, Misery, Gloom, Anguish	Despair
Shame, Blaming, Remorse, Humiliation	Guilt
Hopelessness, Weak, Wretched, Useless, Helpless	Powerless

Beginning at the bottom of the column "Feelings in Play," work your way up and consider what tier best describes the thoughts that tend to predominate in your life. Look across the chart horizontally to discover the descriptive level of your present vibration. The Emotional Level reveals your vibrational set-point.

Reference the Emotional Index frequently, this gradient understanding allows you to more easily recognize the way your subconscious mind is coloring new incoming data. The emotional tier you are now experiencing reflects your subconscious self-view. These are the lens through which you view the world and the lens through which you view yourself.

When one devotes themselves to the process of thinking higher vibrational thoughts, each upward shift is accompanied by a significant increase in personal power and a corresponding rise in happiness.

It's All *Thought!*

Chapter 7

PERSONALITY ARCHETYPES

"By being happy we sow anonymous
benefits upon the world."

Robert Louis Stevenson

Materialism

Happiness does not come from material things. We often
confuse material success with happiness. They are not the same
thing. External accomplishments and the accolades of others may
feel good and motivate us on to other achievement, but these feel
good sensations are usually fleeting. Happiness is a mental state,
not a condition of the outside world.

Every day, in a myriad of ways, we are told that happiness is
available to us if we'll just buy some particular thing or participate
in some activity or other. Much of the difficulty in our advanced
materialistic society comes from seeking happiness through own-
ership of things, and other external accomplishments. There is
nothing intrinsically wrong with being in shape, owning your home,
driving in comfort, and having good investments. These types of
things are wanted by most, but they are still physical things; and
to say they will make us happy is to confuse pleasure and security
with happiness. According to an ancient Hindu proverb,

> "Pleasure is only the
> shadow of happiness."

Pleasure is sensual. Pleasure is temporary. Happiness is an internal state of being. It is an emotional, virtually spiritual, condition of the mind, and it can become a permanent facet of one's life.

Happiness is an internal state of being. It is an emotional, virtually spiritual, condition of the mind, and it can become a permanent fixture of one's life.

All of us are able to draw pleasure from exciting, beneficial, attractive, external circumstances. And yet, if we depend upon things, or others for our happiness, what would happen to us if they were all gone? Are those things or people responsible for our happiness? After all, who decides when you will be happy? It's you, isn't it? So, doesn't this imply that your individual happiness is a choice? In the final analysis, you choose how you shall respond to any given situation.

Happiness requires that we look deep inside, and give careful attention to what our inner self, our very heart and soul, has to share. The dilemma here is that most of us have become experts at ignoring the "still small voice" from within. We are fascinated and totally distracted with the outside world. It is not there that our individual happiness resides. Happiness has little to do with the physical things in our lives. Happiness has everything to do with our attitudes toward life. Whether we deny it or not, eventually we will discover that nothing in the external world can make us happy. In the words of the Buddhist Lama, Dilgo Khyentse Rinpoche:

> "Those who seek happiness in
> pleasure, wealth, glory, power,
> and heroics, are as naive as
> the child who tries to catch a
> rainbow and wear it as a coat."

The key to our personal individual happiness resides within each one of us. The source of our happiness does not reside in someone else. No one else can be happy for me. Only I can do that for me.

Beliefs

The state of being we call happiness amounts to attitude. Attitudes are habits of thinking. Attitudes reflect our perceptions on how we view our world. Our habitual ways of thinking are the basis of our belief system. Beliefs are simply the thoughts that we have thought again and again. They are those thoughts that we do not challenge. Most of our fundamental beliefs were firmly established in our subconscious well before we were old enough to challenge their accuracy. In Chapter 6, we reviewed that many psychologists claim that 75 percent or more of our initial programming, our belief system, was complete by age six. If this is so, or if it is even close to being so, what does that say to you? Beliefs are the thoughts we rarely question.

Beliefs are those undergirding thoughts that govern everything we think and do. Most of us will have heard that something like 95 percent of our thoughts, reactions, and interactions, are governed by our subconscious beliefs. New evidence suggests the number is more like 99 percent of all our bodily functions, actions, thoughts, and feelings, are the result of subconscious monitoring, and our automatic response to the world we perceive.

Subconscious beliefs form the internal operating programs that run our lives. These beliefs are those critical perceptions and thought processes of which we are essentially unaware. Each of us is pretty darn sure that our particular common sense understanding of things (our belief system), represents the truth of what constitutes the "real" reality around us. As a result we rarely challenge our beliefs. Only rarely do we even glimpse the reactionary programs that automatically steer us through life. They are hard to spot because they have usually formed our immediate response to things subliminally before we give conscious consideration to whatever it is we are then considering. Our natural tendency is to not take responsibility for the thoughts and actions we have that are not really serving us. Life is the ultimate scapegoat.

Beliefs are thoughts that trigger emotions. Put another way, we literally feel our most cherished thoughts; both the good and the not so good. With few exceptions our egos are almost entirely in charge of everything we do, or don't do, what we think, or don't think, what we feel, or don't feel.

With few exceptions our egos are almost entirely in charge of everything we do, or don't do, what we think, or don't think, what we feel, or don't feel.

Our egos convince us that we are right in the way we view things. The result is that whatever we believe must in fact be so. Truly, how often do you consider that your particular way of perceiving things might be wrong? Or at least, that there may be another, fully legitimate way of seeing any given situation? And yet, it is well known that millions of people die each year for their beliefs. In fact, there is a growing body of evidence that suggests that we all eventually succumb to our personal perception of the way things are, which may have little to do with truth. We review this in greater detail in Chapter 10.

Our beliefs form the lens through which we habitually view the world, and our place in it. Most of us have some conscious idea of what we deem to be our spiritual beliefs. This is generally true, whether one is religious or not. Strangely, personal religious beliefs are grounded on those thought patterns that are most often subject to reconsideration. Whereas it is true that most people do not question their most cherished beliefs, at least they are aware that religious thinking represents a belief system. The larger problem is not our personal religious convictions, but the other beliefs we cling to that form our bedrock thinking. Why? Because these are the beliefs of which we are usually unaware. If we are unaware of the most fundamental premises upon which are lives are playing out, how can we examine them for their real impact?

One's spiritual practice is hugely important to one's overall internal point of reference, nevertheless this collection of thoughts comprise only a small portion of the actual programs that underlie each of our individual realities. What is vitally important for us to grasp is that it is the composite of all our beliefs that will determine the amount of happiness we will ultimately allow ourselves.

> **It is the composite of our beliefs that will determine the amount of happiness we will ultimately allow ourselves.**

Again, religion and spirituality represent only a small segment of the total of our underlying beliefs. So, let's be clear that this discussion is not about what religious group or institution we may or may not see ourselves affiliated with. The real issue bears repeating; most of the beliefs that shape our understanding stand outside of what we typically consider to be our beliefs. We explore religion, spirituality, the meaning of life, and similar ideals, in the chapters of Section III. The point I wish to develop here is this: Happiness is the result of our thoughts and feelings, and is ultimately governed by our internal belief system.

> **Happiness is the result of our thoughts and feelings, and is ultimately governed by our internal belief system.**

To be happy, really happy, not just temporarily immersed in a pleasurable experience, requires we refine our approach to thought. Thoughts, thought upon for any length of time, with some degree of acceptance, are the basic ingredients of our belief system. It is important to recognize that our belief system is considerably more than what we usually want to think it is.

Thoughts

Thoughts always precede feelings. Change our thoughts, and we change our emotional response to both old and new thinking.

This entire concept may feel a bit uncomfortable about now. We are so conditioned to believe our emotional responses are the result of someone else's actions that learning we're the ones in charge may be a hard pill to swallow. As I began to fully appreciate the essence of this understanding, my tendency was to keep saying, "Yes, but the government is engaged in lying to the public," Yes, but there is massive governmental abuse," or "Yes, but the Justice department is not just" "Yes, but - you fill in the blank.

Notwithstanding my natural and immediate resistance to wanting to accept full responsibility for my own feelings, eventually I began to see the truth of it all. What this really means is we can change the way we feel about virtually anything, assuming we are prepared to examine our thought processes and adjust them as needed. So, to improve our level of happiness, we must rework our thinking. That's the basis of it all. There is not a series of actions we must perform. Only a host of thoughts we must rethink. The really good news here is that by changing the way we view the world, we can dramatically affect our happiness right now!

The really good news here is that by changing the way we view the world, we can dramatically affect our happiness right now!

Realizing that happiness is all about what's going on in our heads, then improving our habits of thought about life can bring us greater joy almost immediately. However, in order for joy's exuberance to expand and mature into lasting happiness, we will need to raise the standard of our thinking. We must choose to focus on gratitude, love, and self-acceptance. Isn't that what we want more of in our lives?

There is a fundamental law of life that seems to have been irrevocably decreed in heaven, which simply stated says: like attracts like. In other words, we attract into our lives that which we are most focused upon. So, whatever it is that you are wanting, focus upon that. Do not focus on the lack of it, but rather on the abundance of it. In several later chapters this will be more fully developed. But, for now, it is important to recognize that it is our choice to rework the feelings that surround our current and prior negative emotions. And yes, by doing so we CAN be happier and more productive, right now. That's because happiness is a choice. It's *your* choice, not someone else's, not mine. It's for you to choose!

Dr. Tel Ben-Shahar, a renowned teacher of positive psychology at Harvard University, divides personality types into four archetypical quadrants. (An archetype is an ideal example of a type.) Dr. Ben-Shahar lists his four archetypes as: Rat Race, Hedonism, Nihilism, and Happiness. He then asks us to evaluate our lives to determine where we spend most of our time.

While my reflection and experience mirror Dr. Ben-Shahar's thinking in several ways, I have always preferred to view these personality manifestations in terms of where these archetypes predominately dwell in their thinking; the past, present, or future. The depressive personality tends to live in the past. The pleasure-seeker, or hedonistic personality is focused on the now to the exclusion of everything else. Those caught on the treadmill of life are in the business of postponing their joy; they live for the future. The fourth archetype I think of as the enlightened. These are those who practice the secrets of a robust and happy life.

Each of us lives, to some degree, in all of the four quadrants. And of course, most of us enjoy various pleasures, and some degree of happiness along the way. However, there is a huge difference in the peace, joy, and centered disposition of the enlightened, versus the majority of humanity. Let's consider these archetypes more carefully.

Pleasure-seekers

The Pleasure-seeking personality is essentially selfish. When we are in this mode of thinking we believe (consciously or not), that our desire for self-indulgence trumps everything around us. We are focused on our personal gratification in the present, while ignoring the potential adverse implications of our actions downstream, and/or to others. We want everything, and we want it now.

Pleasure-seekers have lost contact with an effective working definition for happiness. They typically believe that pleasure is happiness, and they believe that all happiness is sensual and transitory. Instant gratification is the hallmark of the Pleasure-seeker; their motivation is based on whether or not some thought or action feels good now. This mindset, buttressed by the need for constant stimulation, requires that the Pleasure-seeker continually be on the lookout for new ways of arousal, excitement, and satiety. Jumping from one extreme to another in sports, sex, food, alcohol, and drugs, is typical of the hedonistic Pleasure-seeker. The pleasure seeking personality lives a roller-coaster life of constant ups and downs. They are always reaching for what they cannot obtain through the constant pursuit of pleasure to the exclusion of legitimate happiness.

There is nothing wrong with pleasure, in and of itself, but when pleasure seeking becomes the primary objective to one's life, that person is doomed. Without purpose, life has little meaning. Without challenge, there is nothing for us to accomplish. Those who make a habit of distracting themselves with the pursuit of pleasure, eventually erode the happiness they might have had, in both the present and in their near and long-term future. Pleasure-seekers inevitably slide down that slippery slope of self-indulgence into misery.

Pleasure-seekers inevitably slide down that slippery slope of self-indulgence into misery.

Treadmills

I suspect that the Treadmiller represents most of us, or at least, most of us who would take the time to read this book. This is the personality type that has bought into modern materialism. Few of us really question that the good life awaits those with money, influence, and good looks. Most of us live in this make-believe world, the majority of the time. Business owners, professionals, and career-oriented individuals of every ilk, are particularly susceptible to the seduction of living for tomorrow's happiness. We look forward to happiness, believing subliminally that it is another future goal for us to achieve. Happiness is out there. It is in our future. We will one day access that euphoric peace, just as soon as we get past the now. The trouble is we never really get there. Our goal is believable, but strangely just out of reach.

When we are focused primarily on the future we're always looking towards the goal, hoping for it, wanting it, but not yet experiencing it. For those trapped on the treadmill of life, the present is nothing more than a flashing moment between the movie of our past and the directing of our future.

> **For those trapped on the treadmill of life, the present is nothing more than a flashing moment between the movie of our past and the directing of our future.**

Early on most of us were thoroughly programmed to jump on the treadmill, to postpone our current happiness in exchange for some real or imagined future benefit. Our culture reinforces the belief that, in order to be successful, we must sacrifice the present for some distant expectation. As a result, most of us have learned to focus on future achievement instead of experiencing joy in the here and now.

Quite often the Treadmiller is reasonably successful, at least when measured against the yardstick of society. Yet, increasingly, those who have achieved the "good life" discover it is not nearly as good as it appeared from a distance. The trade off for our so-called societal success is that we've sacrificed joyful enthusiasm, peace, and self-acceptance, for what we believe are worthwhile future benefits. Gifts of the spirit have been traded off for the material goods we inaccurately believe are the very source of these good feelings.

In my former life, meaning before I was interned in the monastery, I found myself functioning as counselor (and to some extent confessor), to a large number of multimillionaires. During this time it became quite clear to me that it was better to be poor and unhappy than it was to be wealthy and unhappy. Why? Simply because the poor and unhappy believe money will fix their problems. They have *hope* for a better future. Those that are wealthy and unhappy have already learned that money is not the underlying ingredient for sustained peace and joy. The wealthy and unhappy have lost hope, often triggering depression. At least the wealthy have the money to pay for anti-depressants.

Those on the treadmill of life have bought into the belief that once they do such and such, or accomplish this or that, then they will be happy. The problem with this pervasive belief is that new goals always appear to replace the ones approaching fulfillment. Now that's generally a good thing, but when our thinking is skewed, it serves to continue our postponement of the happy state. There are always new projects, new needs, new musts with which we must deal. Linking our happiness to their fulfillment is the problem. The mantra (actually sutra), for those on the treadmill sounds something like this: "I'll be happy when - fill in the blank."

When we allow ourselves to believe that happiness is a destination we've missed the point. If we truly believe the stories we tell ourselves when we say "I'll be happy when, we are out of debt," or "when the car is paid off," or "when I get new carpet," or anything else we can think of, then we have not yet recognized that we will continually find ways to quietly postpone the WHEN of our own happiness. We postpone our happiness because we repeatedly attach the belief that "I'll be happy when" to a stream of new hoped for outcomes. "I'll be happy when I find the right partner," or "I'll be happy when my kids are back in school," or "I'll be happy when I get that job I want," or "I'll be happy when I lose 20 pounds," and on and on it goes. We postpone our happiness without ever even realizing we've done it.

Happiness can only be experienced in the present. True enough, you can call up a pleasant experience from the past, and thoroughly enjoy reflecting upon it, but you are doing, what you are doing, in your now - in your immediate present. Rarely do we really grasp that happiness is the journey not the destination.

**Rarely do we really grasp
that happiness is the journey,
not the destination.**

Our culture does not celebrate our personal journey, nor does it applaud our progress towards a more enlightened state. Instead, we are only recognized for things we've completed, plans we've accomplished, objects obtained, goals achieved. As strange as it may seem, particularly given our societal programming, it is the quality of the journey, not its completion that dramatically impacts the excellence in our lives. Think of happiness as an ever unfolding process, rather than a place of arrival. It is a false dichotomy to say that we arrive to a happy state. The real truth is that we must decide to live in a place of happiness. That place is in our heart and head. Happiness is an inside job. There is very little external to it.

Depressives

Society tends to consider the Depressive personality as something of a hero. Someone soldering on, doing that which our particular cultural support group believes is noteworthy. Many single mothers live in this place, and some single men. Numerous men and women that are actually well-married, with good homes and families, feel trapped in a world of overwork and under appreciation. Most alcoholism and drug addiction emanate from this sink hole of despair. Drugs and alcohol provide temporary escape from the Depressive's negative state of mind, hence the reason for their great demand.

Many mothers sense themselves caught up in the need to be all things to all people. They believe they must be Super Moms, upward mobile career women, all the time feeling the pressure to be model beautiful, and sexual bombshells. Men have their own insecurities. They are bombarded with the need to earn more, have more, be in better shape, and focus on the sensual. Instead of encouraging strong partnerships, our materialistic over-sexed society is driving men and women further and further apart.

Instead of encouraging strong partnerships, our materialistic over-sexed society is driving men and women apart.

Commercialism tends to endorse fractured lifestyles dressed up as elegant options for persons of discerning taste. This approach to life is doomed to generate insecurity, despair, and disease.

Those whose thoughts and conversation are focused primarily on the past tend to be depressive personalities. Ask those people whether or not they are happy and you'll likely get a blank look. Depressives have frequently given up on happiness. They don't seem to believe that life has much meaning. Recognize that where there is a lack of meaning in one's life there will be an existential vacuum.

Most of us know a few depressive personalities, and sometimes we know them intimately, because we are they. The negativity that a Depressive exudes can be quite powerful. A person that is seriously down can quickly affect the happiness index of almost everyone with whom they come in contact.

A tendency toward criticism is the foremost mask of the Depressive. The Depressive covers up their own feelings of inadequacy by pointing out the flaws in others. Those that are constantly complaining, about everything from injustice (real as it may be), to their boss' unreasonableness, to their spouse's insufficiencies, to their children's poor attitudes, are slip-sliding their way into a misery pool that can be extremely difficult to escape. Ultimately the Depressive is haunted by the fear that real happiness does not exist, or if it does, it will never be available to him or her.

Enlightened

To Hindus, Zen, and Lamasery Buddhists, the term "enlightenment" is a high level of ascendance, the place to which the evolved have arrived. I use the term much more loosely, defining it as anyone who has begun to unravel the knots of our humanity.

These are those who have learned to genuinely enjoy and appreciate the now, whilst maintaining a bright hope of expectancy for the near and continuing future. According to Lama Sury Das,

> "Enlightenment means spiritual
> illumination, realization, freedom,
> and the ultimate actualization
> of all that we are and can be."

In both the Tibetan language and the ancient Sanskrit of India, the words translated into English as "enlightened" means "to awaken," or simply "awake." From what do the enlightened awake? From the delusion that happiness is anything other than a series of choices, as to how we view and function in the world. We must wake up from ignorance, confusion, and self-inflicted suffering. The enlightened understand that their thinking is not the actual out there reality.

**The enlightened understand
that their thinking is not the
actual out there reality.**

Our thoughts about any situation represent our attempt to interpret what a given situation means to us. Each such interpretation triggers an emotional response based on our belief system. These responses are not about what happens to us, they are, instead, simply a result of our thinking and beliefs. The enlightened person understands that he or she can be happy under all kinds of conditions.

**The enlightened person
understands that he or
she can be happy under
all kinds of conditions.**

For most people, their happiness levels go up and down with their external circumstances. But, once again, it isn't the situation or circumstances that generate their happiness, or unhappiness, but rather their mental interpretation of what those circumstances mean to them. This is why almost identical situations can represent such different things to different people. The enlightened recognize that negative thoughts are the source of distress, anger, self-doubt, and misery.

> **The enlightened recognize that negative thoughts are the source of distress, anger, self-doubt, and misery.**

Negative thoughts are not truth, but simply the thinker's attempt to interpret events. Most negative thinking is mere noise. It is the ego-voice in our heads spinning out possible scenarios. It is a form of mental static, the blather of an undisciplined mind. In the words of Shakespeare: It is "a tale told by an idiot, full of sound and fury, signifying nothing." The enlightened know not to energize casual thoughts with emotion. Thoughts flow in and thoughts flow out all the time. If we observe without judgment, without attaching meaning and emotion to them, we shrink their impact.

Only someone trained in meditation seems to be effective at suspending his or her mental traffic. For the rest of us, it is important that we recognize that everyone's mind produces a steady stream of what-ifs; a constant flow of mentation. Everyone is occasionally subject to aggressive thought attacks. These are those times when you can't shut off the voice in your head. There is nothing to be gained by listening to our egos' unwanted, unhealthy chatter. To invest our focus in negative thought patterns will always lead to distress and unhappiness. Yes, ugly thinking sporadically jumps into our conscious mind. To neutralize this, we need to observe that we're having a negative thought, and dismiss it.

Enlightened souls are centered, calm, joyful, loving, harmonious, wise, and kind. They are secure, positive, playful, and fun. They are fundamentally happy and they are at peace with the world about them. When one is at peace with the world, one has discovered how to be at peace with one's self. These people know who they are. They have a strong sense of why they are here, and a positive expectancy about where they are headed. For the enlightened among us, life is good. Life is lovely. Life is wonderfully abundant. These are those who nurture and maintain a childlike wonder and express curiosity at the beauty and complexity of the universe.

> **For the enlightened among us, life is good. Life is lovely. Life is wonderfully abundant. These are those who nurture and maintain a childlike wonder and express curiosity at the beauty and complexity of the universe.**

Each of us is fully capable of finding and developing this new sense of ourselves. We seem foreordained to this purpose. It should be the legacy we leave to our family and friends. This remarkable appreciation of beauty and an overwhelming sense of gratitude and love; awaits us all. We have but to change our habits of thinking, and learn to choose a better way forward. So who decides what's right for us? We do. The truth has always been in us. Our source of happiness resides entirely within our hearts and minds.

The heavy programming of man's consciousness by negativity has meant that most people will never really find the brilliance, peace, love, and profound compassion that await us if we would but seek it out. The radiance is within. The choice is yours. True happiness is an inner power, natural, loving, abundant, healing, and always available. It is up to you to claim it!

Approaching the conclusion of Chapter 6, the following thoughts were posed:

Science is now telling us that our beliefs are important to who we are, how we live, and what we may become. From the hormones that regulate, build, balance, and repair our bodies, to our basic immune response, human belief is a major factor in quantum biology.

We live our lives based on our beliefs. These are the paradigms through which we experience our world. Our beliefs define our relationship with ourselves. And, they define our relationship with God. Thus it is, that the great question at the core of your life is, what do you believe?

What do you believe?

Not what do you think you believe, or what would you like to believe, but what do you truly believe about yourself and the world about you? These vital beliefs are in firm control of your entire life.

It can be confusing figuring this all out, and putting things into a new perspective. You're pretty darn sure you want to be happy. And, yet, you're probably not real clear on just what that is. The next chapter addresses just that subject.

It's All *Thought!*

Chapter 8

WHAT IS HAPPINESS?

"Happiness is man's greatest achievement; it is the response of his total personality to produce orientation toward himself and the world outside."

Erich Fromm

Happiness

Happiness; everyone wants it, but confusion abounds when we try to define it. The American Heritage Dictionary defines "happy" as: (1) Lucky or fortunate, (2) Enjoying, sharing, or marked by pleasure, (3) Well adapted or felicitous, (4) cheerful or willing.

People tend to use the term "happiness" to describe their feelings, beliefs, and physical sensations. For some, the term "happiness" has moral consequences. For others, it is strictly an emotion. Saint Augustine wrote, in his work *On the Happy Life:*

"The desire for happiness is
essential to man. It is the motivator
of all our acts. The most venerable,
clearly understood, enlightened,
and reliable constant in the world is

> not only that we want to be happy,
> but that we want only to be so.
> Our very nature requires it of us."

Our desire for happiness does indeed underwrite our every act, our every thought, our every word. It is so automatic and unthinking it is like the very air we breathe. We seldom actually think about it. It is simply our natural way.

What is It?

For at least 3,000 years, philosophers and theologians have waded in on the subject, usually doing little to clarify a definition. Speaking on happiness, the philosopher, Robert Misraki, presented a unique and effective definition:

> "Happiness is the radiation of joy
> over one's entire existence, or
> over the most vibrant part of one's
> active past, one's actual present,
> and one's conceivable future."

Christian scholars of the middle European period took vastly different positions on this topic. They ranged from the premise that happiness could not be achieved in this life, but was rather a reward for living virtuously, to its almost exact opposite, suggesting that happiness in this life was the result of living virtuously. Others preached the sort of happiness they thought their parishioners ought to want; this served to further confuse the issue.

By the fifteen hundreds, as the western world began its rise up and out of the Dark Ages, a consensus on the concept of happiness was beginning to consolidate. No less a pivotal figure than Martin Luther once wrote (in a letter to Prince Joachim von Anhalt):

> "I, who have hitherto spent my
> life in mourning and sadness, now
> seek and accept joy whenever I
> can find it. We now know, thank
> God, that we can be merry with a

good conscience, and can use God's
gifts with thankfulness, inasmuch
as he has made them for us and is
pleased to have us enjoy them."

Luther had preached in a sermon some years earlier that,

"Sin is pure unhappiness,
forgiveness pure happiness."

This is a thought-provoking idea, particularly in light of modern research. We now know that the crucial issue of forgiveness is the critical step in shifting one's demeanor towards a more fulfilling, and happier life. John Locke, the famous English philosopher, while living in Holland in the late 1600s, stated emphatically that,

"The highest perfection of our
nature lies in a careful and constant
pursuit of true and solid happiness."

Joseph-Marie Lequino, a French lawyer of some renown in the late 1700s, was an official in the revolutionary government. He gave a powerful sermon in a cathedral, which was then being rededicated as Rochefort's "Temple of Truth." Lequino's government-approved speech included these words:

"Brothers and friends, I am going
to speak to you today about that
which interests you all, about an
object for which you all yearn and
sigh, and toward which all our
actions tend. What does each of
you want? What do we all want?
What do we search for from the
first instant we become capable
of desire until the time our blood
runs cold in our veins and our
needs are annihilated? All, in a

word, whoever we are - big or
small, strong or weak, young or
old - we all dream of happiness;
we want only to be happy, we
think only of becoming so."

More History

Throughout history, we observe great thinkers endeavoring to grapple with the concept of happiness. Some believed that happiness was found in the absence of something, such as pain or hunger. Both Hindu and Buddhist literature addressed this philosophical precept. Well before Christ, the Buddha instructed his followers that happiness was the ultimate enlightenment; the rising to Nirvana. However, Nirvana itself was seen as essentially the release of the soul from suffering, and its final dissolution back into the cosmic ocean from whence all things have their origins.

The seeming contradiction that the Hindu and Buddhist approach to happiness presents (the final dissolution of our personality as one merges back into the cosmic ocean from whence all things arise), at least for those with a western philosophical bent, is that in essence, we must ultimately lose our individuality in order to achieve ultimate happiness. This idea begs the question, how can WE be happy if WE no longer exist as what we think of as US? One might argue that this is simply an issue of semantics and that we are simply trapped in words and definitions. And, of course, that may well be true. But words are how we express ourselves, and they reveal our thoughts and our state of mind. So, whereas I am thoroughly impressed with much of what Buddhism in particular has to offer, the concept of individuality needs further clarification before most of us raised in the west will easily receive this message.

A rather curious observation about our understanding and use of the word "happy," is that when it is followed by the words "that" or "about," the writer or speaker is rarely declaring their feelings of happiness, but instead expressing a philosophical position about something. For example, was one to say something such as: "I'm happy they hung Saddam Hussein," is he or she really happy about this culmination of events? I'd say it was unlikely. In cases like these one is merely emphasizing his or her philosophical position.

So, what do you think? Can a murderer be happy? How about the man who beats his wife? While I'll admit these questions are severe and not meant to stimulate you into resolving a real answer, they do heighten the question's meaningfulness to you personally. Indeed, what is happiness? And seriously, how important is it to you personally?

Defining It

Martin Luther may well have been onto something with his curt observation, "Sin is pure unhappiness, forgiveness pure happiness." Other than the use of the "sin" word, a term loaded with religious overtones, Luther's statement is a valid philosophical position well worth considering. For many years, I have thought that the word "sin" might better be defined in today's language as simply "poor choices." Looked at in this way, the statement would better read, "Poor choices lead to unhappiness, forgiveness leads to happiness." When one realizes that all poor choices arise from wrong thinking, this begins to sound like a pretty good definition. Here's another definition that has merit: Being happy is learning to love oneself, imperfect though one may be.

> **Being happy is learning to love oneself, imperfect though one may be.**

Think on that for a while. To love one's self is to love life. Therefore, to love oneself and yet be imperfect is to continually come from a place of forgiving. Learning to love one's self is not about selfishness or egocentrism, although it may sound like it. Why? Because abiding happiness arises from deep within, and only as we develop sincere gratitude for the blessings in our own lives and in the world generally.

There is a contagious high vibrational energy that emanates from us as we focus on gratitude and love. It moves us to help others discover greater meaning in their lives. This recognition may lead us to modify our definition of happiness to say something like: To love one's self is to love life. To love life is to be happy.

To love one's self is to love life.
To love life is to be happy.

Happiness radiates from the good-hearted. From those focused on gratitude and who are willing to love. It just so happens that we are literally unable to love others unless we are able to love and accept ourselves. We are literally unable to love anyone if we're holding tight to personal grievances or focused on what's wrong. In other words, when we're being judgmental about anything, we are *not* in a place of love. It follows then, that we have a very real need to forgive others, AND we absolutely must learn to forgive ourselves.

The truth is we cannot love ourselves unless, and until, we have forgiven all those around us for whatever it is that we believe they've done inappropriately. Put another way, we must forgive others their bad choices before we'll give ourselves a pass on our own poor choices. Bottom line, you cannot be happy while holding a grudge. It does not matter why you may refuse to forgive. It just matters whether or not you will forgive.

You cannot be happy while
holding a grudge. It does not
matter why you may refuse
to forgive. It just matters
whether or not you will forgive.

Most of us have been so thoroughly brainwashed at the altar of materialism that we have great difficulty separating happiness from economics. Invariably we confuse pleasure with happiness. Pleasure is a physical sensation. Happiness is a psychological or spiritual sensation. It embodies euphoria, a high positive energy, and feelings of gratitude, love, joy, goodness, peace, fulfillment, and satisfaction.

Pleasure is a physical sensation. Happiness is a psychological or spiritual sensation. It embodies euphoria, a high positive energy, and feelings of gratitude, love, joy, goodness, peace, fulfillment, and satisfaction.

Pleasure, is a temporary sensual thing. Happiness is an internal condition that can be sustained and expanded upon. As most of us recognize, happiness begets more happiness, just as misery begets misery. And yes, "misery does love company." It is important that we remind ourselves that happiness does not consist of things, but rather in the feelings we associate with our affection for those things.

If we look to material possessions for our happiness, we will live unhappy lives. There is no exception to this rule. Stuff never makes us happy. Author Victoria Moran once wrote,

"Happiness comes from inside. Most people start looking for happiness through what they can get, and eventually realize that it comes instead from who they are."

Outside Inside

Nothing outside of us can make us happy. Happiness is an inside job. It's in our head and heart. This does not mean we need to renounce material things, and live like monks, although some have done this with great success. What it does suggest, is that we need to reevaluate why we want what we want. When we face squarely the "why" of the things we do and say, we are headed in the right direction. For example, studies indicate that most of our focus on material things arises from our desire to look good to others.

Studies indicate that most of our focus on material things arises from our desire to look good to others.

Whether we admit it or not, we are all affected by what we think other people think about us. (Note: I didn't say what others *actually* think about us, but rather, what we think they think about us.) It seems that deep down inside, we believe that others will think more highly of us when we're surrounded by the right stuff.

It seems that deep down inside, we believe that others will think more highly of us when we're surrounded by the right stuff.

This claim may sound shallow, but shallow or not, it is undeniably true. And, perhaps what is worse is that the accumulation of stuff, when allowed to become a life priority, is destined to ensure that we cannot have that which we truly desire: unabashed happiness. Somehow, we have become confused, thinking that if others believe we're happy because of all our stuff and the places we can afford to go, that this will somehow make us happy. At this point, we are in a real fix, as we've transferred the responsibility for our happiness to what we think others think about us. It's really a wicked cycle. But the larger problem is that we secretly believe that happiness is rare, and only goes to the successful in life.

Our ego-self is fond of comparing ourselves to others. This process allows us only about as much happiness as we surreptitiously believe we deserve, based upon our internal comparisons. This scenario is the lurking enemy to our discovering of unreserved joy. We need to renounce comparing ourselves to others. And, it probably wouldn't hurt to reduce the stuff we seek to own, right along with the stuff we already own. Of course, this latter approach will not work for everyone, because most people are so thoroughly programmed to obtain, that try as they might, they can't break the relationship with their stuff. So, is this philosophy feeling a little uncomfortable about now? Ask yourself, do you really want to be happy? How serious are you? What wouldn't you trade to be legitimately happy, to be free?

In my analysis of the term "happiness," it can be defined as something like:

A profound sense of meaning coupled with an evolving healthy mind that thrives on gratitude, love, and self-acceptance.

Happiness above all else, is a love of life. It could be said that to lose our reason for living is to spiral into a chasm of continual suffering. But, there's good news! You can throw off the chains that bind and hold you down, and ascend to a higher vibrational place. You can be happy!

Doing It

Happiness is both a choice and a point of view. To be truly happy you must dedicate yourself to relishing life, to finding reasons - right NOW - to be joyful, to love, to let go, and to just have fun. You must choose to turn away from frustration, stress, anxiety, fear, anger, and distress. You must choose to let your energy rise within you. You must allow yourself to feel good, to laugh without guile, to be thankful for this very moment. And yes, I mean this exact moment. Right now while you're reading this very sentence. You see, everything in your life can be so much better. It requires that you decide to experience freedom from self-doubt, and that you allow your spirit to soar. Happiness is the high road. It is the highest spiritual path. Happiness is the whole end and aim of life.

Happiness is the high road. It is the highest spiritual path. Happiness is the whole end and aim of life.

You can start being happier than you've ever allowed yourself to be. "Sure, but what about all the crap in my life?" you say. Okay, we're going to look at that, and you are going to learn a bunch of new stuff that will change your world. That is...if you let it. But for right now, and yes I mean this very minute, SMILE as big as you can. Is this hard to do? Yes? No? Of course I'm serious. Try it. Okay, now smile again...this time bigger. Now laugh. Yes, right now. Laugh out loud. It doesn't matter about what. Can you laugh without a reason? Okay now, try a giggle. Is this embarrassing? Is it fun? If you cannot really manage a big smile, a giggle, or a belly laugh, what does that tell you about you?

Is it possible that you're too taken with who you think you are? Or, perhaps more correctly, who you think others think you are? After all, life is a serious matter. Isn't it? Okay, let's say that's true. So what? How is that philosophy working for you? Could it be that you're afraid to do something weird. Or, has it been so long since you just let go that you've forgotten how to feel innocent. You know, like children, before they learned how to judge themselves and others. Can you laugh out loud just because it feels good? If it doesn't feel good, why is that? If you can laugh on your own and loosen your grip a bit, it's a darn good thing to do.

We were born to be happy. It brings out the very best in us. True happiness is a marvelous and beautiful thing. When we are happy, we glow with an attractiveness that is powerfully magnetic. And, every person who takes the time to rise in levels of vibration to a higher, more loving place is also impacting every other person towards this improved place of being. Intentionally or not, we are each continually signaling everyone else as to how we think and feel, and affecting them with our vibrational signature. Everyone around us can sense and see this phenomenon. And, everyone benefits from being happy. Now, consider the exact opposite. Literally no one's life is improved by your being miserable.

Everyone benefits from being happy. No one's life is improved by your being miserable.

The lives of everyone with whom you come in contact are enhanced by your genuine smile and the glow that emanates from within you. When we have consciously committed ourselves to love and happiness, a higher quality of people gravitate toward us. They want to be around us, to plug into our positive energy. They are mesmerized with the buoyancy of our step, the ease of our living, the play, the fun, and the childlike wonder and excitement we reflect. To those not yet pledged to the high road of enlightenment, they struggle to understand our lack of defensiveness, and the optimism and spontaneity with which we are able to conduct our affairs. When happiness is the hallmark characteristic of what you have become, everything else in life tends to improve right along with it.

A happy person is one that has unlearned much of what our society has inadvertently taught. The truly happy among us have set aside worry and anxiety, and taken up kindness, generosity, trust, and love. The world is so magnificently better when seen through the eyes of one who is fully present in the NOW; with one who is dedicated to goodness and is grateful for the experiences life provides. Heaven accompanies the happy wherever they go. Hell follows those unable or unwilling to discover the good around them.

> **Heaven accompanies the happy wherever they go. Hell follows those unable to discover the good around them.**

The ones unable to discover the good around them are those disinclined to be grateful for their blessings. Those experiencing hell on earth are focused on what's wrong in their lives; they simply cannot see what's right.

> **Those experiencing hell on earth are focused on what's wrong in their lives; they simply cannot see what's right.**

Responsibility

Paramahansa Yogananada, the first Hindu Yoga to live permanently in America, was one of the most gifted and prolific sages of the past century. He took up residence in California in 1924, after meeting with the President of the United States by special invitation. Yogananada was extremely well received throughout America as he spoke to record-breaking audiences everywhere from the major lecture halls of the largest universities, to some of the country's most significant religious congregations, to Carnegie Hall. He frequently spoke on the basic fundamentals of Christian teachings. Yes, that's right, a Hindu Swami, a guru of the highest order, was a Christian biblical scholar. His several books are both insightful and a joy to read. His essential counsel to everyone everywhere was continually:

> "No matter what you are
> doing, keep the undercurrent of
> happiness. Learn to be secretly
> happy within your heart in
> spite of all circumstances."

It is within us to discover that one of the "secrets" to a truly wonderful life is that we have a choice as to how we view the world. We either focus on injustice, outrage, discontent, and unhappiness, which are clearly all around us, or we can choose to concentrate on gratitude, love, kindness, peace, happiness, and joy. Proverbs 15:15 teaches:

> "For the despondent every day
> brings troubles; for the happy
> heart, life is a continual feast."

Motivational speaker Keith D. Harrell says: "'The key to happiness is realizing that it's not what happens to you that matters, it's how you choose to respond." In fact, the approach we take to almost anything is an automatic response from our prior habits of thought. We either expend the energy to develop happy habits of thinking, or we do not. Alexandra Stoddard, contemporary author, put it this way,

"Happiness must become a
habit, a way of looking at and
appreciating life, the door we are
always opening to let in more
light and richer experiences."

The 19th century American writer-philosopher Elbert Hubbard summarized this philosophy in just a few words, "Happiness is a habit – cultivate it." The famous Greek scholar Aristotle was even briefer, "Happiness depends on ourselves." And so it is. Happiness does depend upon our self. No one can do it for you. In the end, it is only you.

Earnie Larsen, nationally known author-speaker and pioneer in the field of drug and alcohol recovery, suggests that one must completely accept responsibility for one's own happiness by repeating this kind of affirmation:

"I accept responsibility for my
own happiness, for the obstacles
I put in my own way, and for
the happiness substitutes that
I use to distract myself."

This statement is concise and to the point. Do we, or will we, accept personal responsibility for the substitutes we use to distract ourselves from truth? Those of us who are used to the "doingness" of life may now be thinking something like, "Okay, okay, just tell me what to do." But the truth is, it is not something we must do, it is our thinkingness that must be changed. It is time to let this insight seep deep down into our subconscious.

We must continually expose ourselves to improved ways of thinking. Let these more positive thoughts build upon themselves. In effect, you have planted a good seed by just reading this material. It now needs nurturing to grow. Once the product of the seed begins to break the surface, the results begin to show up in your life. Then you must be diligent to weed the garden of your mind, so that which you do not want is cleared from your thinking, and the good seed may grow and take deep root. As you do this, the process becomes easier, yet you still must be diligent to care for this new way of being. It takes time to weed your mind of poor thinking, to cultivate yourself and plant and grow new habits of thought. Yet, anyone can do it, if they'll make up their minds and apply themselves. As Abraham Lincoln wisely said,

> "Most folks are about as happy as
> they make up their minds to be."

Matthieu Ricard, a Ph.D. in Cellular Genetics and Buddhist monk, writing on happiness, provided this valuable advice:

> "Wealth, pleasures, rank, and
> power are all sought for the sake
> of happiness. But as we strive, we
> forget the goal and spend our time
> pursuing the means for their own
> sake. In so doing, we miss the point
> and remain deeply unsatisfied. This
> substitution of means for ends is
> one of the main traps lying across
> the pursuit of a meaningful life...
> Happiness is not given to us, nor is
> misery imposed. At every moment,
> we are at a crossroads and must
> choose the direction we will take."

In Chapter 1, summaries garnered from a myriad of psychology and medical surveys were presented. We learned that happy people live longer, healthier lives. Deepak Chopra, physician, author, and nationally recognized speaker, comments on this particular aspect of happiness:

> "...happiness, which simply means
> having happy thoughts most of
> the time, causes biochemical
> changes in the brain that in turn
> have profoundly beneficial effects
> on the body's physiology."

Chopra is telling us we can be physically healthier simply by thinking more healthy thoughts. Amazing? Everyone wants to be happy and everything else they want is essentially a means to that end. So, notwithstanding life requires we recognize what's wrong from time-to-time, the fact is that focusing on what's wrong rarely improves conditions. In truth, it almost always does the exact opposite.

So, what will it be? It's pretty certain that you've already decided to make changes, or you would not have read this far. Yet, even though you really do want an abundance of love, wisdom, health, wealth, and happiness, you're still not really sure how to make all that happen. In the next chapter we'll cover some of reasons why it can be so easy to lose sight of our commitment to improve.

It's All *Thought!*

Chapter 9

WHY AREN'T WE HAPPIER?

"You attract what you believe you deserve. Thus, not only do you enjoy as much happiness as you believe you are worthy of, but you suffer as much pain as you believe you are worthy of."

Dr. Robert Holden

The Simple Answer

Why aren't we happier? It's a simple question. And, believe it or not, there's a simple answer. *We are only able to enjoy about as much happiness as we deep down believe we are entitled to have.* What?! That's it?! Yes, that is it. But it will likely take some review before most of us can begin to grasp the real significance of this statement, and accept the responsibility that goes along with it.

When we are feeling really up about ourselves, happy feelings are a natural response to the internal belief that we're fundamentally good, that we're headed in the right direction, and that there is purpose in our lives. However, most of us secretly fear that perhaps we're *not* really worthy of lasting happiness. And, that's because our lifelong mental conditioning has instilled within us a deep-seated guilt, and a belief that we're never quite good enough.

Our lifelong mental conditioning has instilled within us a deep-seated guilt, and a belief that we're never quite good enough.

Oh sure, we enjoy portions of life's little pleasures, but will we allow ourselves to love, relish, and delight, in sustained happiness? How much joy can you handle? How much love and attention will you accept before you get antsy? How long will you permit yourself to bask in unlimited freedom of thought before your practical nature requires you to focus on what's wrong around you?

Paradigms

Our paradigms, the mental programs that form the lenses which sift, shade, and filter all incoming information, are the models of reality our brains have constructed. It is through these paradigms that we view and understand the world. We are rarely aware of the internal models through which we compare and judge everything, and we only rarely question their accuracy.

Paradigms are the mental programs that form the lenses that sift, shade, and filter all incoming information.

It's important that we fully grasp that our mind views everything through the mirror of past experiences. The mind filters all new incoming data through our political, social, scientific, and religious predispositions. This is very important, because many of our views are flawed.

Historians will grudgingly admit that probably 90 percent of everything we think we know of history just isn't so. As a would-be historian, I personally struggle with this thought. What I think I know of history I really do want to be true. I mean after all, I've spent much of the last fifty years learning, relearning, and trying to remember it. Yet the real truth is, human history is pretty much opinion and propaganda. Of course, it's not just the history we think we know that is inaccurate, our subconscious mind is literally plagued with defective paradigms. The larger truth is that if we're willing to be blatantly honest with ourselves, we'd have to say that the vast majority of what we believe is not particularly accurate. This is not to say that we are unable to function with false paradigms; people lived for thousands of years believing the world was flat.

Holding on to defective concepts and imperfect beliefs interferes with our ability to fully experience happiness; at least to some degree. So, if finding and experiencing happiness is the ultimate underlying motivation of all the actions of man, what about the pursuit of truth? How does this play into the picture? Let's suspend this question for the present and ask a slightly different one. Why don't we simply stop right where we are, and just *decide* to be happy? Well, duh, why don't we? It is a good idea, and for some it might just work. But surely for most of us, we're going to have to undo some flawed habits of thinking and replace them with improved ways of being. In other words, we need to get a better grasp on the truth. Furthermore, finding happiness probably has a good deal more to do with "undoing" than doing. This is a lesson we will likely relearn a number of times before we really get it.

New information integrated into our personal paradigm becomes knowledge we can use. Increased knowledge expands the mind, and stimulates our creativity. When we are in a creative state of mind we are generally at our best. Positive thoughts are flowing, new ideas arise, things seem easier to accomplish. Creativity is a beautiful thing. More and more information points to the conclusion that we are designed to create. And, that's certainly true of our personal lives, because whether we are ready to admit it or not, we are the creators of our reality. Further, there is compelling evidence to support the contention that we literally exist to create new experiences through which we may grow and evolve.

**We literally exist to create
new experiences through
which we may grow and evolve.**

Our imagination is stimulated when we integrate new experiences and new insights. We begin to consider what the new information might mean, how it might be used, what actions or new opportunities we might pursue as a consequence. With fresh discernment we are able to stimulate new dreams and dare to consider moving outside the current boundaries of what we believe we are capable of. This, in turn, expands our paradigm, and frees us from a form of mental bondage. If we could face it, we'd realize that many of us are chained down and in prison. A prison every bit as daunting as the one I experienced for several years. You see, the truth is, the most limiting prison of all is the one we've constructed in our mind.

Living with Lies

Some of this information has been covered in prior chapters but it needs repeating so we can really get it: Most of us will fail to integrate new incoming information. We discount it without much thought, or we filter it out completely. The sad truth is that most people would rather live comfortably with a lie than go to the effort of integrating new information. Ouch!

**Most people would rather
live comfortably with a
lie than go to the effort of
integrating new information.**

Is that too in your face? Is that too scary? Do you want to deny the truth of it? One may be able to admit that for someone else, but when it comes to us personally, we almost always think it's the other person who isn't getting it. To improve the way we see things, to adjust our paradigm if you will, we must decide to allow ourselves to think outside our self-imposed limitations. We must determine to get the blinders off, to see outside our day-to-day experience. Only then can we embark upon a new life of discovery. It is central to our improvement that we recognize that each of us is already living the life we have chosen, or at the least, we are living the life we have allowed someone else to choose for us.

> **Each of us is already living the life we have chosen, or at the least, we are living the life we have allowed someone else to choose for us.**

It's easy to blame others for our current situations. There is a certain comfort in being the "innocent" victim. In this way we are never at fault, and people will pay attention to us and our dilemma. The ego views this as a double win. But the blame game is for those who are destined to be unhappy. To experience true joy and happiness, we must accept responsibility. There is no need to shout it from the roof tops, or confess our past stupidity to anyone, other than perhaps to those we have harmed. But in order to become the happy, balanced, evolved, person we deep down really wish to be, we must take responsibility for all the circumstances of our lives. By now, it should be anchored in your brain that, that which stands between us, and our greater good, is the way we think. That's the real truth.

> **That which stands between us, and our greater good is the way we think.**

It is not the outside world we need to change, although we may do just that, instead it is our own mental reactions to the world we live in. Most of us refuse to admit it, but the unhappiness we experience we have subliminally sought out. You see, there is a certain social comfort in being treated unfairly. Being the "righteous" victim has benefits. Deep down, we are "in effect" paid off for bathing in the sympathetic understanding of others. We like to talk about our troubles, and indulge a little (or a lot) in self pity. Hey! We're only human, right?

Money

The insidious belief that things can make us happy, and that the absence of things can leave us unfulfilled, is a lie; pure and simple. By all means, enjoy the things you have, but do not buy into the common belief that things can make you happy. Happy people don't need to buy status symbols. Status seeking is a weakness. The insecure have always attempted to surround themselves with validations of their self-worth. They distract themselves from looking deep inside. They are afraid. They mentally take the position that they must be okay, because look at all their stuff. Those who can't afford the stuff are driven on by the false belief, that money will fix their problems. It is not true. Hundreds of studies have proven that money does not elicit happiness. And yet, throughout society, we are convinced that more money will make the difference.

Money is simply a facilitator it is neither good nor bad. We all need it, we all want it, at least to some degree, and we all use it. It impacts much of what we do throughout the majority of our lives, it shapes a considerable amount of our thinking, and it sparks much of our action. Oddly enough, very few people really know how money is created, and what that actually means to them. The recent Wall Street debacle, followed immediately by the banking industry meltdown, is clear evidence of this point. For the most part, people look to money as security, both physically and emotionally. This emotional security tends to emanate from our tendency towards class distinction. It is a sign of status, when we have money. We tend to feel better about ourselves, when we have more than sufficient for our needs. Money is false security. Yet, we ignore it to our detriment. Where's the balance? Suffice it to say, that money is in our way when it interferes with our personal growth. In my experience, those with economic surplus tend to have a problem with humility. It's not always so, but it seems to be the major test in life for those who are financially successful.

Happy people gain their status from within. They are comfortable in their own skin. They feel greater confidence by having a grasp on knowing who they are. They are internally validated, through pursuit of worthwhile objectives and work well done.

Anyone can choose to be happy. It does not require money. Anyone can choose the course of their lives. While unhappy people may not believe that it's possible to achieve happiness without large sums of cash, happy people resist the fear, and decide how they will live. Those who are happy with who they are, will always decide what shall, and shall not, constitute the purpose for their existence. If money is one's purpose, they are way off track. Mahatma Gandhi left us with this insight:

> "Happiness is when what you
> think, what you say, and what
> you do is in harmony."

Addiction

There is a real chemical payoff in our body when our subconscious stimulates the release of short chain amino acids, peptides, or what most of us know as hormones. These are powerful drugs that begin to flow almost immediately when we wallow in negative thinking. One of the most vigorously potent of these hormones is connected with that state of mind best represented as "victimhood." It is oh-so-easy to become addicted to this internally generated juice. Without knowing it consciously, we create situations whereby we are victimized, and our body gets its fix of the hormone it is seeking.

All of us are addicted to one or more of our internally produced drugs. Marathon runners are a good example of this curious, but little discussed phenomenon. For years, my wife Cheri was a long-distance runner. When in training for the uphill 50k Alaska marathon, she ran four miles up a mountain and back down, four times a day, for a total of 32 miles. She laughingly renamed her training mountain, "Mount Orgasm," because of the huge endorphin release she would get about the time she got to the mountain top. The addiction to endorphins keeps a lot of runners running. We may laugh, and call that a socially acceptable addiction, but do we really want to live in a place of addiction?

Dr. Joe Dispenza, recognized authority on the mind, brain function, and body chemistry, defines an addiction as anything you do that you don't really have control over. What parts of your life are so automatic and routine you don't really know how to change it? What are you addicted to? Some might call love an addiction. Even so, virtually all of us would believe that is a good thing. Well then, what about sex? All of us know people who are literally addicted to sex. The entire pornography industry, a $13 billion dollar business on the internet alone, is based on this powerful addiction.

By observing our own conversations carefully, we can discover the extent to which we push our internal buttons in order to get our hormone fix. There are a number of peptides produced in the hypothalamus, the little hormone factory in our brain. These hormones have a direct correlation with our most powerful emotions. The hypothalamus regulates food and fluid intake along with a number of other functions addressed in Chapter 11. There is a peptide release for love, and one for lust, one for happiness, and another for anger. There is one for depression, and one for victimhood, and so forth. Many times, the subconscious develops situations where we kick a whole cascade of these hormones into our system. The thing is, we are not just psychologically playing out developed habits of thinking; we are literally addicted chemically to certain forms of behavior.

We are not just psychologically playing out developed habits of thinking; we are literally addicted chemically to certain forms of behavior.

Pay attention to how many people complain about their headaches, their heartaches, and the dilemmas of their friends. We complain about all kinds of problems with everyone, including business, government, and world affairs. Cable News Networks specialize in driving hormone addictions. If we are not careful, we can easily become news junkies. We all know them, and we may know them intimately, because as the comic strip *Pogo* once said: "They is us."

To sense the depth of the problem, simply consider how often you hear news media expressions of joy, happiness, and enthusiasm for life. How often can you count on hearing positive excitement from your friends, your family, or yourself? Observe your words - they deeply matter. Every word we speak is backed by a thought, and it is thought that drives the creation of our reality.

All of us have a host of past injuries, errors, and pain. Dwelling on them perpetuates and deepens the damage they do. As we revisit these experiences of hurt, embarrassment, or guilt, it strengthens the bonds that bind us. Unless we are specifically revisiting negative memories in order to give them a higher vibration, we should be careful at dredging up the past. Typically, we excuse ourselves the perverse bathing in past upsetting memories by suggesting we'll learn from it. And perhaps there may be some truth here, but there is a huge difference between briefly looking backwards, and taking up residence there. The majority of the time, when people are focused on past experiences they are dwelling on negative situations rather than those that are inspirational. According to the Australian writer Stefan Zweig:

> "Regret does not bring back a
> lost moment and a thousand
> years will not recover something
> lost in a single hour."

Forgiveness

Forgiveness can wipe the past clean of misery and guilt, if we will allow it. Those who do not know how to forgive are destined to lead less happy lives. And, if they hold too tightly to past hurts they'll endure more of the same, leading inexorably to greater distress, anguish, and unhappiness. So, unless we learn to forgive others their trespasses against us, we are philosophically and emotionally unable to forgive ourselves. It's the way your mind works. Argue with it, refuse to believe it, or insist that you're above this happening to you, but none of this will change the way our subconscious mind is designed to function. Forgiveness is vital to happiness. Without forgiveness happiness is impossible.

Forgiveness is vital to happiness. Without forgiveness happiness is impossible.

Forgiving allows us to put the past behind us. It stops us from being a victim. It empowers us to rise above our petty grievances and it gives us back our lives. In the words of Stephen M. Pollen and Mark Levine in the book, *It's All in Your Head*:

> "It's another of those spiritual ironies: Once you stop trying to control your past and just let it go, you'll find the past no longer has control over you."

Consider the programs being constructed in your subconscious mind as the result of the tenor and influence of the negative flow of information in your brain. Step outside yourself and observe your interactions neutrally. You're likely to discover that there is a heavy weighting of data flowing into you which powers up negative emotions. This would be as compared to those emotions that are up-lifting. It is critically important for us to realize that, no one can thrive, physically, mentally, or emotionally, by dwelling on the negative.

No one can thrive, physically, mentally, or emotionally, by dwelling on the negative.

Okay, so that sounds like a rational statement, and it does make sense, but most of us don't really believe that engaging in gossip, growling about our work, family, lack of money, lack of appreciation, and whining about what's wrong with our bodies, actually affects us. Instead, our addictions - and they are real addictions - rationalize for us. Just like the alcoholic who can "hold his liquor," or the guy who denies drinking more than in moderation, we barrage ourselves with a battery of similar rationales. For the most part, we deny the possibility that we are responsible for our problems, most of the time because we simply didn't know any better. Until we get this figured out we'll continue to shift the blame on anything or anyone but ourselves.

A rather typical response when someone really gets this negativity thing for the first time goes something like: "Even if I did admit there is some truth to this concept, how could anyone function in the real world by avoiding the news and not engaging in day-to-day conversation?" Grasping the depth of our dilemma is always unsettling. The real questions should be: How do I control my thoughts? How do I interact with others? How do I live in the real world?

To deal with our addiction to negativity we must first admit, at least to ourselves, that we do get a perverse payoff when indulging in what amounts to a whining session. We need to recognize that our obsessive interest in many television shows, celebrity magazines, and radio talk programming, comes from our desire to bathe in negative gossip, and be titillated by what's wrong with others. To fix it, we need to really know what the "it" is.

Let's use the garden analogy again. No one ever intentionally plants weeds in a garden. But weeds show up anyway. They are pervasive. Before your garden will produce what you've planted, the weeds will do their best to take over. In the early stage, when shoots are just beginning to come up, you need to identify the stuff you want, from the stuff you don't. And then, you've got to get busy weeding.

Guilt

Next to a lack of forgiveness, the most toxic weed in your mental garden is guilt. If you want to be happy, you'll need to eradicate this automatic response program right where it lives. It resides deep in our core; in our secret inner self. As we have reviewed elsewhere, psychologists tell us that somewhere around 75 percent of our mental operating programs were developed by the time we were six years old. As adults we are often running around, busy living lives of frustration, disappointment, and defeat, because we view our world and circumstances through the eyes of an under-developed child. Yes, it's incredible, but it's also quite true! You see, guilt unravels good. Guilt will neutralize happiness. Guilt destroys peace. And guilt encourages all kinds of disease. Feelings of guilt erode joy on contact. We seldom realize this insidious subconscious paradigm is the cankering worm undermining us, as we proceed through life.

Guilt is a sense of wrong. It represents our deep-seated belief that we're not good enough; that we don't really deserve more than a miserly share of happiness. Guilt is all wrapped up in the "sin" world. We learned in childhood to store feelings of shame for childish misbehavior, misdeeds, and errors in judgment. Guilt has imposed an upward limit on our happiness thermostat. We pursue happiness, but early on we "learned" that we're not really good enough. Besides, isn't it awfully selfish of us to want all this happiness? Hint: That's our guilt speaking.

Real happiness, that marvelous state of being where we see life as incredible, love as magical, and beauty all around, requires that we suspend our internal judgment. We must learn to quiet the monkey mind of our negative thoughts. We must learn to love and enjoy our own company. So then, why aren't we happier? Because we don't know a better way.

"Everything is based on mind,
is led by mind, is fashioned by
mind. If you speak and act with
a polluted mind, suffering will
follow you as the oxcart follows
the ox. If you speak and act with
a pure mind, happiness will follow
you as a shadow follows form."

The Buddha

It's All *Thought!*

Chapter 10

JUDGMENT and the EGO

> "Judge not, and ye shall be not judged:
> condemn not and ye shall not be
> condemned: forgive, and ye shall be
> forgiven."
>
> Luke 6:37 KJV

Viewing Things

Most of us take it for granted that we see life as it really is, and therefore rarely question our view of things. We automatically attach qualities to both people and things. As a result of our subconscious conditioning, we decide rapidly what is beautiful and what is not, who is good and who is not, what is right and what is wrong. We rarely look much deeper in order to recognize that this is our ego-mind superimposing attributes and making instant judgment on everything with which we come in contact.

How many times have we heard that the only thing constant in the universe is change? And yet, we ascribe permanence and solidarity to things through our labeling of them. If we fail to challenge our snap judgment of others, they remain frozen in our memory banks in concert with the label we have given them. We cling to our labels, isolating people and things into our own mental cubicles. In effect, we stick people and things into psychological pigeon holes, labeled with the primary emotions we've attached to them. We judge things as enemy or friend, helpful or not, nice or unkind, and without our ever recognizing it, we quietly judge whether every event, situation, person or thing, adds or subtracts to our happiness.

> **Without our ever recognizing it, we quietly judge whether every event, situation, person or thing, adds or subtracts to our happiness.**

Logic tells us that the person who just cut us off on the highway; the one we've just called a "jerk," is probably loved by others. And, if we can bring ourselves to admit it, those others who love our erratic driver surely have a much different opinion of this person than the one that our snap judgment just labeled him. With only a moment's extra thought, most of us should be able to admit to ourselves that we have, in the past, become a friend of someone with whom we originally thought poorly. Most of us received this training when still in elementary school. But never mind this more lofty understanding, because in the moment that we snap judge and label someone, our ego-mind is busy generating what we're convinced is the only one true reality.

We are *addicted* to believing that what we think must be true. This truth of which we are so certain is merely the projection of the attributes we've assigned to everything we come in contact with; the whole of our perceptions to date. If we dare ponder this for awhile, we may grasp that every day, and at all times, we're constantly faced with a simple question: Do we love or do we judge?

Do we love or do we judge?

Underlying much of our unhappiness is our immediate reaction to critically define. That response is our unconscious tendency to judge and find life and all experiences in it, not quite good enough. Even as we enjoy a particular event, we frequently vocalize what would make that event better. Without thinking, we have judged the event somehow lacking. Why do we do this? Because our ego-mind is typically in charge; calling the shots.

Ego

According to psychologists it is the ego that generates most of our thoughts. The ego is the program running in our brain that insists on endless analysis. For the most part, this internal scrutiny is based on emotional content filtered through prior perceptions and conditioning, then colored by fear. Everyone has had the experience of trying to shut off the voice in their head that will just not stop editorializing. Most of us only recognize this as a problem when we're trying to sleep and the voice in our head won't shut up. Have you thought much about this? Are there two of you in your head? Is one of you listening while the other is constantly telling you what's going down?

The ego identifies with the body, mind, and emotions. We all have it. It is the internal program running at the base of the brain that is concerned with physical survival, emotional pleasure, and personal gain. The ego is focused almost entirely on self-interest.

> **The ego is concerned with physical survival, emotional pleasure, and personal gain. The ego is focused almost entirely on self-interest.**

The ego-mind is that part of our psyche or self, which automatically controls basic responses. The ego rules the fight or flight mechanism, along with sexual thought and behavior. It is focused primarily on the body. It is critical by its very nature, scanning its surround, ceaselessly searching for what is wrong. Ego is wholly narcissistic.

The ego invariably insists on being right. In fact, it is so focused on being right it will argue on ad nauseam, rather than admit to being wrong. Being wrong or making a mistake, is a direct threat to one's ego. That's why it is so hard for most people to sincerely apologize; the ego is in control. Psychiatrists, psychologists, and neuro-biologists, argue that the ego program is our most primitive self-protection device. It is the internal mechanism that governs primal instincts, including the instinct for survival.

Scientists refer to the root of the brain, where the fight or flight mechanism is located, as the reptilian brain. Admittedly, the reptilian control center may have saved some of our ancestors from being destroyed before they could pass on the gene pool that resulted in us, but it does not serve us particularly well in a more developed society. Being constantly on the look-out for the negative is detrimental to our well-being.

Humans are the only living things on planet earth with significantly enlarged frontal lobes. This is the part of the brain that resides just behind the forehead. It is the largest component of our brain; it is the seat of creativity and reasoned thought. The frontal lobes constitute our higher thinking center, and this is the place that can signal an override of our primitive emotional reactions, our ego driven responses. We override unhelpful emotional overreactions all the time; we do this routinely when we are being objective. However, if we are not in an emotional space of objectivity, the ego-mind runs amok.

When the ego is running the show, it's almost as though we are afraid to give life too much approval, believing that if we do, things will somehow not get better. It's not unlike how some parents literally can't seem to quit telling their children everything to be careful of, for fear they'll ease up and not keep their eye on the ball.

We have a tendency to judge everything we see, hear, or experience. And, because the majority of our thinking is controlled by the ego, that means we're judging most of the time. Remember that none of us view things as they really are, we only perceive and understand them through the lens of our pre-existing paradigms - the models through which we view our world. As a result, the ego's judgments are never entirely accurate, and are likely inaccurate more than we would admit.

The ego-mind is our physical protector and that is a good thing, but if left unchecked it expands to a place of hyper sensitive to both real and imagined slights. To our ego-self there is no difference between physical vulnerability and imagined emotional vulnerability. And, for those not clearly and specifically committed to transcending the ego-self, their animalistic self-interest will direct all thought, emotion, and automatic reflex mechanisms. This is the space where most people exist.

When we're ruled by ego we're in an emotional place that is not very evolved. Most of us recognize that we need to know more about ourselves, what makes us tick, why we react the way we do. All of us recognize there are times when we've done things out of pure selfishness. We can do great damage by stupid, thoughtless comments and actions. If we dare to look at what drives us, right at that moment we are in a space of personal discovery and development. The ego's domain is not a place where light, freedom, and real happiness can exist. Yet even here, where the predominantly self-possessed reside, there are constant glimmers of insight available leading up and out of this space of anxiety, fear, and disease.

For those devoted to self-transcendence, it is valuable to really appreciate that most thinking is of egocentric origin. The ego's primary function is commentary. A primary obstacle to happiness is the constant mental chatter that our ego produces. This lower narcissistic self of ours seems to grab control, and spew a never-ending stream of opinion, rationalization, judgment, and critique. The ego is captivated by its own stories. After all, we are the central character in its play. And, the world is all about us... Well, isn't it? ...Our ego-voice is certain of it.

The ego presumes the right to interrupt and interfere with our peace whenever it wants, which is much of the time. It makes observations and delivers opinions on everything. "Look at her hair!" "I'm getting fat." "What an ugly shirt." And, on and on it goes. If we are feeling too peaceful, the ego will fairly soon get our attention by presenting some kind of potentially fearful scenario. In order to develop balance, and really grasp what's happening within, it is important to understand that the ego's stock and trade is fear. This includes insecurities of every description: alarm, phobias, timidity, anxiety, worry, apprehension, misgiving, mistrust, doubt, suspicion, loss, fright, dread, terror, dismay, panic, and things of a similar nature.

The ego's stock and trade is fear. This includes insecurities of all kinds.

The vibratory frequency where our consciousness routinely resides is reflected in our experience. Feelings are the result of a given quality of thought. For example, if we are easily motivated (perhaps *manipulated* would be a better word), by feelings of insecurity - *fear* by another name - we will experience anxiety and dwell in a place of unresolved emotional stress. When this happens, we tend to withdraw and interpret much of the happenings in the world as frightening. We feel overwhelmed, as our fears beget more fears.

How do we know where our vibratory level of thinking is predominately resonating? Listen to how our closest friends are speaking. Then if you're really brave, listen to the words you are using in routine conversations and especially those conversations where feelings are attached. Take note, whenever one is complaining, blaming, angry, upset, hateful, depressed, or feeling shame, despair, or humiliation, we are projecting our egocentric negative energy onto others, and setting ourselves up for more of the same.

Whenever one is complaining, blaming, angry, upset, hateful, depressed, or feeling shame, despair, or humiliation, we are projecting our egocentric negative energy onto others, and setting ourselves up for more of the same.

In human ego psychology, that which we give severely negative labels to is all too often something suppressed, repressed, or denied within us. The way the ego deals with suppressed or confused feelings is frequently to accuse or project these obsessions onto others. These others may include individuals, groups of all description, businesses, institutions, governments, and even God.

When the ego has significant control over us, it will develop new enemies again and again on which to project its own guilt, self-hatred, and unloveableness. The really scary part of all this is that the ego would rather make us sick unto death than to admit it is wrong or seek forgiveness for its excesses. An uncontrolled ego will not accept responsibility for its own acts of negativity. It will always search for a way to hang its misery on others. The ego's primary escape mechanism to accepting personal responsibility is to be a victim. The antidote to an over-controlling ego is humility.

The antidote to an over-controlling ego is humility.

The ego hates humility. It demands to be right. Like a spoiled child it stamps its foot and refuses to apologize. However, when we learn to view our ego from a more enlightened place, we recognize that while it is a useful tool for protection, we are perfectly capable of transcending its selfish games. To ascend beyond the ego's grasp, we must live in a place of gratitude, forgiveness, kindness, compassion, love, and most of all HUMILITY. It's easy to say, but a tall order for most people. Humility brings to the fore, the very opposite feelings that the ego uses to influence us. And, even once we've learned the lesson that humility pays huge results in our own personal power, peace and happiness, it seems we must learn the lesson again and again in order to override our prior conditioning.

Judgment

Every time we reflect on a situation and decide how we feel about it, we are impacting our emotional equilibrium. In other words, when we decide something is bad, or not good enough, this is a direct instruction to our emotional control center. This is important to understand, because we literally feel our judgments.

We literally feel our judgments.

Decide something is bad, and shortly we'll be feeling that way. Judge something as good, and we will soon be feeling better. As we think about the judging process, the essential truth of it begins to reveal itself: we cannot focus on negative thoughts about anything and simultaneously feel good. Our basic operating system will not allow this dichotomy.

> **We cannot focus on negative thoughts about anything and simultaneously feel good. Our basic operating system will not allow this dichotomy.**

The basic truth about how we function usually comes as quite a shock when we see it for what it is. Each of us has something akin to an internal thermostat that monitors the amount of happiness we will subconsciously allow ourselves. This is a function of our emotional control center. In order for us to raise our internal happiness setting, and allow ourselves to experience greater joy, we must deal with this judgment reality. Are we able to grasp the fundamental principal that whenever we judge anyone or anything, it is ultimately us that will experience the effects of our judgment?

> **Are we able to grasp the fundamental principal that whenever we judge anyone or anything, it is ultimately us that will experience the effects of our judgment?**

The quote at the head of this chapter records Jesus as saying:

> "Judge not, and ye shall not be judged: condemn not and ye shall not be condemned: forgive, and ye shall be forgiven."

> Luke 6:37 KJV

What's this? If we don't judge others, we are not judged ourselves? How can this be? Could it possibly be true? If we do not condemn others, we ourselves will not be condemned? Of course, we've all heard this kind of thing before. But what does it really mean? And honestly now, do we believe it?

Perhaps you are aware that much of the world's ancient wisdom literature contains the same philosophical idea that *when we forgive, we are forgiven*. Okay, so others have come to the same conclusion, but does that make it true? Modern psychology confirms this dramatic concept taught by Christ (which is a title name meaning "The Anointed One"), over two thousand years ago. The Buddha (which is a title name meaning "The Enlightened" or "Awakened One"), taught this same principal over 2,500 years ago. It is clear that inspired ancients thought this was an important philosophical concept, but still the question hangs out there, what does it really mean?

Let's consider a little more carefully the remarkable notion that to forgive actually allows forgiveness. Can you see that you may be angry at your father, but it's *your* nervous system that experiences that anger? Anger flows from negative judgment, but all of that is going on inside you. Remember, we see nothing as it is, only as we perceive it to be. And, most of those perceptions are based on emotions, so in effect we literally *feel* what we're thinking.

The Buddha is reported to have said, "All things are created in our minds." Modern quantum physics, neuro-biology, and psychology agree. The act of seeing, hearing, sensing, considering, and evaluating, are all functions of the brain. Much of the time, these functions are judgments of a sort. When we judge, we are focused on lack. It is our lack of the acceptance of things as they are, coupled with our ingrained habit of criticizing that creates our internal conflicts, our pain, our fears, depression, and disease.

> **It is our lack of the acceptance of things as they are, coupled with our ingrained habit of criticizing that creates our internal conflicts, our pain, our fears, depression, and disease.**

When we release ourselves from the drive to continually pass judgment on things, our level of consciousness is able to rise. On the other hand, if we are feeling the "hate" of something, such as "I hate this or that," we have automatically triggered the process of aggression within us. Usually this is unconscious response, and not one that we intended. Feelings of aggression trigger anger subliminally, and when this happens it is not long before we find ourselves being antagonistic. All kinds of negative emotional sensations can flow from a single act of what we want to believe is nothing more than a casual observation.

Our deepest felt fears, wants, and intentions, create the experience we are - or shall soon be - having. Our choice to engage in judgment generates a cascade of affects in our emotional control center. If we've judged things in a positive way, we are rewarded with a greater sense of joy, peace, and happiness. As we focus on negative judgments, we almost instantly impact our happiness quotient in a downward fashion. The truth of this basic function of the self is again set forth in the Bible:

> "Judge not, that ye be not judged.
> For with what judgment ye judge,
> ye shall be judged: and with
> what measure ye mete, it shall
> be measured to you again."
> Matthew 7:1-2 KJV

This process of ceasing to judge resulting in our not being judged - is actually an automatic one. It is an internal process with a predetermined result. When you judge others, your subconscious judges you; when you cease to judge others, the subconscious ceases to condemn you. As we learn to suspend judgment and accept others as they are, *only then* are we able to begin the practice of accepting ourselves as *we* are. "What?" you might say. "Accept myself as I am, even with all my imperfections?" Absolutely. We deny ourselves our own acceptance, and withhold our own forgiveness, until, and unless, we are able to forgive others.

**We deny ourselves our
own acceptance and we**

**withhold our own forgiveness,
until and unless, we are
able to forgive others.**

Whether we wish to acknowledge it or not, the above statement is an accurate depiction of our basic emotional and subconscious programming. Interestingly enough, it sounds a lot like a paraphrase from the Lord's Prayer: "...and forgive us our trespasses as we forgive those who trespass against us..." Humans are hardwired this way. Wanting it to be different will not change it. We simply cannot hold a grudge, or feel anger, bitterness, etc., against someone else and expect that it will not impact us personally. We can deny it, but how will that help? The bottom line is that in order to unravel our own depression, our pain, much of our physical disease, and all of our unhappiness, we must forgive ourselves our past poor choices. In order to do this we must first forgive everyone who we perceive have done us wrong. There is really no exception to this rule of life. We are simply unable to accept ourselves until we cease judging others.

**We are simply unable to
accept ourselves until we
cease judging others.**

Suspending Judgment

The subconscious mind does not know the difference between you and me. When we make a negative statement about anyone or anything, our subconscious mind accepts that as information about itself. Oh sure, consciously we are absolutely certain we know the difference, but our consciously spoken words and our consciously held thoughts are the programming code that is being fed to our subconscious mind. Our subconscious mind is, in effect, our own personal auto-pilot.

Let's recall that somewhere around 99 percent of all our functions, whether physical, mental, or emotional, are taking place without our ever recognizing the processes that are in motion. Our subconscious mind — our auto-pilot - is running the show.

What we think and what we say are always impacting how our subconscious programs process new and upcoming experiences. It is vital, therefore, that we improve the way we view things. If we do not take conscious action, to change the programming we are continually feeding our subconscious, then we'll continue to get the same emotions we've always got. We do this through becoming more aware of why we do what we do, then shifting our thoughts and redefining our beliefs. Our lives cannot get better until we suspend judgment, of others first - because it is this shift in thinking that begins to change the code that controls our emotional control center. Happiness is an emotional response to a love of life.

If we forgive others, in order to unravel the painful, distrustful, unhappy, emotions we have been holding on to, what does that imply regarding our relationships with those others we need to forgive? Must we be their friends? Must we continue some form of relationship? We are not required to enjoy those we choose not to be with. We do not have to endorse them, live with them, or do business with them. On the other hand, we cannot afford to hold grudges, or wish others ill will. If we do, we are withholding our own happiness. It's this simple: stop being critical, or continue to pay the price. We must learn to let things go. Can you see that complaining is the enemy to your own personal happiness?

Stop being critical, or continue to pay the price. Complaining is an enemy to your happiness.

We frequently think negative banter is funny. After all, we're only kidding; right? The problem is that our auto-pilot does not get the nuance. It does not get the joke. To be happy requires you change the way you interact with the world. Stop focusing on the negative. Stop thinking and talking about your past hurtful, painful, and frightening experiences. Consider the type of jokes you enjoy. What do they say about you? What message are you sending yourself? All of us are continually re-programming "Auto." We just do not realize we are doing it. Now you know. And, now you can choose to change it.

To be happy, joyful, and fun, requires we give special attention to releasing those deep down grudges we've been holding on to. We would be wise to face down those hurtful things from our past, the unfairness of betrayal, those heart-stopping financial fears, and anything else that's trapped within us. Let them go; no matter what. We need to put ugly thoughts out of our minds; to clean this stuff out of our subconscious. No exceptions. It is really very unhealthy to say you'll forgive Suzie for so and so, but you will never forgive that dirty rotten ex-son-in-law, for such and such. Holding on to emotionally stressful feelings are a cancer to your spirit; a destroyer of your peace. Furthermore, there is mounting evidence to suggest that a cancer in your thinking may well be the source of a cancer in your body. Several recent books have made the case that our emotional dis-ease is the cause of much of our disease. Now pause…and think about that.

The biblical John recorded Jesus as saying:

"Ye judge after the flesh; I judge no man."
John 8:15 KJV

This quote is short, simple, and to the point. It is clear and succinct. Or is it? Christ says, "I judge no man." Did you know that? Read it again. It acknowledges that we are the ones doing the judging. Jesus tells us in the most straight-forward manner that he is *not* judging us. So why do so many church-goers carry around a load of guilt, secretly fearing they are unworthy, and constantly being judged by their savior? The way to offload this internal sense of unworthiness is to forgive others. When we forgive others, our subconscious mind quits searching for unworthiness within. Remember in Chapter 5, when we introduced the universal phenomenon "Like Attracts Like?" When we quit focusing on what's wrong with life, and instead focus on being grateful for the good around us, we begin to manifest more of that - the goodness we observe and are then focused upon.

Beating ourselves up, just like holding bad feelings towards others, is simply not helpful. Jesus says he's not judging you. You are judging you. Guilt and its closest ally, shame, are powerful motivators to hold people in line with social mores. Of course, guilt can move us to change, and that may be a good thing, but being consumed by it, and carrying it around in our subconscious, is an extremely unhealthy form of a lack of forgiveness.

How do you suppose it is that so many religionists have shifted a clear and concise statement like the biblical John quotation above into its seeming opposite? The truth is that we do this all the time, generally by listening to others rationalize their given thoughts on some subterranean meaning that obviates the entire message. We tend to assume that others must know, especially when they are people we admire. Further, we assume that people for whom we have good feelings must be right in their thoughts about such things. Because we admire them, we listen to them without critical analysis. Soon enough, we find ourselves repeating what we've heard them say, what they think (or what we think they think), and what they do. Most of this learning process is done at a completely subliminal level. As a result we are wholly unaware it is even going on. Before long our thoughts and ways of viewing the world are pretty much like those we have listened to, read about, or thought upon, for any length of time.

That is not to say that there are not wonderful people all around you, some with good advice and positive things to teach us, but wouldn't it make more sense for you to rethink your working paradigms for yourself, from a more enlightened point of view?

Each of us ought to re-examine our programming in light of the new things we've learned. Can you see that the failure to forgive is unhealthy? Can you see that if you are harboring guilty feelings about yourself that this is just another form of failing to forgive? Many good people do not understand this most basic principal: A guilty feeling not immediately dealt with is deeply unhealthy. Unresolved guilt cankers all our thoughts and feelings. Further, it appears that those feeling the most guilt, for whatever reason; tend to preach guilt with the greatest fervor. Do not invest in guilt. Forgive others; forgive yourself; move on.

Do not invest in guilt.
Forgive others; forgive
yourself; move on.

Ultimately, it is our judgment of ourselves that really matters. The strange thing is we simply don't usually know we're doing it. In my observation, the lower the evolution of our individual consciousness, the more likely it is we will insist we are not judging... ourselves or others. We trick ourselves into thinking we are not judgmental of character. But stop and think about it. If you were not burdened down with negative feelings, and you felt free, full of light and excitement, wouldn't you consider yourself happy? If you're not feeling light, free, and full of excitement, why not? At this juncture, you surely know that to point outside yourself to external circumstances as an excuse for unhappiness is fallacious. So, your unhappiness is a function of the way you think. And, unless you are pretty darn happy, the way you are thinking must be critical, skeptical, and judgmental.

Each of us is routinely deciding just how much happiness we will allow ourselves. We decide how much pain we shall endure. We decide how depressed we believe we must be, or how hard we must work. We decide how much we shall suffer before we allow ourselves the beauty, peace, and delight of unrestrained happiness.

Those that are unduly critical of themselves are those who do not believe they are worthy of love, yet they still desire attention. Like the child who acts up in order to get attention from her parents, those among us will forever be attracting notice through any means they can. If we're not careful, the ego will convince us that even negative attention is more important than no attention at all. And, there are some powerful psychological studies to indicate, that we really do believe that negative attention is more important than no attention at all. But, you can love yourself. You can give yourself understanding, kindness, and care. To gain and hold on to a happy state requires we recognize that judgment is the origin of our misery, remorse, grief, sorrow, and shame. The antidote is humility, forgiveness, and acceptance.

> **Our very happiness requires that we recognize that judgment is the origin of our misery, remorse, grief, sorrow, and shame. The antidote**

**for all of these is humility,
forgiveness, and acceptance.**

All of us make mistakes. We know this, and usually we are in the habit of forgiving others for whatever we consider to be a "legitimate mistake." Yet, frequently we don't extend ourselves that same ease of forgiveness. Not sure that's true? Listen to your self-talk. Listen to those thoughts that descend upon you when you least expect them. Thoughts like: "I'm not good enough;" "I'm not thin enough, strong enough, pretty or handsome enough, smart or worthy enough;" "I don't make enough money;" "My success is an accident." And on and on it goes. This is self-judgment whispering in your ear. Neutralize it. Suspend criticism and cease complaining. Forgive others. If you do not do these things, you are simply unable to forgive yourself. Forgive others so you can forgive yourself. Then you can step up to accepting yourself. Forgiveness is the opposite of critical judgment. Step past judgment and begin to love. Unhappiness in all of its various disguises is the absence of love.

**Unhappiness in all of its various
disguises is the absence of love.**

Fear and unhappiness are correlatives. Each spawns the other. Each is dissolved by love. Fear powers unhappiness. Shame powers unhappiness. The same is true of grief, anxiety, depression, jealousy, anger, and the pain of failure. All are states of mind, judgments made and clung to. All are a plea for love; as is all unhappiness. Love nullifies each and every obstacle to our happiness. Learn to love, starting with yourself.

**Grief, anxiety, depression,
jealousy, anger, and the pain of
failure, are all a plea for love.**

As soon as we are prepared to stop judging ourselves, and stop bathing in what we believe to be our personal misery and unhappiness, our lives will improve. We must decide to change our critical thinkingness, and catch ourselves when we slip back into our former way of reflection.

At the end of the day, nothing can actually make us unhappy. Only we decide how each event, thought, or action, shall be identified and the emotional attachment we assign to it. If we think a situation that is around us, or about us, is bad, evil, or wrong, then we shall automatically end up suffering, a condition we recognize as unhappy. If we suspend our opinions and merely view situations as events, then we are more able to move majestically with the current of life: accepting, loving, and happy.

To judge does not make one wise. Wisdom is not about judging, in fact it is almost its opposite. Remember, all unhappiness is a plea for love. To be wise about these things is to know that we don't really know all we think we do. To be wise is to awake ourselves to ourselves, to observe and accept and decide to be happy. Choose as we need to but do not invest in perpetuating negativity. Because, each time we judge anyone or anything, it is we that will ultimately experience the effect of our judgment.

> **Each time we judge anyone or anything, it is we that will ultimately experience the effect of our judgment.**

The essence of it all is simply, shall we love or shall we judge? We choose. We always have. Perhaps we really didn't quite understand the power of our choosing. Let us now choose wisely. All of us want love.

Eckhart Tolle, in his insightful book, *The Power of Now: A guide to Spiritual Enlightenment* provides this effective summary:

> "The pain that you create
> now is always some form of
> nonacceptance, some form of
> unconscious resistance to what
> is. On the level of thought,
> the resistance is some form of
> judgment. On the emotional level,
> it is some form of negativity. The

intensity of the pain depends on
the degree of resistance to the
present moment, and this in turn
depends on how strongly you
are identified with your mind."

Love is powerful stuff. It can transcend all obstacles. Love is free of judgment and fear. Love will provide all that we require. We need but focus on gratitude, love, harmony, peace, and compassion. Everything else will follow. As the late, great Mother Teresa once said:

"If you judge people you have
no time to love them."

Do we judge or do we love?

It's All *Thought!*

Chapter 11

THOUGHTS ON THOUGHT

"Thoughts are things, so we find that different kinds of thoughts become different kinds of things."

Dr. Ernest Holmes

Creators of Experience

We are the creators of our experience. Each of our lives is developing in harmony with the vibrational signals that radiate from us as a consequence of our thoughts. The longer we think thoughts of similar resonance, the stronger they become. Our focused attention on anything invites that particular thing into our reality. It does not matter whether the thing we are focused on is good or bad, whether we want it or not, whether it is honorable, appropriate, or otherwise. Whatever it is that we are thinking, even in the most private sanctuary of our minds, we are causing to materialize in our world of experience.

Our lives evolve according to our individual patterns of thought. If we are continually focused on struggles, failure, ill-health, bad relationships, and lack of trust in others, should we be surprised that we are constantly plagued with these same kinds of things? Whether it is a comfortable thought or not, it should be relatively clear by now that we are the author, the designer, and the builder of ourselves. We are the consequence of the thoughts we have placed our attention upon. At this very moment we are the sum total of every thought we've ever thought in our lives.

At this very moment we are the sum total of every thought we've ever thought in our lives.

The really good news about this sobering understanding of things is that we can change ourselves if we're not now happy with who and what we have become. We can decide to evolve. We can decide to become anything we'd really like to be. We are the creators of our own future. Think on that...

Everything is Thought

Everything mankind has ever done began with thinking. Everything begins with a thought in someone's mind.

Everything begins with a thought in someone's mind.

Stop reading for a moment and look around the room you find yourself in. Every object you see, from the walls to the floor, from the furniture to the lights, from the ceiling to the colors around you, were first thought about and then so constructed or organized. It is thus with whom we are. Whoever you are, whatever you have become, how others relate to you generally, your character, your net worth, and your value as a human being, is largely a result of the total of all the thoughts you have ever thought in your life. If this concept is still strange to you, think on it. Focus your thought on this single point of insight.

Yes, of course, things happen outside your control. Wars happen, famine happens, stray events seem to flow in and out of our lives. What does that mean? Does it mean anything? Are the evolving events of your life all of your making? Are some of them? Are most of them? I sense there are three points of view regarding the so-called chance events of your life:

1. Accidents and random incidents are meaningless. They just are.
2. Events are not random. You've pre-chosen to be here to experience these opportunities for growth.
3. Everything is an illusion. Everything is a construct of your thought.

Dozens of relatively recent books can be found on the subject, taking one or the other of these positions. And, each of these books, just like this one you are holding now, provides some kind of evidence to support the author's point of view. From my perspective the answer must be either (2) or (3) or perhaps it is actually the sum of the conclusions of numbers (2) and (3). We'll cover more about these and related questions in the Chapters of Section III. But for now, let's at least consider that you are the creator of your thoughts, and what is working well you'll probably want to keep, and what is not you'll probably want to change. Henry David Thoreau once said,

> "It's not what you look at that
> matters, it's what you see."

And, Ralph Waldo Emerson observed,

> "People only see what they
> are prepared to see."

Perhaps the most important thing to recognize right now is the absolute reality that we are the only ones who decide what to think, how to think it, and what emotional attachment we shall give to each thought we think.

Numerous challenges arrive in our lives unasked for. Can we afford to create more because of the way we think? Every thought has a consequence, and in fact, behind every experience are the thoughts that were that particular experience's source. All things in our lives are preceded by thought. Thought is at the core of everything. If we dwell on poor thinking, if we nurture evil or ignorant thoughts, misery and pain will be attracted to us. Of this we cannot escape. As our thoughts are lifted to higher ideals, and we center ourselves on healthy, joyful, and loving things, these will soon arrive and become a larger part of our reality.

As we learn to change the content and tone of the thoughts behind the things in our lives, we can transform ourselves into an improved and happier us. We can permanently improve our lives by changing our thought patterns. We can be more joyful today by refocusing our thoughts right now. It is remarkably simple to say. But, how hard is it to do? That is also a decision based on thought. The truth of that question is in the answer you are ready to provide. It takes what it takes. Whether that is hard or easy derives from your point of view. Yes, it requires careful focus, and improved awareness to make any appreciable changes, but whether that is hard or not is entirely based upon how you think about it.

To improve our lives, we must internalize this essential truth: Our experiences in the living world are the direct result of the stuff we entertain in our minds. Therefore, it is vitally important that we make our thoughts behave.

> **Our experiences in the living world are the direct result of the stuff we entertain in our minds. Therefore, it is vitally important that we make our thoughts behave.**

The Hypothalamus

The hypothalamus controls the release of at least 8 major hormones, plus multiple mixtures of these, and is involved in the body's temperature regulation. It is in charge of the body's food and water intake, sexual behavior, and it controls our daily biological cycles. The hypothalamus administers our basic behaviors and mediates our emotional responses. As we learned from Chapter 10, this chemical-producing organ, located in the center of the brain, charges our system with specific hormones that relate to the thoughts we are keenly focused upon. Every time we dwell on emotionally-charged thoughts we trigger the hypothalamus.

If we're dwelling on the negative, and experiencing an emotional response to these thoughts, the hypothalamus may trigger the release of hormones that intensify our discomfort.

Medical and biological science tells us that these hormones, or neuropeptides, are powerful chemicals. Studies demonstrate conclusively that we can easily become addicted to these internally produced drugs. If we keep thinking the kinds of negative thoughts that trigger the release of correlated hormones, we become stressed out, our minds become clouded, and we frequently will not act in concert with our best interests. It's simple, think more negative thoughts - continue to feel bad. What is so wonderful about knowing this is that the reverse is also true.

Thoughts are Contagious

Thoughts, the foundation of all emotion, are contagious. Much of the time we secretly love to be around someone who is happy and joyful. We typically feel better the moment a happy person turns a radiant smile upon us. When someone is stressed out, and sharing their misery and fears, we should be extra careful to not be swamped in their negative emotions. After all, haven't we all had a toxic friend?

We draw unto ourselves the essence of whatever we are predominantly thinking. This means that "worry" is the result of using our creative mind to bring into existence the very thing we do not want.

> **Worry is the result of using our creative mind to bring into existence the very thing we do not want.**

Dwell on this thought right now. This is powerful insight. What you think about with strong emotion begins to manifest itself in your day-to-day existence. Rather than allow generic worry to be quietly at work within our hearts and souls, we should focus on what we do want, not what we do not want. To put this understanding to work for us, we need to become aware, to recognize when worrying thoughts are swirling about us. Stop and think a moment and then turn the whole thing around, and concentrate on the outcome we wish to have, not the one we fear.

It is easy to suggest that we learn to control our thoughts. The doing of it is the catch. After all, how do we focus successfully on peace during the atrocities of war? How do we think joy into our reality when we are in the midst of family problems? Are we able to believe in, and concentrate on, abundance while dealing with the ravages of financial meltdown?

Like Does Attract Like

The concept of changing our thinking is so easy to say; the difficulty is in the doing. Nevertheless, the reality of this process is so intricate to our happiness it would be wise to remember this essential principal introduced in Chapter 5:

Like attracts like.

The re-creation of our reality begins immediately with the quality of our next thoughts. If they are negative, disbelieving, sarcastic, or worse, we'll be having more of this in our future experience. However, as we focus on positive, uplifting, caring and kind thoughts, our future begins to look up. This essential principal, "Like attracts like," has been spoken and written about by wise men and women for centuries. A growing awareness of this critical concept has prompted numerous authors to address the subject over the past hundred years.

Ernest Holmes, author and founder of a movement known as the "Science of Mind" in the 1920's was an early champion of the "Like attracts like" concept in our modern era. Many now refer to this guiding principle as "The Law of Attraction," meaning that whatever we think about and give energy to will begin to materialize in our future. Esther and Jerry Hicks have written a number of books on this incredibly significant understanding of the way things work in our universe.

So, how do we give energy to thought? By giving thought our attention. *That's it?!* Yes, that's it. We flow energy simply by focusing our attention. Normally, we do this automatically, without recognizing what it is that we are doing. When we become riveted on a thought, or a group of thoughts, it is because our thinking has triggered an emotional reaction within us. Feelings, which are essentially thoughts combined with emotion, dramatically impact the amplitude of our energy broadcast. Powering thought with emotion is like stomping on our mental accelerator.

> **Powering thought with emotion is like stomping on our mental accelerator.**

Can you see why it is so very important that we constantly monitor our thoughts and feelings? Thoughts precipitate feelings, and always underlie our actions. If you don't yet fully appreciate this important point, stay with it, think deeply about it, grasp the truth of it. Pay close attention to your thoughts and feelings, and keep them centered on what you DO want, not on what you DON'T want.

> **Pay close attention to your thoughts and feelings and keep them centered on what you DO want, not on what you DON'T want.**

There may be little we can do to immediately change the way others think about us. But, we can do a great deal to change the way we think about ourselves. Each of us must learn to form and maintain the best possible thoughts about who we want to become. We must embark upon a program to consciously replace those negative thoughts that just seem to pop into our minds with new uplifting ones. The mind is a mirror. It may be impossible to generate any substantial thought without some reflex action in the mind. The more powerfully we experience a thought the more powerfully it will impact us.

Over the last hundred years, physicists have accumulated powerful evidence, that all of the interactions between objects and materials (all mass), can be reduced to combinations of only four fundamental forces: Gravity and electro-magnetism (light energy), are the two universal forces we recognize at human scales.

The other two forces of physics do their work at the microscopic and submicroscopic plane.

We learn from physics that the more subtle the force as we go down in scale, the more powerful it is on a relative basis. Hence, the nuclear forces (the weak and strong forces of the atomic and subatomic level), are thousands of times more powerful in ratio than gravity or electromagnetism. Many scientists are now suggesting that thought energy is the quintessential force that underlies the universe. Thought is the most subtle of the forces of which we are aware, and it may well be the most powerful.

Change the Plot

Some scientists, psychologists and spiritual teachers, of similar opinion, are now teaching something along the lines of - the world is not done to you; it is being done *by* you.

> **The world is not done to you; it is being done by you.**

Whether this is entirely true or not, we cannot escape the fact that it is our thoughts that form the essence of our lives. So, are you playing the role you would like to be playing in the total immersion movie of your life? If not, why not? You can change the plot. You can tell a different back story by the emphasis you place on the qualities of people and events. You can choose a different plot line. You can choose another way. In the words of my daughter Katie,

> "Life is like a choose-your-own-adventure book."

The logical conscious mind is only able to entertain a single thought at one time. Some people are quite good at multitasking; having the conscious mind rapidly switch back and forth between tasks. If the subconscious mind is engaged in a repetitive task for which it has the learned skills, one can do more. A young person for instance, can drive a car while carrying on a conversation, listening to the radio, and carefully watching a member of the opposite sex walking at the side of the road. How? Because the subconscious mind is driving, while the conscious mind flits between priorities. Just the same, it is important to recognize that the conscious mind can only entertain one thought at a time.

Focus on Time

According to Dr. Joe Dispenza, as seen in the documentary film, *Down the Rabbit Hole*, a person normally focuses for only 6 to 10 seconds on any given subject before flitting off to something else. We may quickly return to that which we were previously focused upon, but as a general rule it's hard to stay absolutely centered on one thing to the exclusion of the myriad of thoughts lining up to grasp our attention. Other scientific experiments indicate that when confronted with new information it must be held in mind for at least 37 seconds before the brain will begin to integrate it into its working paradigm (our mental operating software). The exception to this rule of mental integration is that we must be re-exposed to the new information a minimum of six times before we will store the information in any useful way. (This is why commercials are so repetitive, and explains why the same short commercial is often shown almost back-to-back).

According to Esther Hicks, introduced above, when one is able to focus keenly for as little as 68 seconds on a single thought the mind begins the process of manifestation into our reality. The subconscious is a multiprocessor; it can handle multiple things at the same time. Its nature is to ultimately reflect that which we put our attention upon within the world of our individual reality. If one focuses on being sick; talks about it, thinks about it, reads about it, etc., the creative mind immediately begins to manifest the truth of this thinking throughout the body in such a way as to best reflect those thoughts. This projection of our thinkingness into our real world is very much like the Law of Cause and Effect. Let's recall an earlier concept from Chapter 10: The creative mind does not seem to be able to differentiate between ourselves and someone else.

The creative mind does not seem to be able to differentiate between ourselves and someone else.

This has mind-blowing implications! Think a bad or ugly thought about someone, and the mind sets about reconfiguring our mental programs such that we see ourselves in this light. We must realize that it does not serve us to ever hold angry, mean, or perverse thoughts about anyone. To do so, especially while feeling powerful emotions, is to do ourselves great harm.

As we've reviewed, it is surely no accident that every major religion of lasting impact has put emphasis on forgiveness. In Chapter 10, it was pointed out that The Lord's Prayer is a perfect example of this philosophy. We are forgiven only when we forgive others. But the really fascinating thing is that we are not even able to forgive ourselves, and thereby stop the creation of more pain and sorrow in our lives, until we neutralize the negative energy flow that is driving these problems to begin with. The mirror of our mind is constantly reflecting our thoughts back to us in our day-to-day experience. To forgive someone is to access the delete key so we can erase our own negative programming.

If we find it impossible to forgive, we are stuck in the misery of the experience and cannot evolve. Forgiveness and gratitude are the critical ingredients in our evolution to controlling thought. The simple truth is, that in order to obtain a better reality, we must focus on better thoughts. Everything begins with thought. And, like any other law or natural force, we cannot change the way it works, but we can change outcomes by the way we work with it.

In order to obtain a better reality, we must focus on better thoughts. Everything begins with thought. And, like any other law or natural force, we cannot change the way it works, but we can change outcomes by the way we work with it.

We cannot help but attract into our experience that which corresponds to the sum total of our current state of consciousness.

The law of attraction works automatically. Like a mirror, it reflects the image held before it. We must shake ourselves free from the belief that external conditions are imposed upon us.

We are indeed the creators of our experience. The power to create new, more joyful, happy experiences is within us. Refuse to feel negative thoughts fueled with feeling and imagination. Deprive them of energy. If our negative, fearful imaginings have nothing to feed upon they will shrivel and disappear. Only thoughts that are nourished grow. Thoughts that receive the nourishment of attention must eventually manifest in our physical world in some way. Once again, the point is that we must be careful to marshal our thinking, and be vigilant in ignoring the seductive desire to sink into the ease of negative thought.

We are Beings of Power

James Allen, one of England's premier philosophers wrote nineteen books, and became known world-wide for his leading-edge understanding regarding the power of thought. He summarized his thoughts on thought this way:

> "As a being of power, intelligence,
> and love, and the lord of your
> own thoughts, you hold the key to
> every situation, and contain within
> yourself that transforming and
> regenerative agency by which you
> may make yourself what you will."

Our thoughts are powerful things. As we learn to control our thinking, we are able to direct our lives in the way WE choose. This is the ultimate freedom! We decide what we shall become. No one else chooses for us. Most of us are creating our lives unconsciously based on the autopilot of the subconscious. In turn, the subconscious is responding to the mental belief systems that form the operating parameters that color all incoming data. Our minds make choices based on the skew of that data. The majority of us are completely ignorant of what constitutes the mental paradigms that underlie the lives we live, and the feelings we feel.

So, the real question is: Will you do the work needed to clean up your underlying thoughts and feelings? A failure to choose is also a choice. Let's admit that no matter how intensely we want to believe something that is NOT true, it will not make it so. Investing in beliefs that are not correct will always cripple our freedom. The Dalai Lama once said, "Resistance is suffering." Resistance to what? Resistance to the truth.

Take the time now to establish new habits of thought. Suspend your tendency for automatic judgment. Observe neutrally. Where it is important for you to make choices, align yourself with truth. And remember, just because everyone else believes something does not make it so. For example, were you aware that from antiquity up to the late 19th century, the practice of bloodletting was a standard medical practice? It was believed that the withdrawal of often considerable quantities of blood from a patient would cure, or prevent, a great many illnesses and diseases. Everyone believed it so it must be so. Wrong.

More Thoughts

Science is telling us that the physical universe is essentially nonphysical. Does that still sound strange? Yes, of course it does. Nevertheless, this conclusion is virtually irrefutable. In the words of physicist Peter Russell:

> "Atoms don't really exist. We
> are dealing with elementary
> particles which are only
> potentials for existence."

Let's recall that both Werner Heisenberg and Niels Bohr, each Nobel Laureates in quantum physics, noted that consistent with repeated experiments:

> "Atoms are not things, they
> are only possibilities."

We have learned that the universe and everything physical within it arises from a field more subtle than energy. Many scientists refer to this subatomic plane of connectedness as the

Zero Point Field, or simply the Field. We have also learned that consciousness affects the field. And, we have gained fascinating insight on something else that is absolutely extraordinary about the nature of the universe: everything is somehow connected to everything else. This is the bizarre reality of entanglement.

It has now been clearly demonstrated that atoms, and things so large you can hold them in your hand, can be instantly impacted by other things separated by long distances. In fact, distance makes no difference to the nonlocal influence of entanglement. Why care about how something separated by long distances can affect atoms? Well, atoms are the essential ingredients of all matter and anything that affects matter impacts the stuff of our physical world. So, entanglement is affecting us. In an article published in *Nature*, a premier scientific journal well known for its careful peer review, scientist Vlatko Vedral was quoted:

> "Quantum physics is accepted
> as the most accurate means of
> describing how atoms turn into
> molecules. And since molecular
> relationship is the basis of all
> chemistry, and chemistry is
> the basis of biology, the magic
> of entanglement could well
> be the key to life itself."

Do you recall that one of the fundamental laws of physics says that an event in the subatomic world exists in all possible states (super position), until the act of observing or measuring reduces it to a single state? This process is called the collapse of the wave function. The observer (that can be you or me), could be playing the critical role in the collapse of any given wave function. Two simple questions you might routinely ask yourself: What am I thinking? and "What is the likely impact of those thoughts?

What am I thinking?
What is the likely impact
of those thoughts?

Brain processes appear to occur at the quantum level. The dendritic networks in the brain appear to operate in tandem through quantum coherence. Quantum messaging in the brain takes place through vibrational fields along the microtubules (the skeletal framework), of neurons. Microtubules and the membranes of dendrites (branched filaments in neurons), might be thought of as the Internet of the body. Every neuron of the brain appears to be able to log on at the same time, and speak to every other neuron simultaneously via quantum processes. Thus, we have immense computational power. What might that mean to the quality of your thoughts? Do you have the power to change them?

Conclusions

What have we learned and what conclusions can we draw? Every decision you make is based on some construct of what is real for you. The reality of our five senses looks completely different, and even unrecognizable, when looked at deeply with a microscope. Everything we perceive in the natural world (whether with our senses or through science) comes through the filter of our consciousness, and all of that is determined, to some degree, by the mind's own structure. The structure of the brain is plastic. It is malleable. It can and does change. Changes to the brain are produced by mind; the essence of your thinkingness.

Reality is comprised of different levels; different hierarchies if you will. Body parts are real; cells and molecules are real; atoms and electrons are real. Consciousness is real. There's surface truth, and there's deeper truth. Consciousness and energy create the nature of our reality, and it is our habits of thought - our attitudes - that form the basis of it all. Happiness then is the essence of our thinking.

Our words reveal our thoughts. Our thoughts create our world. When we give thought to the words we use, we begin to create our lives with intention. When we give careful attention to the feelings we associate with our words and thoughts, we attract what we desire.

To be a happy person, we must master our thoughts and create a life by design. We are thinking creatures. However, most of us are not disciplined thinkers. It seems that every moment of every day is filled with thoughts. How often do we really think about the quality of our thoughts? For most of us, the answer to this question is virtually never. And yet, every good feeling we've ever had is the direct result of good and happy thinking. That's because thought precedes feelings. So, if happy, pleasant, good thoughts engender happy, pleasant, and good feelings - and they do - then the reverse is also true.

Consider:
- Every thought vibrates, radiating a signal broadcast on its unique frequency.
- Every thought attracts a matching signal in return.
- We draw to ourselves the essence of our predominate thinking.
- Whatever we give attention to in our NOW unfolds in our future, whether we want it to or not.
- The longer we dwell on specific thoughts the stronger they become. Our attention invites manifestation.
- Our life experience is unfolding in precise response to the vibrations that radiate, as a result of our thoughts.
- Worrying is using our creative imagination to create something we do not want.
- If we want our life to change, we must think different thoughts. What we think, and buttress with feeling, will present itself in our experience because they are a vibrational match.
- Our deepest felt desires, fears, and intentions, create the experience we will be having in our future.
- We should be careful what we wish for, as we do, in fact, have the ability to make it come to pass.
- When was the last time you challenged your thinking?
- Your thoughts are your reality.

Each of us creates our own life, moment by moment, with the thoughts to which we give the most attention. Earl Nightingale famously said:

> "We are all self-made, but only
> the successful will admit it."

Perhaps that is an unsettling statement. But do you really want to ignore the underlying truth that we are the ones that choose just how we will respond to any given situation, and therefore, we are the ones who decide how we're going to feel? Let's remember what Dr. Norman Vincent Peale famously said:

> "Change your thoughts and
> you change your world."

And so it is. James Allen, the English philosopher psychologist, put it this way:

> "You are today where your
> thoughts have brought you;
> you will be tomorrow where
> your thoughts take you."

It's All *Thought!*

Section III

CHARTING A NEW COURSE

Chapter 12

PURPOSE

"The purpose of our existence is to seek happiness."

Fourteenth Dalai Lama

Introduction

In this chapter and the four that follow, we move into areas brimming with strongly held beliefs, judgment and prejudice. In some ways it might be easier to simply ignore issues related to our purpose, religion and spirituality, and discussing aspects of the meaning of life, and who we might be. These are the areas wherein our most cherished concepts reside, and they can be literal minefields of discrimination. Frankly I'd prefer not to step on the reader's triggers. However, to not at least review a few pertinent ideas regarding these sometimes touchy subjects would be tantamount to dishonesty. To a great degree, these elements of our thinkingness are the foundation upon which our happiness is grounded.

According to the Dalai Lama, the purpose of our existence is to seek happiness, to awake, and be happy. If we are honest with ourselves, all of us are relatively certain that we really do want happiness, but most of us have trouble defining just what happiness is, at least for us. For the most part, we are confused about what happiness means, and the more we think about it, the greater our confusion. Could this be due to the fact that we are conditioned to view the world through our unresolved disappointment and stored pain?

Since Childhood

Many of us have become cynical. We are afraid. We are no longer the child who knew how to laugh and play. It may have been a long time since we could unabashedly smile, and giggle at the simplest of pleasures. We're all grown up, and we think that means we must be reserved. We've come so far from that place of unrestrained happiness that we're no longer sure that inner radiance and a sincere joyful disposition is even possible. We are confused. Most of us simply cannot admit, even to ourselves, that our confusion scares us.

What has happened during these years since our childhood is that we have become conditioned to believe that happiness is somehow unique, and perhaps we are not really worthy of it. Yes, we want it, but we no longer believe it can be a way of life. As you may recall, our ego, or lower self, tends to dwell on fear motivation. The ego believes that happiness is conditional, and therefore cannot last.

Subliminally, and perhaps even consciously, we are muddled and perplexed. Not just about happiness; it extends to our beliefs, our purpose, whether there is meaning to life, whether true love really exists, who we are, what or who God is, and virtually everything of real significance. If we give too much attention to our confusion, it is unnerving, so we spend inordinate amounts of time distracting ourselves from the truly important.

To an undisciplined untrained mind, happiness requires suffering and sacrifice. Over time, most people buy into the notion that before we can really enjoy happiness, we must somehow first earn it. We've conditioned ourselves to believe that "life is hard." And, because we are so easily manipulated by fear, we're secretly convinced that we simply do not deserve to be enthusiastically joyful. In fact, many of us have trouble even connecting with the concept.

The route to a new and much happier "us" begins with the understanding that our lack of happiness is a learned condition. Much of what we've been taught in these regards is essentially wrong. We need to know a better way, to take down the dams that hold back our understanding. Then, we can awaken to a greater truth, and start right now to discover a new world where life is fun, exciting, joyful, and full of love, and gratitude. A key lesson to learn is that nothing real blocks our happiness, only misunderstanding and delusion.

**Nothing real blocks
our happiness, only
misunderstanding
and delusion.**

All of our emotional misery, the pain we experience within our hearts and minds, can be released. We can heal and we can be happier than we ever thought possible. Chapter one, paragraph one, of the Dalai Lama's book, *The Art of Happiness*, reads:

> "I believe that the very purpose
> of our life is to seek happiness.
> That is clear. Whether one
> believes in religion or not, whether
> one believes in this religion or
> that religion, we all are seeking
> something better in life. So, I
> think, the very motion of our
> life is towards happiness."

The Dalai Lama, along with many great spiritual teachers of the past, shared with us the special insight that obtaining true happiness is, indeed, the underlying purpose of our mortal lives. This philosophy impresses me, because, as so many of us may have discovered, after reading scores of books on happiness and related topics, the vital issue of "purpose" is often ignored. Or, at least, while the concept of purpose is often alluded to, the subject is all too frequently passed over with glib platitudes. Many authors seem to be afraid to take on this primal question, with all its inherent risks. To what risks am I referring? According to my decidedly unscientific survey, most of the books dealing with happiness have been written by psychologists, including the most recent of the Dalai Lama's books, as it was compiled and written by psychologist Howard Cutler.

The highly loaded question, "What is the purpose of life?" or "What is your purpose in life?" seems to have strayed out of the area of clinical psychology, and moved into the territory where religion exerts great influence. Aside from the fact that it is not generally considered politically correct for psychologists to weigh in on religious matters, it is a topic that a number of these professionals are not comfortable with. As a result, secular authors tend to skirt the topic, rarely engaging it straight on. In my view, this is the equivalent of ignoring the 800 pound gorilla in the living room. Although the subject is critical, at least subliminally, to all of us, the underlying concern for both writers and professionals is this business of coming up against the reader/client's most cherished belief systems. These powerful internal thought patterns are the ones that will make us put down the book, or turn off the counsel of a well-intended professional. So, how do we proceed when we're up against this level of pre-disposition? My approach is to simply ask the reader to temporarily suspend judgment when he or she is feeling those sensations of emotional conflict, and carry on. Does this work? You'll know pretty quickly.

As we consider what our purpose may be, it is helpful to recall that all of us view the world through our own lenses. Remember Chapter 6 dealing with paradigms? Our internal belief system constitutes the paradigm through which we construct our reality. Every experience, every sensory input, all new incoming information, is first filtered and compared through the lenses of our own individual prejudices. These are the assumptions through which we have come to know the world. This process is an unconscious one, yet we live and breathe our embedded beliefs, and all our thinking and interaction is a reflection of them.

Tinted Glasses

As we've learned, all of us are wearing tinted glasses that shade and color everything we see, through the knowledge we've thus far gained. Our minds view all new data only after reflection in the mirror of our past experiences, adjusting, tinting, and harmonizing the information accordingly. Furthermore, we can only see the world that our human sensory equipment is able to see, and that which our internal belief system and emotions will allow us to see. Put another way, we create the world we perceive. And, that's because, the drama on the stage of our lives is what our minds believe it is.

> **The drama on the stage of our lives is what our minds believe it is.**

This concept of vision bears repeating. We view all new information via the agency of the mirror of our past thoughts, choices, understanding, and experience. We automatically color all new input, as a consequence of our political, social, scientific, and religious predispositions. This is really not an issue as to whether or not you are active in church, temple, or mosque. All of us, regardless of religious background or training, carry some form of internal belief system. And, it should also be clear that we are the script writer, the producer, the star, and the publicist of our own melodrama. We've produced the movie of our past, and are now directing the movie of our future.

So, then, what is this thing called purpose? The American Heritage dictionary defines purpose as: (1) An aim or goal, (2) Intention, (3) Determination or resolution. Thus, assuming the Dalai Lama is right, and that the purpose of our life is to seek happiness, then our primary goal in life ought to be to garner happiness. We should intend it! We should be determined, and resolute in its pursuit!

A How To

There is a relatively easy way to plumb our value system, and begin to define ourselves in the here and now; a way to point us immediately towards greater happiness. It is such a simple concept many will discount it. Try it. You'll be surprised. It is easy to begin and easy to do, but it can be dramatically effective in reorienting you towards a happier more satisfied you.

Simply select single words that you would like to represent your primary personality attributes. These individual words should convey a sense of how you perceive yourself, or how you would like to see yourself. Make a list of positive words with which you want to identify more closely, and, if it's helpful to you, write out a sentence or phrase. This is a beginning, and it's more than that; your words may form the basis of a meditative mantra, or act as a set of personal affirmations. Recollect that words have power.

Next, narrow your list of words down, by choosing no more than ten with which you want to closely identify, at least at first. Think of words like: abundance, artistic, cheerful, charming, courageous, creative, dependable, faithful, honest, funny, intelligent, inventive, kind, loving, loyal, secure, and so forth. There are lots of beautifully descriptive words, and once you've made your list, you may want to select them all. However, it is important that you prioritize, as this very act will reveal to you the essence of who you truly wish to be right now.

For me, I've evolved two groups of five words. They form my walking mantra. The term "mantra" is actually a Hindu term from the Sanskrit. Essentially, it is a sound or word (sometimes a group of words called a "Sutra"), the repetition of which can be personally transforming. Hence the reason I refer to these single descriptive words as a mantra. I identify closely with them, and repeat them multiple times every day. I focus on only one group of five words for each quarter-mile around a track, alternating them back and forth. These words are meaningful to me, but chances are, they will not really ring your bell. This is as it should be. We are all wonderfully different. Dare to be yourself. My words are:

Gratitude	Kindness
Love	Wisdom
Harmony	Health
Peace	Wealth
Compassion	Happiness

I use two lists of five words each because I can click them off on the fingers of my two hands. Repeat your list before you drift off to sleep each night. Repeat the words that represent the qualities that are the most attractive to you, right now, at this stage of your life. As a general rule, I would suggest you keep these to yourself, so you do not end up using words that others might find more noteworthy. Your words should represent you, *to you*.

I've actually found myself quietly singing the words I've chosen, putting them to verse and rhyme, exploring different ways of making sure my subconscious is getting this new programming code. By saying your words and clicking them off on your fingers rather quickly, you'll be able to simply glance at a finger and call up the positive feelings you've associated with that word. Repeat your words again and again. Use them in prayer; use them as a mantra in meditation. If you stick with this simple process, it will not be long before you become that which you are now thinking.

> **If you stick with this simple process, it will not be long before you become that which you are now thinking.**

I know this seems all too simple; it's not. Remember the science behind it. Remember how your subconscious works. Begin right now to design the new you. It is really not hard to make it happen, you just need to get started and stay with it. Do it. Do it now.

Our Teachers

In order for us to better understand our purpose, and revel in a life of joy, enthusiasm, and true happiness, we will need to practice sincere gratitude for things as they are, and as they may become. With more mature insight we discover that our greatest teachers are the people we judge to be enemies, and the circumstances we judge to be catastrophes.

> **Our greatest teachers are the people we judge to be enemies, and the circumstances we judge to be catastrophes.**

If you will take a moment and think back with humility about the most stressful experiences in your past, you will probably admit that you learned and grew as a consequence of them. Nobody consciously seeks out stressful situations, yet when they arise it usually requires that we step up in order to deal with them successfully. It is almost always the more difficult circumstances that help us grow. These are indeed our real teachers in life. When one grasps the truth of this concept, we are better able to embrace those who perhaps intend to do us harm. Of course, it may not immediately feel natural to us to this, and it does take a great deal of humility. Notwithstanding, these are they that actually aid us in lifting our sights, in rising above the skirmishes of life. It is in these moments of the here and now that we are able to challenge our predispositions, and decide to override the comfort of being a victim, and instead evolve to a more enlightened space. Remember, it is not what is done to us, but only how we allow it to affect us that truly matters.

It is not what is done to us, but only how we allow it to affect us that truly matters.

How does this help us clarify our purpose for existence? Consider that our time here in the physical world is more than just living; it is learning. When we are experiencing a thing we are immersed in it. We learn much more effectively doing something than in simply discussing it or philosophizing about the doing of it. This is not always true, but it is substantially correct. So again, why consider our struggles in life under the heading of purpose? Because a purposeful life requires that we evolve. Evolving requires that we learn and grow. Growth requires real live experiences. We learn by living.

The truth is we are made to learn. In the prison setting, many men with whom I've worked objected loudly to this concept, at least initially. About half of inmates in the federal prison system have not graduated from high school, and therefore, they find themselves in Congress mandated day-time GED classes. A lot of these students claimed they hated to learn new things, or that they couldn't learn, for whatever reasons it is that they had been telling themselves. But, once we discussed the things they enjoy doing, shooting hoops, playing softball, running the track, lifting weights, talking sports, they begin to grasp that all of these things are related to learning. This realization resulted in a huge paradigm shift among them.

Whether or not an inmate has received much formal education has little to do with what he knows about professional athletes - what they do, how they do it, what kind of person they are, what trouble they've gotten into, what their stats are, etc. In other words, they've *learned* a lot about something. When one is shooting baskets, they're doing it to get better...that's learning. We're made to learn. We want to learn. In fact we love to learn, whether we know this or not. The question is not whether we love to learn, so much as what is it we love to learn? Assessing our desire to learn, and recognizing that we can always be learning if we will allow ourselves, is a big hint as to why we are here, and what our purpose may be.

An essential component on our road to happiness is that we learn from our experiences. We must awaken to the value of all the events of our lives. Relish with enthusiasm every development, every occurrence; see them for what they are, new opportunities to learn and grow.

Happiness, A Spiritual Path

Is it not reasonably clear that what we choose to do in our NOW will affect what we shall become? And perhaps, even more importantly, how we choose to *feel* in our NOW shall unerringly affect our future? Consider again that literally no one benefits by our living a joyless, uninteresting, drab existence. We exist to love and be loved, to thrill to life's opportunities, to smile and enjoy our evolution towards greater light and knowledge. Neither conditions, nor circumstances, determine whether or not we seek to discover the good. On the contrary, happiness and a joyful existence require that we focus on what's right, and that we develop a keen sense of gratitude and appreciation for everything as it is, and as it may become.

Those who believe there is nothing more to existence than to eat, breed, work, and die (important to living but not to life), and who believe in no greater purpose, have no hope for the future, neither for themselves, nor for anyone they hold dear. Whereas it is true that each of us must determine what our individual purpose in this life shall be, there are elements in our discovery of purpose that are common to us all. Fundamental, basic, and undergirding everything worthwhile is our commitment to be happy. This is our highest spiritual path; the route to self-mastery.

> **Undergirding everything worthwhile is our commitment to be happy. This is our highest spiritual path; the route to self-mastery.**

We decide. We choose. We either commit ourselves to the higher road of personal self-realization, or we do not. It is an absolute fact that happiness is a choice in the way we think. It is a decision to evolve along the path of self-mastery and wisdom.

> **Happiness is a choice. It is a decision to evolve along the path of self-mastery and wisdom.**

William James, the nineteenth century philosopher psychologist, said it this way:

> "How to gain, how to keep, how to recover happiness, is in fact for most people at all times the secret motive of all they do."

Does this ring true for you? Recall that at the beginning of our study together we focused on the sixteenth century French philosopher Pascal's powerful summation:

> "All men seek happiness. This is without exception.

Whatever different means
they employ, they all tend to
this end. This is the motive of
every action of every man."

It seems that great thinkers of all nationalities, and of all times, have come to similar conclusions. We all seek happiness, whether we're conscious of it or not. And, as we've learned, happiness is an internal, or mental, state that has very little to do with what we have, what we earn, or how powerful other people think we are. This is because the secret to a joyful life is in our head. Happiness is about attitudes, not actions. And, as we've reviewed several times already, happiness is rarely associated with material things.

Happiness is a mental condition, not a set of external circumstances. Recall that we've also learned that what and who we are is equal to the sum total of all the thoughts we've thought to date. Or, as Gautama Siddhartha (the Buddha), put it:

"All that we are is the result
of what we have thought."

Let's also remember that our words reveal our thoughts. Our thoughts create our world. When we give thought to the words we use, we begin to create our lives with intention. When we give careful attention to the feelings we associate with our words and thoughts, we attract what we desire. To be a happy person, we must master our thoughts and create a life by design. We are thinking creatures. But most of us are not disciplined thinkers. We can become more disciplined by training our thought processes towards creating the life we want, rather than simply responding to what we see as the life we've got.

To be a happy person, we must master our thoughts and create a life by design. We are thinking creatures. But most of us are not disciplined thinkers.

Virtually, every moment of every day is filled with thoughts. How often do we really think about the quality of our thoughts? For most of us, the answer to this question is virtually never. And yet, every good feeling we've ever had is the direct result of good and happy thinking. Why? Because thought precedes feelings. Thus, if happy, pleasant, good thoughts engender happy, pleasant, good feelings - and they do - then the reverse is also true.

Think for a moment. Can you remember a time in your life where you felt literally green with envy, or red with jealousy? You really cannot be envious, unless you dwell on thoughts of envy. You cannot be jealous, unless you allow yourself to think jealous thoughts. So, can you be angry without thinking angry thoughts? Can you be miserable or sad, unless your thinking is focused on sorrowful or similar thoughts? No, of course not. So, why do we permit ourselves to live in an unhappy place?

Generally speaking, we are seldom aware when we are obsessing. It only takes a moment to recall something that irks us. It is virtually always something that we've thought before. This amounts to the vast majority of our thinkingness. Feelings flow from reflection. Feelings felt before validate current thoughts giving them even greater power. The real problem seems to be that we are simply not conscious of these routine mental habits. We tend to believe that our thoughts represent the truth, and that their source is from outside of us. The real truth is far different. All of our thinking comes from within. We produce our thought - no one else does. Thought is what we do, not something that happens to us.

Thought is what we do, not something that happens to us.

For most of us, recognizing that our thinking determines how we feel, rather than the circumstances we encounter, is largely counter-intuitive. We are simply unaware that we are in charge of the thoughts we think. Even when we are convinced intellectually, our conditioned belief is that circumstances determine what happens to us. This kind of thinking is pervasive. Somehow, we really don't believe, most of the time, that it is our thoughts, not what happens around us, that determines whether we are happy or not. Doing so requires we accept responsibility, and we center ourselves in a space of humility. That's not always easy to come by – especially considering our conditioning is typically to blame others, or outside circumstances.

Eternal Nature

Each of us will eventually decide what the ultimate truths are by which we shall live our own lives. This is just as true for the agnostic, and the atheist, as it is for the formal religionist, or individual spiritual devotee. All of us live by faith. The question is only what our faith is based upon. One's faith can be centered on one's own intellect, or upon a current scientific paradigm, a group of religious doctrines, political institutions, wealth, or what have you. Every person lives their lives based upon the principles of a belief system. So the question is, what are yours?

Everything in the universe testifies that nothing is ultimately destroyed. From the four hundred billion to possibly three trillion suns in our home galaxy, and their likely hundreds of trillions of planets, moons, asteroids, et cetera, right on down to the smallest of subatomic particles, we observe change in structure, and shift in function, but never annihilation. Matter may be shifted back to energy, or energy into mass, but the sum total of everything remains in one form or another. The universe is a giant *recycling* operation. Everything is reprocessed.

All of the atoms that comprise your physical body have previously been the ingredients in a host of other things. When you draw breath, some few of the atoms that form the air you breathe may have once been breathed out by the greats of history. Abraham, Moses, Jesus, Krishna, Buddha, Lao Tzu, Socrates, and Mohammed, all breathed the very air, and the same atoms and molecules that you are now taking in to sustain you.

You consist of the everlasting atoms that once made up stars, our planet, plants, animals, the bodies of those who have come before you and other things as bizarre as the dinosaurs and ancient swamps. Long after you are gone, and your body is decomposed, those same atoms will have become parts of the basic structure of other physical things. Our physicalness will be recycled. This is a fact. The larger question is whether or not you are just your body. If, as so many have testified over the millennium, you are a spiritual being having a mortal experience, then this belief will surely impact your thoughts on purpose.

Physicists have demonstrated, again and again, that everything in the universe is constructed of the same basic elements. Perhaps even more impressive is that scientific experiments have confirmed that all the elements of the periodic table are a construct of subatomic particles that arise from a huge energy field that is connected and infinite. There is something in all of us that is not limited by death, space, or time. Scientifically speaking, all of our atoms are essentially eternal. Notwithstanding, each of us is destined to die, at least to the extent that we are no longer viable within our biological body suit.

Huge volumes of literature, from the earliest writings down to the present, testify that after our physical death, we move on, in concert with a greater plan than simple humans can yet fully comprehend. The vast majority of authors on this subject seem to at least have a sense of their own immortality, yet a famous quote of Winston Churchill rather well sums up the lack of understanding that many people have on the subject:

> "A riddle wrapped in a
> mystery inside an enigma."

By almost any form of statistical analysis, the huge majority of living humans claim they believe in a greater power than that of mere humanity. Most call the mind behind the matrix of our existence, God. To put this in perspective let's revisit an earlier quote from Max Planck, Nobel Laureate in physics, and co-founder of Quantum Theory:

> "All matter originates and exists
> only by virtue of a force...We
> must assume behind this force
> the existence of a conscious
> and intelligent MIND. This mind
> is the matrix of all matter."

The word God can be a loaded term, but in all cases, it refers to a power greater than mortal man. When we dare to think deeply and take the time to quiet our minds in solemn contemplation, I believe that each of us is entitled to receive a spiritual witness that testifies of our immortality. You may feel differently and that is as it should be. Everyone must sort this out for themselves. Like refining happiness within, no one else can do this for you. It's up to you to investigate and decide.

Like so many before me, and countless people on the earth today, I have gained a testimony of the immortality and eternal life of man. I am immensely grateful for this revealed understanding. Essential to this personal revelatory experience is the explicit knowledge that we humans are an important part of the universal plan of Deity. And, that God (by whatever name you prefer to use), is interested in each of us, and our individual evolutionary welfare.

In my world view, as we progress along our path towards self-mastery and wisdom, we eventually recognize that our eternal destiny is inextricably interwoven with our discovery and development of true happiness. In the doing of this, we are motivated to share this most joyful of emotions and feel a profound expanding love for all mankind. A quote from an ancient scriptural text, known as the Pearl of Great Price, provides a fascinating window on eternal destiny:

> "...The heavens they are many,
> and they cannot be numbered
> unto man; but they are numbered
> unto me, for they are mine. And
> as one earth shall pass away, and
> the heavens thereof, even so shall
> another come; and there is no end
> to my works, neither to my words.
> *For behold, this is my work and my*
> *glory - to bring to pass the immortality*
> *and eternal life of man."* Moses 1:37

What a marvelous and magnificent thought. Would that it were so, yes? If this were true, what might that say of our purpose? The renowned American poet, Walt Whitman, framed this idea beautifully:

> "There is that in me - I do not
> know what it is - but I know it is in
> me…I do not know it - it is without
> name - it is a word unsaid, It is
> not in any dictionary, utterance,
> symbol…Do you see O my
> brothers and sisters? It is not chaos
> or death - it is form, union, plan -
> it is eternal life - it is Happiness.

If we have not given time and attention to determining our purpose, our daily choices may not be made with an eternal perspective in mind. *Purpose* ought to undergird and overarch all that we are, and all that we hope to become. Without a deeply felt and well-designed model for our conduct, and a defined direction for our development, our moment to moment decisions will automatically default to short term considerations. In other words, we become distracted by a different question on which our choices are modeled: "Does it feel good now?"

We may so easily allow ourselves to become sidetracked with the glitter of temporary pleasure, whilst missing out on the beauty, peace, and joy of happiness in the NOW and beyond. The quality of the life we endeavor to live will always impact our NOW, as well as our near and long term future. The choices we make affect those around us, and often times, many people we may not know. When we respond to our higher self, as it quietly reminds us of our eternal nature, we then recognize that our choices today impact our eternal destiny. When we have a heightened sense of purpose, our routine choices will align themselves with this greater understanding.

What is your purpose? Why are you here? Where are you going? Where did you come from? Who are you? Is there a reason for you to exist beyond pursuing your own selfish pleasure? What do you intend to do with the rest of your life?

This life seems to be a learning opportunity. It is a place where we may grow, mature, and evolve through greater self-mastery.

The poet, William Wordsworth, penned two wonderful verses that suggest the most wonderful things.

Ode on Intimations of Immortality

> Our birth is but a sleep and a
> forgetting; the Soul that rises with
> us, our life's Star, has had elsewhere
> its setting and cometh from afar;
> not in entire forgetfulness, and
> not in utter nakedness, but trailing
> clouds of glory do we come
> from God who is our home."

So now we are here, and we're faced with making choices, all day, every day. From the moment we get up, to the last moment of the day, we are deciding things. And the choices we make determine the quality of the life we live. Underlying our choices is the concept of purpose. Sometimes we make good choices, sometimes we make mediocre choices, and all too frequently, we make some hurtful, harmful, bad choices. The trick is to make less and less of the bad ones, and more and more of the good ones. That is what righteousness must be: right choices made often. But, regardless, they are just choices. Choices based on being able to forgive others their bad choices, which by itself, speaks to our progress towards goodness, caring, honesty, and love. The Buddha gave the following advice to his followers, which seems timely for us.

> Do not pursue the past.
> Do not lose yourself in the future.
> The past no longer is.
> The future has not yet come.
> Looking deeply at life as it is
> in the very here and now,
> the practitioner dwells
> in stability and freedom.
> We must be diligent today.
> To wait until tomorrow is too late.

Chapter 13

RELIGION AND SPIRITUALITY

"Like the bee gathering honey from different flowers, the wise man accepts the essence of different scriptures and sees only the good in all religions."

Srimad Bhagavatam

Introduction

The ancient verse from the Srimad Bhagavatam, quoted directly above, is a commanding declaration. We could hardly do better than grasping its power and significance. It speaks wonderfully of tolerance, acceptance, and the gift of greater understanding. The responsibility of the true seeker after happiness should be to receive truth, let it come from whence it may. Personally, I am a Christian by religious observance, but I deeply value both the scriptural texts and the religious disciplines of all the world's great faiths.

In the course of my life I have been privileged to travel, and enjoy many of the cultures of many nation states. As a younger man I was all too quick to judge and discount the wisdom of more ancient societies. As I grew in understanding, and matured in open-mindedness, my desire for greater insight encouraged me to investigate further.

Over time, I have enjoyed personal experiences in many different countries, and with those of diverse background. I've lived in four countries, and attended widely different religious ceremonial observances, participating to some degree or another, in the spiritual practice of various denominations of Hindu, Buddhist, Muslim, Jewish, and Christian adherents. I have also studied other faith-based belief systems, and traveled to many ancient iconic worship centers. I provide this background merely to say that my exposure to these things has convinced me that there is a seeker in all of us.

Whether we pursue the sciences, philosophy, a particular religious adherence, explore our own unique spiritual path, or do all of these at once, each of us is at some elementary level impugned with a desire to investigate life. This compulsion may take the form of serious questioning of our own religious predispositions, or it may not. But, there is something within us that draws us like a magnet towards a greater knowing. When we suspend distracting ourselves from the physicality of life, our brain, mind, heart and spirit, seem to default into a searching for meaning beyond the mundane.

Similarities Abound

Organized religions and personal spirituality have dramatically impacted the lives of the vast majority of people on the planet. Institutionalized religions are faith-based organizations that seek to provide structured authoritative answers for questions related to the meaning of life. As a student of ancient history and archeology for some fifty years, it has occurred to me, time and again, that as we look back through the corridors of history, the core beliefs taught by most of the great religious leaders were amazingly similar.

Whether one looks at the principles of Hinduism, Buddhism, Judaism, Christianity, Islam, etc., they are frequently analogous. Religious practices, like culturalisms, differ, and sometimes greatly, but the highest values of mankind are universally understood.

As an example, let me share with you an extraordinary and amazing phenomenon that took place over 2,500 years ago.

In the sixth century BEFORE Christ, a remarkable evolution took place in the religious and philosophical thought of the world. For a period of about one hundred years centered around 550 BC, there was an unprecedented explosion of intellectual and spiritual insight that would impact virtually every major advanced culture at the same time, and all around the globe. There is nothing in the previous historical record with which to compare this phenomenon and little since. This remarkable fact of ancient history is so incredible that even today, when scholars and history buffs attempt to wrap their mind around the events of the sixth century before Christ, it staggers one in its overwhelming implications.

The Sixth Century BC

Hundreds of years before either Christianity or Islam, the world's earliest major religious traditions all seemed to get their spiritual bearings at about the same time. Some scholars refer to the sixth century BC era as the "axial" or fulcrum period of the ancient world. According to renowned Mideastern scholar, Dr. Spencer J. Palmer,

> "More of the ... great religions
> began during this period,
> affecting a greater number and
> variety of people throughout
> the earth, than during any other
> period in human history."

The prolific 19th Century writer H.G. Wells wrote: "This sixth century BC was indeed one of the most remarkable in all history." For Jews, Christians, and Muslims, this was the time of the great Hebrew prophets, Jeremiah, Daniel, and Ezekiel. It was the time of Nahum, Zephaniah, and Haggai. It was the time of the departure of the prophet Lehi from Jerusalem, the opening story of the Book of Mormon. It was the time frame where a great religious tradition was to evolve in the Americas. This was also the pivotal time of the first Diaspora of the Jews, when Jerusalem and the country of Judah were conquered by Babylon, their people taken into captivity to lower Mesopotamia, today's Iraq.

In China, during the sixth century BC, the revered sage Lao Tzu wrote the "Tao Te Ching," perhaps better known as "The Book of the Way." The religious practice that grew out of Lao Tzu's teachings is known as Taoism. Many from the west are unfamiliar with Lao Tzu, likely the greatest of the Chinese prophet philosophers. However, most of us are familiar with some of his more pragmatic sayings, many of which are erroneously attributed to Confucius. Below are listed a few of Tzu's over 2,000 proverbs written some 2,500 years ago. Some you will likely recognize:

> A journey of a thousand miles
> begins with a single step.
>
> Give a man a fish and you feed him
> for a day. Teach him how to fish
> and you feed him for a lifetime.
>
> Do the difficult things while
> they are easy and do the great
> things while they are small.
>
> Great acts are made
> up of small deeds.
>
> Great indeed is the sublimity
> of the Creative, to which all
> beings owe their beginning and
> which permeates all heaven.
>
> He who conquers others is strong;
> He who conquers himself is mighty.
>
> He who controls others may
> be powerful, but he who has
> mastered himself is mightier still.
>
> He who does not trust
> enough will not be trusted.
>
> He who knows others is wise. He
> who knows himself is enlightened.
>
> He who knows that enough is
> enough will always have enough.

Until the arrival of Buddhism in China, Taoism was the most important religious and philosophical practice of the everyday population. The philosopher Confucius lived during the same all-important period. Confucius had the greatest influence over China's ruling class, and particularly its emperors. China has always had a huge collective population, greater than most empires. So, the religious and philosophical impact of its two greatest sages, Lao Tzu and Confucius, can hardly be understated. Both of these great teachers lived, taught, and wrote, during the critical axial period of the sixth century BC.

In India, the epic scriptural works called the Upanishads were written in the sixth century BC. Mystics inspired by the ancient Vedas arrived on the scene about this time. They would forever change Hinduism, the subcontinent of India, and much of the ancient world. Today, the philosophy inspired by the great Upanishadic sages has permeated much of the globe's wisdom literature.

Siddhartha Gautama was born in the axial time frame. He would eventually assume the title "Buddha," meaning "Enlightened or Awakened One." Buddhism would divide into three primary schools of thought, with many different forms of practice, and spread throughout Asia, and eventually around the world. People generally believe Buddhism to be a religion, although those involved in Zen would likely claim their practice is one of mental discipline and not religion per se. Nevertheless, Buddhism has had, and continues to have, a powerful influence on the minds of hundreds of millions.

In another part of India, during the critical sixth century BC, Vardhamana, father of Jainism, took the title name "Mahavira" meaning "Great Hero." Jainism is the religious practice of about a fourth of India's citizens today. The genesis stories of both the Buddha and Mahavira are remarkably similar.

In Greece, Solon founded his Athenian schools, as did Thales, the acclaimed Greek philosopher. Pythagoras (of the triangle), was a mathematician and spiritual philosopher who developed a religious following of devout adherents at roughly the same time. Socrates and Plato, two of the most famous of the world's philosophers, also established schools of thought and religious contemplation during the axial period. Socrates and Plato have deeply influenced literally hundreds of millions of people all over the world, and in all eras since their short time on earth.

In Persia, modern day Iran, Zoroastrianism was founded in the sixth century BC. According to scholars this was possibly the most influential of all the religions in the ancient world. Zoroastrians inhabited the land of Babylon during the Jewish exile. Scholars believe that Judaism, and thus Christianity, were deeply influenced by the Zoroastrians. Buddhism and Islam were similarly impacted by the remarkable "Magi" of Persia. And, who doesn't know the story of *The Three Kings*, called "Wise Men," or "Magi," who, having studied the stars, discovered the signs they had been seeking, and left Persia to visit the Christ child? The Zoroasters believed that the Messiah would be born a Jew, and for six hundred years they kept careful records of the movements in the heavens, until they observed the signs they sought.

In the movie, *2001: A Space Odyssey*, the haunting classical sound-track was named Zarathustra after the sixth century BC prophet-founder of Zoroastrianism. Many textbooks on astronomy today credit the Zoroasters with creating the Zodiac, which became widely disseminated, thus stimulating serious study of the heavens.

Historian Mary Boyce claimed that Zoroastrianism did more "to influence mankind directly, and indirectly, than any other single faith." It was the state religion of three great empires and dominated much of the old world. The Persian Empire was the largest empire in all of world history up to this point.

We could go on, delving into Sikhism, a derivative-amalgam of Hindu and Islam, or the foundational religions of the Olmeca and Mayan, which were the sixth century BC high cultures of the Americas, but it is enough to say that the entire world was ablaze with a new religious zeal at almost the same time. Of course it may be that this transcendence of thought, by highly gifted seers and thinkers, was coincidental. Or, it may be that there was a much more significant commercial intercourse between the prominent kingdoms of antiquity than we have heretofore recognized. Whatever it was that drove the incredible shift in intellect and spirituality, it was dramatic and immensely powerful. It would be hard to exaggerate the impact on all of world history that the sixth century before Christ produced. It's as if an inspirational beacon swept across the earth providing light and enlightenment to all those able to receive it.

It would be hard to exaggerate the impact on all of world history that the sixth century before Christ produced. It's as if an inspirational beacon swept across the earth providing light and enlightenment to all those able to receive it.

Each of the more highly developed nations of the ancient world was dramatically affected at almost the exact same time. Many of the essential core beliefs of widely separated nation states were suddenly, and remarkably, similar. Against this backdrop the Book of Mormon records a revelation given to an isolated group, who claimed to have migrated to the Americas in the sixth century BC, by boat:

"Know ye not that there are more nations than one? Know ye not that I, the Lord your God, have created all men ... and I bring forth my word unto the children of men, yea, even upon all the nations of the earth?"

Religions and Culturalisms

From a historical perspective we observe that over time the predominate culturalisms of the separate nations became appended to their various religious philosophies. This made them seem much more different than they originally would have appeared. It is a common occurrence of all religions that over time, their societal traditions eventually become treated with equal authority as their original doctrine.

In the biographies and writings of the great thinkers and religious leaders living within a hundred years of the axial period we learn of their deep sincerity, and belief in personal revelation. Whether they called their source of inspiration God, Krishna, Vishnu, Shiva, or Brahma, Mazda, Allah, Eloheim, Yahweh, or Jehovah, they all revered the spiritual substance of their being. All these divergent religious leaders taught the principals of gratitude, love, forgiveness, self-acceptance, harmony, peace, personal responsibility, kindness, honor, AND that happiness is to be refined within us.

> **All these divergent religious leaders taught the principals of gratitude, love, forgiveness, self-acceptance, harmony, peace, personal responsibility, kindness, honor, AND that happiness is to be refined within us.**

Hundreds of years AFTER the critical sixth century BC era, a new Jewish sect would erupt on the world scene and expand to include those not of the Jewish tradition. This would evolve into the largest religious belief system in the world, and become known as Christianity. Six hundred years AFTER the birth of Jesus of Nazareth, the prophet Mohammed would rise to prominence in Arabia, and reorganize its regional tribalism, Judaism, and early Christianity, into a powerful new form of worship called Islam.

As a matter of historical record, both Christianity and Islam share the same religious mother. Both emerged from a much older religious practice generally referred to as Judaism. However, the most ancient monotheistic religious practices track back at least a thousand years before the Jews actually existed as an identifiable people.

It is significant that Muslims, Christians, and Jews, all identify their ancestral forefather to be the patriarch Abraham. From the biblical record we see that one of Abraham's grandsons was named Jacob. Later in life Jacob's name was changed to Israel.

Israel's children and family down-line were known as the Children of Israel, or simply Israelites. Jacob/Israel's fourth born son was named Judah. Judah was the father of those known as Jews. Before Judah was born, the Abrahamic form of monotheism was a well established religious practice.

Religious Atrocities

Whereas some of the greatest atrocities of history have been orchestrated in the name of religion, these are the acts of *men* who hijacked whatever spiritual discipline held sway over the masses, in order to manipulate them into doing their bidding. Nationalism has always endeavored to influence the entrenched religious bureaucracies that have sprung up based on the prior inspired teachings of a prophet or seer.

Historically, we can observe repeated shifts in doctrinal emphasis by institutionalized religions, once they were elevated to official status by a governing state. In effect, many religions ultimately became an extension of government. Even today this scenario is being played out with the Dali Lama who was exiled from his country of Tibet after it was taken over by the Chinese. The Chinese communist party has made it clear that the next Dali Lama will be appointed by their government. How does that work? The senior worldwide leader of Lamasery Buddhism is to be appointed by a government based aggressively on atheism? Hmmm. In some ways this situation is not unlike the middle European period when French kings were able to appoint Catholic popes.

From history, we observe that as theocratic institutions grow in power and influence they tend towards layered bureaucracy. Over time, entrenched belief systems tend to become frozen into creeds, for ease of instruction to each upcoming generation. All bureaucracies gravitate towards tighter internal structure, which usually requires expanded rules for all aspects of practice and administration. This in turn breeds inflexibility.

Rules for operation and conduct eventually tend to override the revelatory elements upon which the institution was originally founded. To some degree, this will always translate into a loss of focus on inspiration and higher ideals, by putting greater reliance upon internally generated rules. Theologies of every sort, once they evolve to a certain size, commence to govern by internal rules linked to belief systems usually referred to as doctrines. Much of the initial beauty and vision of their founders may become subsumed, through edicts and dogma.

Radical fundamentalists tend to arise in almost every faith. These are those who insist on their way as being the only right way, based on their interpretation of things. Radical fundamentalists are apt to crystallize their positions based on what they believe may be wrong with the policies and doctrines of other religious institutions. This approach breeds militancy, as certain personality types practice a form of negative spirituality. The situation is quite similar to the negative media campaigning we are exposed to during election periods.

The practice of exclusion creates unhealthy tension between faiths, and undermines the peaceful inclusiveness that was a hallmark of the original teachings of most religious founders. To ignore the good in others, because of religious prejudice, is ignorance by any other name. To be happy requires we give up the ignorance of prejudice. We must learn to observe and enjoy without judging.

Science Withdraws

Our sun is one of many stars, and its near twins exist in great numbers throughout the galaxy. For some reason, many religious institutions find this fact threatening. There is no particular ancient scriptural reason, the Bible included, as to why life should not exist off-world, but many of those interpreting scripture have historically taught that the earth was the center of the universe. In an earlier time, scientific icons like Galileo were placed under arrest, and incarcerated for claiming something as outlandish as the earth revolved around the sun. Astronomer Giordano Bruno, a Roman Catholic monk, was put to death for refusing to recant his position, after stating he also believed as much.

Bruno was a highly-skilled mathematician. He demonstrated that the sun-centered model of the solar system presented in 1543 by Nicolas Copernicus (a Catholic Church official from Poland), was substantially more correct than the earth centered model developed by the Greeks many centuries earlier. Bruno was also of the opinion that the universe was incredibly large, and that there must be numerous other worlds peopled by God's children. This was thought to be a great heresy by the religious leaders at the time. When Bruno refused to withdraw his thoughts on the subject, he was burned alive by the inquisition. A pretty drastic response to a new idea, wouldn't you say?

Galileo Galilei also supported the Copernicus model of the solar system. He wrote his thoughts in a somewhat veiled discourse, published in book form. Obfuscation aside, he was still confined to house arrest until the day he died, for daring to question the church's opinion about this matter. Today, Galileo is referred to as the "Father of Modern Science" because of his experimental discipline, his use of mathematics, and his obsession with replicatable (empirical) observation.

The reigning church of the western world once taught that our planet was the literal center of the universe, and notwithstanding Galileo's telescope, and the mounting information to the contrary, it was unthinkable to believe otherwise. Of course, we now know that the Roman Church was dead wrong. The authorities of that time had made a classic error; they had pinned their world views on subjective interpretations of biblical text.

The Bible does not say the earth is the center of the universe. That was an opinion arrived at by church authorities, who had studied the much earlier works of Aristotle and Ptolemy. It is instructive that the ideas originating with Greek philosophers became accepted as fact by high-ranking religious leaders, and eventually these opinions assumed the power of religious dogma. To challenge church leader's ideas about how the universe was organized, was deemed a threat to religious authority, and subjected one to the political power of the Church.

Today the Roman church has admitted its error, apologized, and become an enthusiastic sponsor of a considerable array of astronomical observations. Catholic Church government enthusiastically supports scientific inquiry, and one of its own, Monsignor Georges Lemaître, a Belgian Roman Catholic priest and professor of physics and astronomy, was the original idea man for the Big Bang theory.

A Belgian Roman Catholic priest, a professor of physics and astronomy, authored the concept now known as the Big Bang.

Lemaître applied Einstein's theory of general relativity to cosmology. By 1931, he had secured both Einstein's and Hubble's support for the Big Bang concept. Thereafter, the Big Bang theory became a household name. Some Christians believe the Big Bang theory to be in opposition with their faith. Most scholars do not see it that way, including the pope. So, does that make the Big Bang true? No, not necessarily, but having a widely supported scientific model against which physical evidences may be applied is quite valuable.

Science is very good at discovering re-confirmable facts and then weaving them into a logical hypothesis that can explain known observations. Thereafter, each newly discovered piece of relevant information is weighed against the hypothesis then in vogue. Where new information conflicts with old models, these models must be revamped to include new data, or in more extreme cases, the whole model will be junked in favor of a new concept, that better addresses all known phenomenon. The process allows for a continuing probe of all currently accepted scientific models, whilst theoretically keeping preconceived beliefs off the table. This is supposed to be the scientific method. Suspend judgment and test all feasible aspects of a theory that explains how things have worked in the past, and that is able to predict things that come to pass.

Bullheadedness

It is troubling to see a repeat of the infamous bullheadedness of the 16th century Roman church by many fundamentalist Christian denominations today. The sun centered universe was a hugely heated topic in the early days of the Renaissance. Today, no less a dispute is firing up the passions of men: Darwinian Evolution. Some people feel very strongly about it. They have lots of reasons for why they are sure that the theory of evolution is wrong. Personal opinion aside, the Scriptures are quiet on the subject. To look to the Bible to support a religious bodies' opinion on science is to make the exact same mistake that earlier Roman scholars did to their ultimate humiliation.

> **To look to the Bible to support a religious bodies' opinion on science is to make the exact same mistake that earlier Roman scholars did to their ultimate humiliation.**

Suspend judgment. In your pursuit of truth it would be unwise to prejudge information from any source of reasoned insight. You are not required to decide one source is right and the other wrong. It should be clear that neither science, nor religion, has a lock on the truth, and neither does philosophy, psychology, etc. Should we throw one out in favor of the other? Certainly not. Learn and consider. It is not required of you to judge, or be certain of any scientific claim, one way or the other. With this thought in mind consider the following true story:

Some 300 years *before* Christ, a Greek scientist, Democritus, demonstrated that the world was a sphere. He did this by observing the difference in the length of shadows cast at noon by stakes placed several hundred kilometers apart. Then using mathematics, he demonstrated that the earth must be round. Democritus correctly calculated the circumference of the globe to within an accuracy of 2 percent almost 1,800 years before scholars would begin to root out the false belief of a flat world. When people believed the world to be flat, they often turned to Scripture to support their point of view. Of course they were wrong, but at the time everyone seemed to agree with them, so they were certain that their belief must in fact be the right one.

Up until about fifty years ago, anyone who seriously considered the possibility of life on other planets was scorned by both science *and* religion. Certainly it was true for virtually all scientists, and is still true for some religionists. On a personal note,

I vividly remember the derision and utter exasperation of my 8th grade science teacher, when I suggested the possibility of life elsewhere in the universe. And heaven help you, if you'd have suggested such a thing in most religious circles until more recently!

Philosophy

Currently accepted philosophy is the rule against which most humans tend to measure truth. Basically, people repeat what other people say. Wherever there is a consensus of belief, people treat that belief as true. As in, "it must be true, everyone else believes it."

> **Wherever there is a consensus of belief, people treat that belief as true.**

Just because a lot of people believe something does not make it true. It wasn't all that long ago when physicians were in the business of bloodletting, and both scholars and religionists taught the earth was the center of the universe, and that the world was flat. Beliefs are simply thoughts that one has thought about until those thoughts achieve status as opinion. Opinions held and defended are beliefs. We must sort things out for ourselves, looking to the underlying motivations for alternative viewpoints.

Is it true, is it loving, is it kind? Is it honorable, is it fair, and is it uplifting? Does it encourage us to become better people? Any of these might be a reliable ruler against which to measure worldly issues.

An absolutism approach shuts down new inquiry, as our egos tell us we already know the truth, and that somehow our belief system is the only one that is correct. Some religious organizations have an institutional ego problem. In reality, we rarely know the whole truth of a thing, yet to protect our treasured opinions, we'll take some pretty drastic measures.

Wars are fought over opinions, money, and power. People are killed daily because other people do not value them as fully human. Those who do not value the sanctity of human life without regard to nationality, race, and creed, are certain that their opinions – beliefs, are the ones that really matter. They believe themselves to be the only legitimate repository of truth. The way they think is the only right way.

In general, these types of people excuse themselves, and confuse others with slogans and glib excuses, for otherwise abhorrent behavior. Unfortunately, the very character traits that make motivated persons so sure they are right are the same traits that often make for electable politicians. We want to rally around those we believe know what they are doing. To be sensitive and thoughtful is not a characteristic much admired of leadership. Instead we tend to idolize clear, no-nonsense action; the do-something-even-if-it-is wrong paradigm. The extreme of charismatic leadership is seen in the likes of an Adolf Hitler; a man elected and revered by the people at large. It seems a reasonable conclusion that, when leaders make plausible arguments for death and destruction, they have become the adversaries of human evolution.

Many traditional institutions of religion, be they Judaic, Hindu, Jain, Sikh, Christian, Muslim, Tao, etc., seem to view their own spiritual convictions as threatened by science (although there are some remarkable exceptions to this rule). But why is this? If we believe in God, and believe in God's incalculable superiority to us, why then are we so insistent upon forcing God's methods of doing things into our limited opinions about how such things should be accomplished? In other words, why is it that so many of us insist on God being omnipotent, and yet demand that God must have done things the way we believe they should have been done?

> **Why is it that so many of us insist on God being omnipotent, and yet demand that God must have done things the way we believe they should have been done?**

Isn't it vastly more reasonable to believe that God has perfect knowledge, and is therefore all-powerful and absolutely good with no exceptions? Isn't God supposed to be the embodiment of light, truth, and love? The biblical scriptures teach forgiveness and claim God is our Father in Heaven; do we dare to believe such things? People committed to a religious creed, rather than godly ideals, will frequently rationalize biblical writings, and wrest the scriptures to make them say whatever it is they want them to say. Stay away from organizations that preach divisiveness, lack of tolerance, and hate. These are not spiritual virtues; these negative traits are based on institutional egos.

Is it reasonable to believe that what God does is done within the framework of universal law? Consider that if it were otherwise, God would be a changeable and arbitrary being, like the gods of the ancient Greeks. Ought not our personal pursuit of meaning be the pursuit of truth? What do you think? Are you interested in seeking further light and knowledge toward the end of discovering the greater truth, not just learning the currently acceptable philosophies of men?

All of us are able to learn truth through common experience, thoughtful contemplation, scientific endeavor, and those flashes of insight we might call personal revelation. In the final analysis though, neither physics nor any other science is able to prove or disprove the truth of religious claims. However, there is a great deal of light now being shed on the topic of spirituality and organized religions. A few of the latter seem to flourish in the bright illumination of new scientific discoveries. These are those religious organizations and spiritual thinkers that are expansive enough to accept truth regardless of how it is discovered. Science, psychology, religion, philosophy, and personal spirituality, are all mechanisms for discovering greater truth. Do not be deterred. Use them all.

Compassion

When we allow our beliefs to become narrow and exclusive, we tend towards a loss of compassion and love. The New Testament of the Christian Scriptures refers to charity as the true LOVE of Christ. This we are told is compassionate love. The entire 13th Chapter of First Corinthians demonstrates that Christians are to focus on charity above all else. Chapter 13:2 says:

"And though I have the gift of
prophecy, and understand all
mysteries, and all knowledge:
and though I have faith, so that
I could remove mountains, and
have not charity, I am nothing."

The 13ᵗʰ chapter closes with these words:

"And now abideth faith, hope,
charity, these three; but the
greatest of these is charity."

Respect and tolerance, or perhaps more correctly the lack
of same, particularly as it relates to religious interpretation and
ethnic preference, now tends to shape and define countries, as
much as their historical precedents. For example, consider that
of the fifty-four predominantly Muslim countries and territories,
repressive governments rule all but three. In other words, kings,
dictators, warlords, or militant clerics, administer virtually all of
them. Tolerance for competing political ideologies or religious
views, other than those perpetuated by the state and their pow-
er-brokers, are almost always condemned in these countries.

Just as Christianity was hijacked by feudal warlords in the middle ages to enhance their power and justify their actions, so has
Islam become the tool of political leaders, to gain and maintain
control in underdeveloped Middle Eastern and African countries.
These acts are not about religion; they are about power. Karl
Marx, the author of the Communist Manifesto, maintained that
religion was the "opiate of the masses." Although it pains me to
give him credit for real insight, there is merit in the statement.
(My sister claims that television is the "opiate of the masses.")

Despots of every kind have played on ignorance, and mixed
it with the passion of religion, to gain power over the masses.
Unfortunately, they have done so all too often, without the average person discovering their deceit; at least until after the tyrant
had solidified his control. Interestingly, the atheism that Karl Marx
preached, bore all the hallmarks of the state-sponsored, radical,

religious fundamentalism that we see in a number of Muslim countries today. Yet, just like the Bible, the Vedas, the Upanishads, the Yoga Sutras, the Bhagavad Gita, and a host of other scriptural works, the Muslim Qur'an teaches gratitude, love, peace, goodness, and forgiveness. Unfortunately, that isn't the spin put on it by those anxious to condemn or control others.

Radical fundamentalists of every political or religious persuasion tend to have in common a lack of tolerance for the thoughts, ideas, and opinions of anyone who does not act or think the way they do. This is the diametric opposite of charity; loving compassion. It seems that no matter how valid or vital one's belief system might be, one undermines that system, and ultimately negates it, whenever one becomes rigid and dogmatic in its adherence.

Most of us know active members of various faith-based groups who spend their time putting down other religions. This is misguided spirituality. Instead of extending compassionate love to others not of their particular religious faith, those engaged in this kind of practice are focused on criticism. If unrequited they will become mean-spirited, and project the belief that they are better than others because they somehow have the only truth. That is not a Christian principle, nor does it resonant with most of the world's core religious values. On the other hand, it is clearly reflective of a psychological rung on the ladder of our personal evolution. This is the religious level where the ego is in charge.

Prophets and teachers from all over the world, during many periods of time, and from many different religious backgrounds, have sought inspiration and dared to seek answers to the world's great questions. Consequently, many inspired men and women have found deeply satisfying resolution to life's perplexing puzzles. Looking back through history it appears that no single group has ever had a complete franchise on perfect insight and inspiration. But, be careful to not throw the baby out with the bathwater. To observe critically that no single institution has it all, does not negate the value that devotion provides. Dedication to your own spiritual evolution is paramount, and for most of us, an organized religious organization will help facilitate the journey. To rise above the day-to-day fracas of the mundane, on to the refining of real happiness within, is the very hallmark of spiritual evolution.

At some point in each of our lives, we will likely confront ourselves with questions like these: Shall we live a life of self-centeredness, and never quite be happy because we are so wrapped up in ourselves that we cannot appreciate quiet beauty, the good, and the Now? Or, will we embark upon the highest spiritual quest, the love that leads to a state of happiness?

In my personal view, anything we do to evolve ourselves, and improve the lives of others, is consistent with the core principals of the vast majority of religions. In a work entitled *Ocean of Wisdom*, the Dalai Lama said this quite eloquently:

> "Every major religion of the world - Buddhism, Christianity, Confucianism, Hinduism, Islam, Jainism, Judaism, Sikhism, Taoism, and Zoroastrianism – has similar ideals of love, the same goal of benefitting humanity through spiritual practice, and the same effect of making their followers into better human beings."

It's All *Thought!*

Chapter 14

MEANING

"How to gain, how to keep, how to recover happiness is in fact for most people at all times the secret motive of all they do."

William James

Caveat

The introduction to Chapter 12 and the Author's Note at the beginning of this book both contain caveats of a sort, which I essentially repeat here because it is so important. In this chapter, we continue to explore areas brimming with strongly held points of view. Subjects related to whether or not we believe there is meaning to life encroach on areas where our most cherished and deeply felt beliefs reside. These subjects are rife with subliminal judgment, and as a consequence, they can be literal minefields of discrimination. My intent is not to offend, notwithstanding I shall offer my thoughts and conclusions, as I believe it may add value to the text. As a result, the reader's belief system may kick-in, causing an emotional response anywhere from a vague sense of unease, to skepticism, or perhaps even stronger reactions.

It will help if the reader will remain alert, practicing self-observation, and recognize when one's buttons are being pushed. When that happens, and it will be clear by the way you feel about what you're reading, I recommend you consciously tell yourself to suspend judgment, so you may gain any further insight that might be available to you, by garnering further information without prejudice. Unfortunately, the reading of a book does not provide the stimulating environment where open discussion ensues, as thought-provoking questions are posed. But, if you will simply ask yourself, out-loud if possible, how you feel about exploring certain subjects, you'll find yourself stepping up to a more understanding space. It's a healthier, happier place as you recognize within yourself that you are rising above the embattled arenas of emotionally-charged opinions, and learning to listen, reflect, and observe, without succumbing to conflict.

Personal Evolution

A large part of the personal growth each of us must make, in order to gain a happier state, is in learning to suspend judgment, and allowing ourselves the freedom to investigate life with an open-mind. How else can we learn things outside the box of our existing reality? How may we access new and better ideas to improve our lives, if we pre-judge things on the outside of our current grasp of things, as unworthy, unacceptable, or worse? The walls of our prejudice are real. It is not easy to see the boundaries we've imposed upon ourselves, but they absolutely exist. And that's true for all of us.

The more evolved we become, the less frequently we will be offended by different points of view. It is only our ego that takes exception, gets insulted, or is irritated by conceptual positions that seem to be in conflict with our own. It is fine to have opinions, although if we suspended most of them we'd probably be better off. When we hold opinions, we should not allow them to be so etched in stone that we cannot neutrally reflect on other perspectives. This is especially important where contrary points of view are sincerely made, and based on thoughtful consideration.

Is There Meaning?

Few things have the power to impact one's sense of value, and hence one's happiness, like the question "Is There Meaning to Life?" The mere asking of this question points directly to the issue of one's personal spirituality, or lack of same, and/or one's religious observance, convictions, social obligations, and so forth. These highly sensitive elements of who we are have great influence over our automatic response system.

From my perspective, those without a sense of meaning in their lives are adrift on the fickle sea of public opinion. This is not a statement about religion, but it is a statement about one's own spirituality. Those without meaning are without an anchor properly set in safe moorage. When the sea changes of our external life, combine with the tides and currents of our unresolved insecurities, we are in danger of capsize. There are times in all of our lives where the winds of diversity blow and howl about us. Where there is confidence born of meaning, we are able to hold fast and avert disaster. Without a sense of meaning we are lost.

When our life is bound up in the external world, and we've not developed a pure place of peace and calm within us, adversity produces pain and suffering. This understanding is mirrored in an interesting message from the Dalai Lama:

> "Pain is inevitable,
> suffering is optional."

Left unaddressed, the loss and lack of meaning in our lives can degenerate into our losing all reason for living. A sense of meaning is critical for a good life.

Viktor Frankl, was perhaps the best known psychiatrist, of the last several decades. His memoir, *Man's Search for Meaning* has riveted generations of readers. Within this particular book, of the 30 he wrote, Frankl describes his life in the Nazi death camps. Before the camps were liberated by Allied forces, 27 out of every 28 persons so interned would die. Every person was confronted with their own likely death, every day. This unimaginably horrible, and dramatically stressful environment, spurred the genius of

Dr. Viktor Frankl. Frankl was to observe, again and again throughout his life, that without meaning we are not fully human. Without meaning we slide into animalistic proclivities, losing grip on the most uplifting of human attributes. Like Siddhartha Gautama (the Buddha), twenty-five centuries earlier, Frankl argued that all of us will encounter suffering, but what it does to us is our decision.

One particular insight of Frankl's should be of special interest to Americans:

> "A statistical survey recently
> revealed that among my European
> students, 25 percent showed
> a more-or-less marked degree
> of existential vacuum. Among
> my American students, it was
> not 25 but 60 percent."

Insecurity

Why do Americans appear to be less emotionally secure than their European counterparts, even though they enjoy a more financially secure environment overall? Frankl argued that it's because Americans have more of everything tangible, but have less meaning in their lives. Notwithstanding America's collectively high religious participation, there is a subconscious fear amongst a great many of us that life may have no real meaning.

There is a subconscious fear amongst us that life may have no real meaning.

Where there is a lack of meaning in people's lives, it is frequently covered over with a desire for power. Our egos believe that if we have power then others will respect us. This chain of thought continues with the belief that when others show us increased respect we must have greater value. It is a fundamental tenet of psychology that most of us garner our sense of who we are, and our sense of personal self worth, through *what we think others think about us*. We've addressed this before but it needs restating nonetheless. It is not what other people think about us that so powerfully affects our sense of self worth, it is what *we think* others think about us, that is so forcefully impactful.

The most primitive form of the will to power, other than the obsession with physicality, is the will to money. Money is the subliminal source of power. For those desperate to prove their value, both to themselves and to others, the accumulation of wealth is subconsciously seen as the most direct route. Most of us will have also observed the reverse of the possession obsession. Take away a man's source of income, and you may see something akin to the collapse of his personality. A man's feeling of self-worth is typically a function of his ability to earn.

Although it is politically inappropriate to say it, up until just a few decades ago women tended to traffic on their looks, men on their pocketbook. Men sought the "trophy" wife as confirmation of their prowess. Women tended to seek the security of a man's wealth and the influence of his position. Many men feeling monetarily inadequate stormed the gym to put on muscle, believing this was the second best way to attract a trophy woman. These tendencies still continue, notwithstanding the huge gains in education and employment made by women, in particular. So, what's the point? If one looks at this situation with some honesty, we observe that those who are *obsessively* focused on wealth and physical appearance are essentially insecure. This insecurity is a strong indication that these personality types have no real sense of meaning in their lives.

> **Those who have become *obsessively* focused on wealth and physical appearance are essentially insecure. There is no sense of meaning in their life.**

Insecurity is Fear

This is not meant to offend. The intent here is to have us face underlying truth. Insecurity is a form of fear. Fear is not a source of meaning. When we operate from a place of fear, we can get things done alright, but it does not engender peace, and it is not the source of happiness. Do you dare ask yourself why you do what you do? Are you able to honestly and sincerely confront yourself? Would a powerful conviction that there was greater meaning in your life help you sort through this kind of thing?

The human brain is so structured that we are more easily motivated by fear than we are by the desire to improve. All of us are motivated by fears to a greater or lesser degree. So, what fears are having the greatest influence in your life? Can you see them? They're not always easy to recognize. Most of us are so used to suppressing our fears we don't look at them. In fact, most of us refuse to admit, even to ourselves, that there are subliminal fears controlling much of our behavior. We are so used to justifying our behavior to ourselves that we frequently do not even know why we do what we do. Let me share a personal story to illustrate this point about self-delusion.

Hypnosis

Almost four decades ago, my wife Maureen, and I, sat in John Mackey's living room. John was a close friend, and we were in the habit of spending a good deal of time together. John was a scientist with PhD's in both physics and mathematics. (Years later he would go back to school and get a law degree.) Many nights we came together exploring ideas about science and religion. The camaraderie was palpable, upbeat, and the atmosphere conducive to open communication and thought-provoking discussion. On this particular evening, my wife Maureen commented that she had been trying to give up smoking, with little success, and was considering going to a hypnotist. John's wife, Lana, gave John a knowing look and shared with Maureen and me that John was actually a trained hypnotist. This was a real surprise as he had never mentioned this before. John then shared with us his concerns over the startling developments that had sometimes taken place with subjects under hypnosis. He had been seriously shaken by a few of these events. After several years of experience he quit practicing altogether, and determined to not let others know of this past skill, so he would not be called on to perform parlor tricks.

John allowed himself to be talked into assisting Maureen, but only if all of us were present. As it turned out, Maureen was a good subject. Three nights in a row John put Maureen under three times each evening, allowing her to recall all but a few minutes of the half-hour or so she was experiencing deep relaxation. On the third, night two additional friends, David and Peggy Wilson were there, in company with the four of us, when Maureen commented that, while she was enjoying the restful aspects of each hypnosis session, she was certain that she could remember everything that transpired, and confided that she had actually never really been fully-hypnotized.

Discussion ensued about how to best demonstrate to Maureen, once she was awakened from a session, that she actually had been hypnotized. If in fact, she had been. Under hypnosis, Maureen was told that when John said the word "blue," after she was fully awake, that she would feel thirsty, and ask Lana for a glass of water. The first swallow would taste like orange juice the rest of the glass would taste like normal water. It was a somewhat silly, but fun, experiment. After being told to come completely awake, Maureen was again certain she had not been fully hypnotized, and could remember everything that had taken place. Actually, she could, except for the specific time when John had given her special instructions about the water, and then asked her to block it out of her conscious mind.

Sometime later, amongst the small talk that seems to be self-generating when good friends get together, John mentioned the color blue quietly, without the rest of us even noticing. Maureen turned, and asked Lana if she would be kind enough to bring her a glass of water. Alerted by the request, the rest of us pretty much froze, waiting to see what would happen. Lana asked Maureen why she didn't just get a glass of water herself. Maureen leaned over, and began to rub her ankle, saying she had a cramp. Lana got the water. Maureen took her first sip, and immediately spewed it back out. She was shocked. What had Lana done to the water? Lana said she had done nothing. John encouraged Maureen to take another sip. Now it was water. Maureen was shaken and embarrassed. When she was told why what had happened had happened, she simply did not believe it.

Maureen was convinced that we had all come together and rigged something on the lip of the glass to change the first taste of water. When asked why she had insisted that Lana get her the water, she had a ready answer. It was Lana's house, and Maureen had a cramp in her ankle. None of us could convince her otherwise. Maureen's subconscious mind had given her sequenced instructions of what to do, but her conscious mind had come up with a completely reasonable rationale to explain the why of it. The reasons Maureen gave were not the real reason why things happened the way they did, but she absolutely believed it. Not only was she not convinced that she had been hypnotized, and told to ask for the water, but she was actually close to convincing the rest of us with her reasonable explanation. I was somewhat sobered to realize that my wife's mind had literally caused a cramp in her ankle, in order to justify why when she felt thirsty she would ask Lana for a drink, rather than get it herself.

We all agreed to do another experiment, but only after having to convince John to hypnotize her once more. He was concerned that he might inadvertently cause Maureen some downstream emotional damage. Maureen assured him she was fine and truly wanted to go through the process again.

The lights were dimmed, we were all relaxed and comfortable, most of us curled up in chairs, or on a couch with shoes off. Once again Maureen went into a deep trance. John instructed her that at some point, after she was awakened, he would say a code word, which she would now block out consciously, but upon hearing the word later she would gather up my cowboy boots and put them on. Not satisfied that this was odd enough, John instructed her to put the boots on the wrong feet. Once again Maureen was awakened, and was completely convinced she could remember everything that took place during her trance like state. And, again, she did recall everything that took place, except for the direct subliminal instructions John had given, and caused to be blocked from her conscious mind.

John waited almost a half-hour before giving Maureen the code word in the flow of a normal conversation. The Wilson's and I actually missed him do it, and hadn't even noticed Maureen casually slipping my boots onto her feet. When John asked Maureen why she had put my cowboy boots on, it snapped all of us to attention. Maureen replied her feet were cold. John asked why she put my boots and not her shoes. She said they were larger and warmer. He asked why she put them on the wrong feet. She responded, in dead earnest, that "Terry is always telling me to quit turning my feet in towards one another, or I'll breakdown my ankles, so I put his boots on to warm my feet, and put them on the wrong feet, to make sure it kept my feet turned outwards." I was stunned. Maureen was totally convinced that the reason she gave was honest, truthful, and completely rational. The rest of us knew she had done what she did because of a post-hypnotic suggestion. There was nervous laughter amongst us, but in truth we were all pretty shocked.

Maureen's conscious mind had complied with her subconscious promptings, but it had also produced a reason for why she was doing what she was doing. She believed the explanation fabricated in her own mind, and she was pretty darn convincing in her explanation. Maureen would eventually realize that she was fooling herself, but it was not easy for her to simply discount the reasons she had come up with. So, what can we learn from this?

As the years have accumulated, I have remembered this event again and again. Maureen and I would discuss it many times before her death, questioning ourselves as to why we do what we do. It became clear to us that we all participate in self-delusion to come degree. There are many applications for the strange insight gained from this singular event. But, more than anything else, I have found myself left with a series of questions. How often are we fooling ourselves? Can we dig deep enough to know the real truth for our responses to various situations? Do we really want to know, or are we more likely to tell ourselves comforting lies?

Incidentally, John's blocked out hypnotic suggestions to Maureen, that each time she would light a cigarette they wouldn't taste good, and that she would lose interest, and stub them out without finishing a single cigarette thereafter, worked amazingly well. I remember watching her light a cigarette, a couple of days later while sitting in a restaurant (that was 40 years ago) she took a couple of drags and put it out, with a grimace on her face. Part of John's technique was she should not know what he was suggesting, so her conscious mind would not be alert to the ploy. Maureen managed to quit smoking within two weeks, and never returned to the habit again.

Sexual Excess

In addition to mankind's excessive focus on money and fitness, our unresolved desire for meaning is sometimes transposed into the will to pleasure. In this regard, Frankl states:

> "Existential frustration often
> eventuates in sexual compensation.
> We can observe in such cases
> that the sexual libido becomes
> rampant in the existential vacuum."

A lay person's translation of the above might be that when we fail to believe that there is meaning to life, we either become deeply depressed, or we launch into activities powerfully attractive enough that they direct our attention away from what is really going on.

Do you remember from Chapter 10 that it is the ego that is constantly focused on fear and insecurity? It is worth repeating that where there is lack of meaning in one's life, it is frequently offset by a desire for greater power. This is a sobering thought. The obsessive pursuit of wealth and physical fitness says a lot about us. Of course, money is not bad, and neither is good health, and physical fitness, but the obsession with either or both of these is a clear indication that one is subconsciously insecure, and seeking external validation of their worth.

Note: Whenever you hear someone saying "I don't care what others think;" or something to that affect, they are actually attempting to deny their underlying motivation. Secure people have no need to make such a statement. Only when one is feeling fairly insecure about something do they feel the need to say such a thing.

How do we gain an unassailable security? One based on internal values not the fickle shifts in public opinion? Perhaps the best way is to really "get" who we are (the subject of the last chapter).

Another source of unwavering self-worth is to have such a powerful grasp on what we believe constitutes the meaning in our lives that we are devoted to constant personal growth, and our evolving to a condition of self that might best be described as enlightenment.

Time Alone

How many people are literally panicked to be by themselves, with nothing to do for any length of time? To be in a situation where there is no immediate mechanism of distraction terrifies a lot of us. That is, if we care to admit it to ourselves. When left alone without a book, television, radio, or something to distract us, we must actually BE with ourselves.

Do you relish the opportunity to just sit for a couple of hours, comfortable with nothing more than your thoughts? Most people do not. Most people are bored with themselves, and secretly may not like themselves all that much. This leads to other questions: Would you really enjoy being close friends with you? If not, why not? What might you do in these regards to shift your feelings to a better place? What thoughts that you routinely think need to be improved upon?

Many of us are so busy keeping ourselves busy that we lust over the freedom to just be. We are continually speaking to the need for having time for just us. And yet, when the opportunity to "just be" finally arrives, we tend to get a bit disoriented. We don't know what to do if there is nothing specific to focus upon. Women seem to be slightly better at suspending action for brief intervals. Women are generally quicker studies at meditation, and better able to just lie on a beach doing nothing for a while. Men on the other hand, tend to have more trouble with inactivity.

Men subliminally define themselves through actions and results. And, for the most part, men need to find something to do, in order to quickly distract themselves from themselves. We guys are so typically caught up in identifying with what we do, and what we've done, that suspending focus is sometimes impossible. As a group, we're pretty darn good at distraction activity. That can be something as simple as talking sports to mindlessly watching television. Left entirely to ourselves, with nothing much to do but be with our own thoughts, is not *just* a bit disorienting, it can be disquieting to the point of frustration and irritability. In my experience, the only real exceptions to this fear of being alone, with nothing to distract us from ourselves, is when one has cared enough about this issue to learn how to meditate. Not a high priority for the average western male.

Women may be better at sitting quietly without distraction, but neither men nor women are generally able to suspend thought, and just sit for any length of time. The problem is our ego-mind takes over and runs amok. In the East, they call this tendency, "monkey-mind." The simple truth is that the vast majority of us spend our lives distracting ourselves, from considering the deeper questions and thinking deeper thoughts.

> **The vast majority of us**
> **spend our lives distracting**
> **ourselves, from considering**
> **the deeper questions and**
> **thinking deeper thoughts.**

We avoid quiet reflection, because we find it both confusing and disquieting. Most of us are afraid to just be, because this is exactly when questions like, "Is there meaning to life?" bubble up from our subconscious and frighten us with their implications. Other than undistracted quiet time, there are few motivations to direct us to considering the all-important issue of, Meaning, and its correlative question: "Who Am I."

Death, crippling accidents, and things of a similar nature, usually demand we stop the constant distraction for a moment, and consider more deeply the meaning of it all. But even then, how many people do you know that will go way out of their way to find a reason to not attend a memorial service? Aside from self-absorption, what does that say about a person in this situation? Can't face death perhaps? And, why would that be? No underlying belief in the meaning of it all? Another exception to our tendency to avoid the deeper questions is church, synagogue or temple attendance. But even then, most of us secretly view regular religious observance as more of a social obligation, than an opportunity to be with our creator. Of course, there are those among us who truly do relish time to commune with themselves, usually in a natural setting of some sort. God's cathedrals, as it were.

The majority of us will at least acknowledge some desire, or yearning to watch the sunrise, the sunset, visit a quiet forest glen, or be one with God and Nature from a secluded beach, the deck of a sail boat, or almost anywhere we can quiet our internal voice, and commune with spirit. All of us want a sense of meaning in our lives, but when we are afraid that there really are no satisfying answers, we are most likely to avoid the matter. It is almost axiomatic to observe that without foundational meaning, we are simply lost. We know this. That's why we avoid focusing on uncomfortable questions. So...how long will you stave off dealing with the underlying questions that haunt you?

Meaning Requires Spirituality

When I first outlined the classroom presentations upon which this book is based, I thought I would be able to avoid the use of the "God" word. Clearly, it is a highly charged term, with different emotional associations for persons of divergent backgrounds. To speak of God is to convey concepts at a spiritual, philosophical, emotional, and psychological level. And, although you may not think so, the word "God" means different things to different people.

This is something of a conundrum, as an atheist may have, and probably does, a very different God paradigm than might a Christian Scientist, or than does a Roman Catholic, a Protestant, Greek Orthodox, Buddhist, Muslim, Hindu, New Ager, Evangelical, Mormon, and so forth. Nevertheless, to honestly and openly discuss the basics of happiness, and its most important correlative (the importance of meaning in one's life), and then to disregard the spiritual aspects of human experience, is to ignore the elephant in the living room. That's like pretending religion and spirituality doesn't have anything to do with our personal happiness. It does. We know it does. Scientific research has proven this point, again and again. We can deny it, but some form of spirituality is a vital component for virtually all of humankind. When we ignore it, the price is dear.

Over the course of my forty plus years in the adult world, I have spent time with a great many different people. In addition to thousands of business clients, over a thousand employees, and large numbers of persons I've interviewed in schools, community, and religious organizations, there are the many hundreds of prison inmates with whom I have been intimately involved. I share this as preface to a conclusion drawn from personal experience.

As much as I have tried to avoid the spiritual question outside the religious environment, it has become clear to me that some form of spiritual underpinning is essential, for ultimate confidence that there is significant meaning to life. By that I mean, every single one of us needs to find a spiritual center. And, whereas it is not absolutely necessary for one to attend a formal service of some sort, it is certainly a more practical approach. If we claim spirituality, whilst saying we are not religious, we may more easily fail to align ourselves with a set routine of spiritual focus. Far better to align one's self with a group suited to your emotional and spiritual progress, and become fully participative. Spirituality requires devotion. The routine of regular service attendance typically helps us form improved habits. On the other hand, for some, routine involvement seems to generate a "have to" rather than a "want to" mindset.

Knowledge Increase

Science has provided us with a large cadre of ever increasing information. In the ancient world, the sum total of all the information available to mankind doubled approximately every 500 hundred years. Notwithstanding the education slippage of the Middle European period, better known as the Dark Ages, by around the middle 1800's, new information was coming at us at such an accelerated rate that we saw all the discoveries and scientific knowledge of mankind doubling every 100 hundred years. This was followed by a huge steepening of the knowledge curve, as the total unique data of mankind began doubling in fifty years, then twenty, and finally every five years. Once the internet arrived and had become the effective communication tool that it is, the curve steepened once more. We now have good reason to believe that the total aggregate knowledge of the world is doubling every ten months!

Technologists continue to industrialize new scientific discoveries, thereby providing us with a constant flow of newly developed goods, particularly in the world of electronics. However, neither science nor technology is able to answer the great philosophical questions that have intrigued all societies on earth during all periods of time. The great questions are generally considered to be: Who am I? Where did I come from? Why am I here? Where am I going?

> **The great questions are generally considered to be: Who am I? Where did I come from? Why am I here? Where am I going?**

There are many other important questions to be sure, but these four seem to be *the* critical ones upon which everything else rests. Underlying these questions is the unspoken, but clearly inferred question: Is there meaning in life? Or perhaps, stated differently: What purpose underwrites our existence?

> **Is there meaning in life?**

For some, the answers to the great questions seem to be that we are simply a transitory sentient being, comprised of materials made in the core of stars and that there is no purpose for our life. This point of view says essentially: We're going to die, and physical death ends our existence. In other words, there is no meaning. Vladimir Nabokow, the author of the once controversial book *Lolita,* sums up this position thus:

> "The cradle rocks above an abyss. Common sense tells us that our existence is but a brief crack of light between two eternities of darkness."

Common sense may tell Vladimir Nabokow that there is no meaning or purpose in life, but that does not reflect the common sense of most people. According to recent surveys, over

90 percent of the world's population believes in Deity. In addition, more than 50 percent of scientists polled say they believe in God, or some definition of God, that would reflect the underlying intelligence that science itself is now revealing as present throughout the universe.

Science should no longer be viewed as an enemy to spirituality. Science, religion and personal spirituality, are finding reconciliation and real peace in the hearts of many, and that group is growing. True enough, science and religion remain in conflict at the level of the zealots in either camp who see their private belief system as threatened by the other. These are those who are focused on what is wrong, rather than what is right about the other camp's point of view.

My recommendation is that we not buy in to the science verse religion conflict. Rise above it. Open your mind and your heart. Dare to examine the essential beliefs that underlie your thinking, and don't worry so much about what you believe others are thinking and believing. Focus on your own growth and development, and let others do the same. Help one another as you can, but decline to engage in battles of opinion, as they are rarely productive and frequently destructive. Recall that it is important for us to be focused on the positive, not searching for what's wrong with someone else's point of view.

Virtually every study done by psychologists, where religion or spirituality are reviewed, report that that those involved in spiritually focused activities are physically and emotionally healthier than those who are not. Let's revisit Dr. Martin Seligman's (1998 president of the American Psychological Association), statement from his book entitled *Authentic Happiness*:

> "Religious Americans are clearly
> less likely to abuse drugs, commit
> crimes, divorce, and kill themselves.
> They are physically healthier and
> they live longer…Most directly
> relevant is the fact that survey data
> consistently show religious people
> as being happier and more satisfied
> with life than non-religious people."

We may never know how everything in the universe works, but we can apply our understanding of what works to the benefit of our personal lives. Everyone is benefitted by deep introspection, and a reverence for life, and things greater than themselves. We all have a deep down desire for some element of spirituality. Honesty dictates we recognize that sincere spirituality yields major dividends to the practitioner. It does not make any difference whether you are a scientist, an intellectual, philosopher, psychologist, or any other label you wish to brandish. You ignore spirituality to your great loss. On the other hand, just how you define spirituality, and what it consists of, is your choice.

Keep in mind that one does not have to understand how things work in order to benefit from them. How many people know how a microwave oven works, or how their DVD player operates? Most folks do not know how these things work, although millions know how to make use of them. The same could be said of spiritual practice. Why it works have psychologists baffled. Whether it works or not is no longer a scientific question. Spirituality can make a huge difference in the quality of one's life.

It is probably important that we remember at this point that there is some form of hierarchy in the universe. Most of us can grasp that energy becomes physically material through some process. Science tells us that some part of light-energy progresses into becoming subatomic particles. These particles come together to bind into atoms. Atoms are very small, in fact, there are approximately 1 billion atoms in the period at the end of this sentence. That's small. Yet we know that atoms collect and compound themselves into molecules. Molecules combine to become the basic elements. Sometimes they aggregate to become living cells. It appears to be at this very point in the evolution of energy (some may call it "spirit"), that energy either lives, in the classic physical sense, or is formed as inert mass.

We know that arms and legs exist. We know that cells exist. We know that atoms exist. We know that sub-atomic particles exist. And, we know that below these particles, all is energy. What does it mean? I don't know. Yes, I do have ideas, some of which I will share in the next chapter, but no I do not know. On the other hand, no one knows why gravity works the way it does.

We do know that gravity works in certain and specific ways, and we can predict with absolute accuracy how things will be affected by the gravitational influence of mass. In a sense, spirituality is a bit like that...we can see that it can be a powerful influence for good, and we can share our opinions on the why of it all day long, but the truth is we do not know the why of it, we only know that it does affirmatively impact us.

If you are willing to face the great questions, then you are likely already involved in meditation practice, religious study, church, synagogue, temple, mosque attendance, or you are involved in some form of spiritual endeavor. All of these spiritually focused approaches are effective as avenues through which to garner greater meaning in one's life. Most religious institutions are organized around their ability to provide answers to the disturbing whys and wherefores of our lives. However, as education levels rise, and more people feel compelled to ask deeper questions, some of the more dogmatic religious groups find it hard to support rigid spiritual interpretations.

There is much confusion in the religious world. Christianity alone has hundreds of different organizational bodies, many claiming different doctrinal positions. For the most part, each one of these "churches" takes the position that their interpretation of Holy Writ is the correct view. For the western world, Holy Writ usually means the Bible, but there are differences of opinion regarding even what constitutes those prophetic writings.

For most of us, our religious denominational affiliation was determined by our parents. We've generally accepted what we were taught at a young age, and most will feel comfortable and secure in this place. On the other hand, there are determined investigators who seem driven by the nagging fear that no one really knows who we are, where we came from, why we're here, and where we are going. We can always ignore the deeper questions. But, eventually we figure out that the most obvious alternative to seeking spiritual enlightenment is the same position that paleoanthropology espouses: There really are no answers to these questions, because we are only evolved animals sitting atop the food chain. According to this view, we have no particular purpose other than to live, breed, and die. Hence, there is no meaning to life.

There are those who are truly atheists, or at least honestly agnostic. Many of these are perfectly wonderful people, highly-educated, thoughtful, and sometimes a good deal further along emotionally than many religionists. On the other hand, the agnostic position has always been an attractive one for the emotionally guilty, those wanting to suppress conscience and justify actions. After all, if there is no higher moral authority, one is free to do virtually anything without pause, provided one does not openly violate society's laws...or at least get caught at it.

Peck's Phases of Growth

The typical way out of the religious/spiritual dilemma for most people is to simply not think about it. Others side step critical thinking by glibly claiming they believe in spirituality, but do not believe in religion. Whereas this is a valid position for some, for most it is simply a clever twist of terminology. According to author psychiatrist M. Scott Peck, there is a common pattern or evolution of spiritual maturation as follows:

Scott Peck's Phases of Spiritual Growth

Stage 1: Chaotic, antisocial
Stage 2: Formal, institutional
Stage 3: Skeptic, individual
Stage 4: Mystic, communal

Stage 1 represents our earliest stage of growth. Children are naturally self-focused and manipulative. Many never grow out of this developmental stage; they simply fail to graduate into social responsibility (the keenly narcissistic fall in to this category, as do many of those in prison.) For those wearing atheism as a cover for activities inconsistent with social fairness, they have not actually progressed to Stage 3, but are still firmly rooted in Stage 1.

Stage 2 is where many of us accepted our parent's religious affiliation, and evolved some concept of God. We likely felt spiritual promptings to some degree and saw God as the source of good and fairness. It is about this place where we develop fear of the judgment of God. Viewing God in terms of judgment and reward is where most begin their spiritual path. If stuck here, we remain as children, never gaining the greater insight that leads to the peace and happiness that exceeds all understanding.

When Stage 3 arrives, as the result of honorable thinking, it is often because one challenges the goodness of God and fails to find meaning in life, i.e.: "How could a loving God allow all the unfairness in the world?" Many traversing the avenues of higher education get caught here. This is not an accident. Greater knowledge raises more troubling questions, and many shrug their shoulders, quitting the pursuit of a broader grasp of the universe and our place in it. Eventually those in Stage 3 tend to move on to Stage 4, provided enough of their more disturbing questions about faith are addressed to their own satisfaction. There are few thoughtful, honorable, atheists that make it to the threshold of death without reconsidering the question of "meaning" within the context of life. The more one's life develops in the direction of love and compassion the more likely that a person will move through Stage 3, and eventually arrive to a place of spiritual confidence.

Scott Peck's clinical experience demonstrates that there are people stuck in all three stages of spiritual development. Some are blessed to find the greater peace and happiness that only Stage 4 can provide. Some may be put off by Dr. Peck's use of the term "mystic," in his Stage 4 explanation, as they observe correctly that this word is the root of "mysticism." Prejudice abounds surrounding the use of this term. The renowned psychiatrist explains his use of the word mysticism, thus:

> "Mysticism," a much maligned
> word, is not an easy one to define.
> It takes many forms. Yet through
> the ages, mystics of every shade of
> religious belief have spoken of unity,
> of an underlying connectedness
> between things: between men
> and women, between us and the
> other creatures and even inanimate
> matter as well, a fitting together
> according to an ordinarily invisible
> fabric underlying the cosmos"

Peck's explanation sounds a lot like the concepts of entanglement, the root mysticism of Quantum Mechanics.

Agnostics and Atheists

An agnostic is one who *doubts* the existence of a higher power. Atheism is the doctrine or belief that there is no god. To put Dr. Peck's Stage 3 in numeric perspective, according to the December 2007 issue of the National Geographic magazine, 14 percent of the world's population is atheistic or agnostic. That number is largely due to the position taken by certain Communist governments, i.e.: China, etc. In the United States the percentage of atheists/agnostics, is less than the world average. In the Baylor Survey of Religion (2006), 5 percent of Americans are atheists, or about the same percentage as the worldwide rate, if one discounts China. It reports that 92 percent of Americans believe in God, and that 90 percent have a religious belief in God coupled with a specific faith-based affiliation.

In my analysis, based on the research provided from both of the studies cited above, those that are numbered in the atheistic-agnostic group seem to break into three broad based categories:

(1)   Those claiming atheism due to governmental edict: North Korea, Cuba, China, and communist states generally;

(2)   The intellectual elite, who take the position that the bio-chemical evolution of life forms has pushed God into the realm of mythology; and,

(3)   The criminal and seriously disenfranchised of all societies, whose justification for violating law is their belief that there is no higher moral authority. (Prisons are filled with these people.)

It is interesting to note that in each of the world's most populous countries a different belief system dominates: China is atheist by government edict; India is predominantly Hindu, America is largely Christian, Indonesia is 94 percent Muslim. Christianity is the largest religious affiliation amounting to 33 percent of the world's total population. Muslims are the second largest religious group. Muslims account for approximately 21 percent of the world's population. The third largest religious grouping falls under the collective moniker of Hindu, accounting for about 13 percent of the world's population. Buddhists are the fourth largest religious grouping accounting for 6 percent of the earth's total population. The remaining 12 percent of the globe's population is comprised of a mix of other religious organizations and affiliations. The National Geographic *States of Faith* article, also in the December 2007 issue, says:

> "In the 20th century, seismic political forces altered the geography of religion when communist regimes declared millions of new atheists, and Europe's Jews were dispersed or killed. Now the ground shifts again: Christianity is on the rise in Africa, China, and Russia, while Islam grows in Europe."

All religious institutions are considered faith-based groups. However, even the serious atheist must conjure considerable faith in something, i.e.: science, military power, money, influence, etc, in order to believe whatever it is he or she has decided to believe. Belief in science, to the exclusion of everything else, is still just a belief system.

Almost anyone can point out that science is incapable of "proving" some of humankind's most basic of experiences. For example, the emotion of love has been experienced by most, but it is impossible to put love in a test tube and prove its existence. From a strictly scientific paradigm, one would therefore be forced to say there is no such thing as love because science has not been able to prove its existence. And, remarkably enough there are a few who actually take this position. But, if you take this position you must then admit there is no such thing as happiness either, and seriously now, isn't the desire for happiness the reason you're reading this book?

Maps Verses Territories

The study of world religions from an historical point of view does little to give one much confidence that mankind has a solid grip on the great questions. However, individual study, prayer, and deep reflection on the great wisdom literature (the scriptural works of different religious disciplines), is another matter entirely. Remember, to learn about something is a mental or thinking function. We are then gaining information upon which we will usually form an opinion and possibly an eventual belief system. On the other hand, to immerse oneself in the experience of spirituality is to understand it from an entirely different point of view. The two processes are akin to studying a map verses exploring the territory.

One might study the John Muir trail for example, learn the distances, consider the effort required to walk, carry, and camp, and then come to a conclusion as to the value of the actual experience. This would be in contrast to walking the deep forest glade, smelling the pines, crossing the streams, hiking the mountain trails, breathing the fresh clean air, seeing the mountain peaks reflected in the high clear lakes, spending nights in quiet reflection huddled close to a campfire. The first learns the turn of the trail by projected experience, the second by the doing. The first thinks he knows the experience to be had, the other knows he knows. One process embraces all the senses including thought and emotions. The other is opinion based on thought alone.

Thoughts thought upon to the point of some form of conclusion progress to become opinions. Opinions replayed enough become beliefs. But thought alone is a function of thinkingness; it is not validating experience. Experiences that involve the senses, and the doing of some sort of activity, are immensely more satisfying to us. To know something experientially provides us with strong internal confirmation, in other words, the proof of the pudding is in the eating.

Learning about pudding is a very different thing than eating it. Discovering meaning in your life is an intensely personal experience; literally no one else can do it for you! It's something like explaining pudding to someone who has never eaten it. You can discuss the texture and taste of pudding, you can memorize recipes and become an 'expert' on the ingredients, but until you eat it, everything is purely conjecture.

The example directly above might be analogous to the bible scholar who has gone to seminary, can quote chapter and verse for all manner of subjects, knows the map, can quote the recipe, but has never walked the trail or tasted the pudding. One cannot study themselves into spirituality, although it may surely help in one's preparation. One must take the plunge, and experience what it is like to go deep within, to be open without prejudice, to turn down outside distractions and listen for the spirit, to quietly mediate and await the answers to reveal themselves. This is walking the trail. This is the tasting of the pudding. Everything else is learning the map or studying the recipe. To evolve, we must be prepared to both study the map *and* explore the territory, the latter being more important than the former.

The majority of people have probably had spiritual promptings at one time or another. Typically, rather than follow these prompting on to the obtaining of greater knowledge and enlightenment, we get sidetracked by the world, lose focus and become hopelessly mired in our work-a-day circumstances. Most of us, without really thinking about it, immediately give more credence to the outside world of our expected experience, than we do the inside world of our translated experience. Perhaps that's because most religious participation consists of studying the map. Good but not great. True spirituality is found in the tasting of the pudding, living the deeply reflecting experience, walking the talk.

A Personal Understanding

My father was an educated man, schooled in the sciences, mathematics, history, and English. He claimed to be an atheist, although, in actuality, he was more of an agnostic. My father did not attend any form of religious activity, nor did he study any kind of religious material. My mother was also well educated; she was a generic Christian, not dogmatic or doctrinally focused, but definitely dedicated to honorable principles and regular church participation. My only sibling, a sister 6 ½ years my senior, is a brilliant woman. In addition to being one of the most wonderful women I have ever known, she holds double masters and double doctorate degrees. Her religious leanings are Judeo-Christian, Buddhist, Hindu, and Shamanistic. I share this personal information as background to the next four paragraphs.

In my reality, there is powerful and significant meaning to each of our lives. To believe we have no eternal destiny is actually in direct conflict with the intuitive understanding each of us have felt strongly at sometime in our life. Turning one's back on the belief that there is significant meaning to our existence literally forces one to tamp down what our subconscious quietly tells us to the contrary.

I believe there is immense meaning to our reason for being; probably much more than one can appreciate through traditional ways of learning. I did not gain my witness as to the meaning of life entirely through books, lectures, or church attendance, although they all serve a worthy purpose. Rather, I received a personal and powerful spiritual witness that there is indeed extraordinary meaning to our lives. This undeniable witness of the spirit has come in many ways, and at different times, but most potently within deep meditative (prayerful), states that result in what is now frequently referred to as an OBE, out of body experience. Shocked?

Many with children have surely experienced how they can play the strings of our heart so completely that we may sometimes find ourselves embarrassed by tears when there is no reason to be crying. I cannot explain this kind of love, but I know that it is real. (Of course, you do not have to have children to have had this experience.) I cannot address this intensity of emotion with any kind of rational argument, but I have felt it move through me with great power. It is thus with deeply moving spiritual experience; you may not be able to explain it in terms understood by those who have not felt it, but there is no question that it is authentic.

Those extraordinary and uniquely mysterious revelations we may be privileged to have are beyond all languaging, yet in my experience they are completely genuine. In many ways, the unfolding of my most intimate spiritual moments still feel more vivid than anything that has transpired in my physical life. Therefore, speaking from direct experience, I offer my witness that there is purpose in our existence. And, I've come to recognize that the meaning of life is absolutely saturated in love and beauty. I further testify that WE are the critical component and reason for everything in our physical world.

> **There is great purpose in our existence. The meaning of life is absolutely saturated in love and beauty. We are the critical component and reason for everything in our physical world.**

So again, why all this discussion about spirituality in a chapter about meaning? Because the vast majority of us will at least partially define "meaning" in terms of a religious association, or path of spirituality with which we can identify. And, this is good, provided we are careful to not allow our prejudice to misdirect our thinking into becoming critical of other's spiritual path. Criticism and judgment do not constitute spirituality.

The great religious leaders, those whose works and words have withstood the test of time, whether they be called Mystics, Lamas, Sages, Philosophers, Magi, Prophets, Apostles, Priests, Gurus, or Swamis, have each taught that the outside world does not hold our happiness. We are to seek happiness, the meaning of life, and the kingdom of God, deep within our very selves.

In order to discover greater meaning in life and experience the enduring peace of happiness, we must shift our focus to one of profound gratitude. In order to do this we must suspend our immediate tendency to judge (criticism by another name). Once we learn to accept things "as is," we'll discover the capacity within us to truly love. This means we'll want to forgive everyone for whatever it is we are holding against them. As we forgive others, we are automatically releasing our self-criticism. Then, and only then, are we able to love ourselves. Once love begins to shine forth from within, we will surely seek ways to serve others. As recorded in James 1:27:

> "Pure religion undefiled before God and the Father is this: To

visit the fatherless and widows in
their affliction, and to keep himself
unspoiled from the world."

When we are doing good the Law of Attraction will unerringly return good for good. Focus on helping others and set aside life's melodrama. It is only then that you will begin to realize that the meaning of life is creation, love, and happiness. Love is the power of creation. Happiness is the result.

The MEANING of life is love
and happiness. Love is the
power. Happiness is the result.

VERBUM SAT SAPIENT

It's All *Thought!*

Chapter 15

THINK HAPPY THOUGHTS

"What being is there who does not desire happiness?"

Socrates

Basic Truths

Think happy thoughts, the wisdom of Peter Pan. In its simplicity, it's an insightful pronouncement, and a darn good idea. Think happy thoughts is a great statement for living. Yet, no matter how simple and true, we'll need to continually re-expose ourselves to the myriad implications this statement so succinctly summarizes before its value can likely take hold.

Multiple times we've reviewed another simple fact, happiness begins with gratitude. Why is that? Because we must appreciate the good around us, or no matter how good our good fortune really is, we simply cannot be happy. If we can't see it, sense it, touch or taste it, we will not feel the peace, the positive expectancy, and the expanding joy, which is available to us. In my personal world-view, we exist to live in a place of unbounded love and blessedness. Surely, we all want to experience a state of abundance, harmony, and fun. This place really does exist. It is within each one of us.

By now the reader should be familiar with these three essential truths:

1　How we respond, to what we perceive to be the outside world, is actually a choice we make within.

2　We are the ones who decide the experience we will be having, as it is a direct consequence of the thoughts we think.

3　Happiness is not about how much stuff we accumulate, or what we've accomplished, rather it is primarily about gratitude, love, and self-acceptance.

Gratitude, love, and self-acceptance, is where we must live at our core, if we sincerely want to be in that time, space, and place, of genuine happiness. These are the measures of our inner self that describe who we really are. When we've got this right, heaven shines from within. When they're seriously out of whack, we live in a hell of our own making.

Heaven or Hell

When gratitude, love, and self-acceptance are not anchored firmly in some understanding of "Who we are," or some sense of meaning, happiness can only be a temporary respite from unease, dis-ease, discontent, and eventually depression. Of course if one is really good at distraction, the results of postponing your inner investigation may not impact you right away. "Who Am I?" is the subject of Chapter 16, however, at this stage of our growing understanding we ought to recognize that whether we live in heaven or hell, or find ourselves caught somewhere in between, is literally an emotional response to who we are within.

> **Whether we live in heaven or hell, or find ourselves caught somewhere in between, is literally an emotional response to who we are within.**

A Holographic Universe?

Do you recall that much of our focus on the outside things of our world is a subconscious attempt to distract us from deeper issues? Most of us are extremely reluctant to focus within, essentially believing as we do, that everything is from without, and therefore, we are virtually helpless in regards to the greater events to which we are exposed throughout life. However, ongoing experiments in the quantum field, along with the results of exploratory mind-body research, suggests that not only are we each responsible for the world we experience, but there may be much more to it than that.

One theory gaining ground suggests that the energies that comprise our existence are actually three-dimensional projections. A number of recent books and scientific papers put forward the notion that our universe is actually holographic. What does that mean? In the movie *Star Wars*, the adventure begins when a light is projected from the robot R2 D2 creating a three-dimensional likeness of Princess Leia, asking Obi-wan Kenobi to come to her assistance. That's a hologram.

Technologically, we now know how to create and project three-dimensional pictures, with the aid of a laser and sophisticated software, and were it not so incredibly expensive, it would be all the rage in a new going-to-the-movies fad. Talk about getting lost in the picture, can you even imagine? It's easy enough to lose yourself in a normal theatre experience. In some ways, a movie is like a waking dream, but what would it be like to actually be in the middle of the show with the characters, objects, and sound all around you?

It's a pretty certain bet that if one can lose track of a couple of hours of daily reality by sitting in a dark movie theatre enjoying a well-made movie, then our senses of reality would be even more overwhelmed, if the sets were three-dimensional. Adding other senses would be just a function of wireless brain stimulation. As it is, all of our physical senses are simply quantum impulses experienced within our brain. We have the experience of things being out there, but everything we actually experience is processed within our heads. That is not conjecture; it literally is the way it is.

Understanding the implications of how easy it is to create brain wave stimulation, and considering new ground-breaking insights on the ways by which we experience all that we do, is at least a partial validation that we are all living our own illusion. A number of scientists have already weighed in on the astounding conclusion that everything in our world of experience is indeed projection and that the entire universe itself is a kind of giant hologram, a splendidly detailed illusion. To quote Michael Talbot, the author of *The Holographic Universe*:

> "Put another way, there is evidence
> to suggest that our world and
> everything in it - from snowflakes
> to maple trees to falling stars and
> spinning electrons - are only images,
> projections from a level of reality
> so beyond our own it is literally
> beyond both space and time."

Whereas this information is certainly interesting, and in fact may be true, whether it is, or it is not, is not the point here. What I want to emphasize is that what we do know about our mental make-up is that, we are the ones who decide to live in heaven or hell.

**What we do know about
our mental make-up is that,
we are the ones who decide
to live in heaven or hell.**

We are the ones in control, whether we acknowledge it or not. This is truly the way things are. If you are miserable right now, that's probably the last thing you want to hear. On the other hand, it is the most important thing you can learn. Do not avoid it, internalize it. Your life can change quickly once you get this understood and integrated into your thinking processes. If you put it off, your life cannot dramatically improve. Yes, there may be temporary respites from struggle, but overall nothing will change substantially. And, that's because everything we experience is actually experienced within us. No exceptions. It is the way it is.

Perhaps it is helpful to recall that in the New Testament of the Bible, the Apostle Luke records Jesus as instructing the Pharisees with this insightful statement:

"...behold, the Kingdom of God is
within you."

Luke 17:21 KJV

What a profound statement! The Kingdom of God IS WITHIN
US! What does it really mean? As a religious declaration it sounds
more like Sufi wisdom, or perhaps a Hindu Vedic, Upanishadic, or
Yoga Sutra, philosophical position. When viewed from another
perspective it sounds like a scientific treatise coming from the
architects of the holographic universe theory, two of the world's
pre-eminent thinkers: physicist David Bohm, protégé of Einstein's,
and Karl Pribram, a neurophysiologist at Stanford University.

Those familiar with Buddhism will recognize a similar teaching to that found in the New Testament, and as recorded in the
Gospel of Luke above. In the Kalachakra Tantra, the Kingdom of
Heaven is the internal Shambhala, mistranslated in Western literature as the mythical paradise on earth, known as Shangri-La. It
exists in two places...first within, secondly in another reality, not
yet observable by man.

The Kingdom of God, Heaven, Paradise, or whatever name
we wish to identify that perfect place, that virtually all religious
disciplines speak to, first and foremost must be discovered within, only then can it emanate into the external world of our experience. Does it surprise you that most of the world's historical
religions have taught this same foundational principal? As we reviewed in Chapter 13, our spiritual expectations are much more
alike than what we have been taught to believe. From the ancient
Hindu scriptures known as the Upanishads, comes this insight:

"You are what your deep driving desire is.
As your desire is, so is your will.
As your will is, so is your deed.
As your deed is, so is your destiny."

Upanishad IV. 4.5

We're in Charge

Our deepest desires, in fact all of our desires, reside within us. Where else would they be? Our will, the driving force behind all our actions, is also a function of the inner self. Neither desire nor will, come from without; both radiate from within. With only a little reflection it should be obvious that no one tells us what we will think. They may influence, it is true, but only you decide what to focus upon. Only I decide for me. No one else is able to decide what you or I shall think. Perhaps others can control your exterior for a time, sometimes rather dramatically as happened to me, but only you - and you alone, make the internal decisions as to what you are thinking, and what emotions shall color those thoughts. The catch is that most of us don't really understand this critical principle. Now you know. We are in charge of our lives. We do have the power to change.

We are in charge of our lives. We do have the power to change.

It cannot be overstated that each one of us ultimately decides the emphasis, or the lack thereof, that we assign to every situation, to every occurrence. We are in command of our feelings, albeit few there are that will accept the responsibility. The vast majority of people are simply reacting to their feelings in concert with their childhood programs and experience driven paradigms. Very few will take the time to recognize and strictly understand that, we are the ones running our own emotional control center.

The greater our unhappiness, the greater the likelihood we will deny that it is our very selves that decide how we shall react to external stimuli. Our ego will always demand that we find something, or someone to blame for our misery. But, again, it is you who determines the value you assign to each thought. It is you who determines the emotional content attached to each thought you think. And, it is you who thinks any given thought in the first place.

Admittedly, those who are capable of turning off thought are far and few between. In the east they refer to these remarkable few as "Masters." Masters of what? Masters of themselves.

Self Mastery

Anyone can move towards self-mastery, although throughout world history only three have been specifically honored by civilization, as having complete mastery of themselves. But here's the important point to grasp: We do *not* have to be masters to live in a happy state well over 90 percent of the time.

> **We do not have to be masters**
> **to live in a happy state well**
> **over 90 percent of the time.**

What must we do to live in this place? I suggest you address the following with a singleness of purpose: Develop a meaningful sense of who you are. Focus on gratitude, love, and forgiveness. Be aware. Quit judging. Cease the negative chatter, and get out of your past and live in the present. There is more to do, but these alone will put you in a state of happiness, most of the time. Again:

1. Develop a meaningful sense of who you are;
2. Focus on gratitude, love, and forgiveness;
3. Be Aware;
4. Quit Judging;
5. Cease the negative chatter; and
6. Get out of your past and live in the present.

Recall that each of us ultimately determines the meaning of the things in our present, as the result of viewing everything through the lenses of our past reality. This situation guarantees we will have the same reoccurring "issues," whether they actually exist or not. When we overlay our mental lens on the images, we predict for our future, we project the past forward. Is that what you want? If not then you must find a better way. Cease to plan your future by your past!

The recipe for happiness requires we learn to live in the present. We must unhook our obsession with predetermining our present by our feelings of inadequacies from the past. It is only when we get out of the past, and stop trying to live in the future, that we can deeply experience the NOW. It's only in the NOW that we are able to enjoy happiness. In the words of Ralph Waldo Emerson,

> "What lies behind us and what
> lies before us are tiny matters
> compared to what lies within us."

Let's remember that the biblical Proverbs has summarized this basic understanding in just a few words:

> "For as he thinketh in
> his heart so is he."
>
> Proverbs 23:7

Living in the Now

We've addressed it before, but still, could it possibly be this easy? Change your thinking and change your world? We simply decide? Is our state of mind *really* the ultimate source of happiness? The answer to each of these questions is an emphatic yes! When we recognize the potency of learning, and actually choosing to be happy in the NOW, as well as how to feel good in the NOW, we begin to grasp the power by which we can attain to any state of being.

If you've read this far I absolutely guarantee that you have both the capacity, and the means, with which to garner peace, harmony, wisdom, health, wealth, and happiness. You can be certain this is true. Vibrationally you have been attracted to this information. Vibrationally you have been pulled towards a deeper grasp and more clear understanding. What you are exploring is a core teaching of all the avatars. It is the gospel (a term which simply means "good news"), of living. We are born to be happy, its pursuit is our highest spiritual path, but to refine bliss within, we must wake up to the truth. The truth is in every one of us: look within. We can suspend our tendency to judge, we can forgive others, and we too can be forgiven. We can look up towards higher realms of living and be grateful for the good that is all about us. We can smile and laugh and enjoy the very now. It is the natural state of our natural self.

We were born to be happy. It is the natural state of our natural self.

When we are happy, life is joyful, and there is beauty and purpose in everything to which we turn our attention. Just as misery clouds our vision and poisons the fun of even our most cherished activities, heartfelt joy adds brightness, color, and delight to even the mundane. It bears repeating - because we need to be crystal clear in our understanding - that happiness is not about the tangible stuff we have accumulated, or what we wish to accumulate, and it's not about what we have or have not accomplished, it is about gratitude, love, and self-acceptance.

> **Happiness is not about
> how much stuff we have, or
> what we've accomplished,
> it is all about gratitude,
> love, and self-acceptance.**

The Sikh's are a monotheistic religion of India. They have combined both Hinduism and Islam in a unique way. The Sikh Bible, the *Granth*, says,

> "God is in thy heart, yet
> thou searchest for him
> in the wilderness."

Isn't that the truth? Aren't most of us searching outside of us for truth? We look hither and yon, but rarely inside. The *Tao te Ching*, the Bible of Taoism, the ancient philosophy and religion of China, teaches this same principle. The *Bhagavid Gita*, the *Dhamapada*, the *Qur'an*, the old and new testaments of the Christian Bible, the *Book of Mormon*, and all the great spiritual philosophies of mankind, have arrived at the same conceptual understandings, which might well be summarized as: Our relationship with God, and ultimately our individual happiness, can only be discovered within us. The space-time for that discovery can only take place in our NOW.

> **Our relationship with
> God, and ultimately our
> individual happiness, can
> only be discovered within**

**us. The space-time for
that discovery can only
take place in our NOW.**

Being Thankful

It is important to keep reminding ourselves that without a sense of thankfulness, it is impossible to be happy. Our habitual focus on worry, and what is wrong with our environment, relationships, health, and so forth, attracts things to our attention that need improvement. There is no end to discovering flaws in our surroundings. After all, this is an imperfect world. But, it is a world that is perfect for each of us to experience sufficient struggles to aid us in our evolution.

Our cultural emphasis endorses the need for critical analysis. Thus, in an effort to make things better, we tend to fixate on what's wrong around us, operating under the theory that we need to discover things to improve. This internal program seems to always be turned on. When it's not focused on the outside world, it's examining us. Ouch!

Our thoughts frequently run away with us. Unfortunately, it's only rarely that they're running in a truly positive direction. As a society, we are plagued with excessive self-judgment, and constant self-criticism.

Behind our pain and illness, our fears and unhappiness, is relentless self-judgment. Our internal chatter, that monkey-mind of self-criticism, rarely stops. It's like a hamster incessantly running in its exercise wheel, never getting anywhere, but driven to continue until exhaustion. We literally wear ourselves out, when we judge, censure, berate, and criticize others, which is really just another form of self-criticism.

Joy arrives when someone smiles, laughs (without guile), and whenever one begins to focus attention on the good around them. All of us have moments of joy and happiness. However, for most, these moments are too few, and the experiences too short, and too shallow. This is because the lack of joy and happiness in our lives flows from the lack of balance in our thinking.

**The lack of joy and happiness
in our lives flows from the lack
of balance in our thinking.**

Wrong Focus

We spend far too much of our time considering what is wrong. This imbalance in our mental process is supported by immense multi-sensory impact. What appears to be wrong around us is constantly broadcast on television, radio, the internet, in our newspapers and magazines. As a result, worrisome talk swamps our general conversation. We eat, breathe, and sleep a continual flow of negativity. Is it any wonder that our typical first response to a new situation is to note what we think is wrong with it?

So, you ask, "What are we supposed to do, become a recluse and ignore the world around us?" Hmmm. That's an interesting thought. Seems there is an old adage about that: *Ignorance is bliss.* Perhaps that's the reason history records so many great sages getting away to a place removed from the helter-skelter of life. In truth, everyone needs sanctuary. But simply sticking your head in the sand, or running off to a mountain-top, or my favorite: disappearing to a jungle-island somewhere, is as impractical a proposal (for most of us anyway), as it may be irresponsible.

We live in a world of dramatically increasing complexity. And our essential biological programming is fine-tuned to scan our surroundings for potential danger. To disable this function is to put us at risk, so the answer is not to turnoff and tune-out, but rather to develop equilibrium. How is this possible when the vast majority of the raw data streaming into our senses seems to be focused on what's wrong with a given situation? To illustrate the enormity of the problem, remember that all advertising is designed to show you what you do not have, and thus what you are in need of, in order to measure-up or be "happy." The basic premise of advertising is to develop a sense of "lack" in those who are exposed to it. Its intent is to generate unease and a sense of inadequacy that may only be resolved by our purchasing a given product.

Can we honestly appreciate that everything in life is based upon one's viewpoint? Can you see that there are usually different ways to consider virtually every new piece of information arriving to our brain through our senses? We really need to grasp that the way our minds' address new input is a function of our individual habits of thinking. Yes, that's it. We're back to habits of thinking! Remember? Habits of thought are better known as attitudes. And it is our attitudes, which form the mind's programs through which all experiences are processed. This is, in effect, the brain's operating system.

The software running in our brains is connected to our emotional reactions. Our emotions both reveal us, and are literally the essence of our lives. Emotions are not bad, emotions are life! We experience all of life through emotion. But remember, emotions are always hooked to thoughts. Thoughts precede our emotional response. Therefore we can change the feelings we feel by changing the thoughts we think.

> **Emotions are not bad, emotions are life! We can change the feelings we feel by changing the thoughts we think.**

"What about facts," some will ask? "Facts are facts," is usually the follow-up line, as if that is all there is to say about it. So, what about facts? Do facts stand alone as bastions of independent truth, or are most supposed "facts" generally presented as irrefutable truths by someone intent upon demonstrating a point they themselves are endorsing? In other words, are not most supposed facts organized by presenters to support a point of view? No matter who you are, where you came from, what your educational background, in the end, everything experienced in life is plainly based upon one's viewpoint. When we think about this for a bit, we will likely recognize that what we believe to be facts, may not really be facts at all. For example, as already pointed out, any historian can verify that the "facts" of history, those things the vast majority of people believed and in many cases were ready to die for, were not what they thought they were. It is often said that throughout history probably 90 percent of the things people were so sure of, turned out to not be true. Now that's a sobering thought!

We are Creators

Each of us is the creator of our own reality. Everything begins with the thoughts we think. Our thoughts determine our actions. Our actions determine our habits. Our habits determine our levels of happiness, which in turn, evolves our character. Our character determines our eternal destiny. Everything we perceive in our world is processed through the filter of our consciousness, and every decision we make is based on some construct of what is real for us. As the Buddha is recorded to have said,

> "All that we are is the result of
> what we have thought. If a man
> speaks or acts with an evil thought,
> pain follows him. If a man speaks
> or acts with a pure thought,
> happiness follows him, like a
> shadow that never leaves him."

It is really not possible for anyone else to create our reality. We do it. Of course, it is true that we can pretend that our lives are the result of other's choices, and perhaps most people do just that. But, this is merely a mental mind game we play with ourselves to deny our personal responsibility for the way we feel. What is true and bears constant repeating is: we create our own reality, even if we do not yet understand that we do it.

**We create our own reality,
even if we do not yet
understand that we do it.**

When we are consciously aware of our thoughts, we are then able to marshal them to support our innermost desires. After all, our belief system and our desires are simply thoughts themselves. And, it is our desire and our most firmly rooted beliefs that will be attracting the experiences we will be having in our future. Remember that whatever we give attention to in our

NOW, infusing it with the energy of emotion, will unfold in some form in our future. And, that's true whether we want it to be or not. We are *always* choosing, even when we are not aware of it.

Every time we think, we are using our creative source. How careful we should be to think constructively. Mental laws are as real as physical laws. The use of our creative power is as natural as the use of electricity, as consistent as the law of gravity. Imagination, and its corresponding creative principal, is entirely reactive to thought. The universe seems to receive the slightest vibration of thought-energy and acts upon it. The process appears to work something like a mirror. As we call up images of thought, they are reflected in the mirror of our memory. As emotions become affixed to thought, they accelerate thought-form which eventually matures into our life experiences.

> **As emotions become affixed to thought, they accelerate thought-form which eventually matures into our life experiences.**

The focus on any form of thought image, or what most think of as visualization, begins the process of bringing that image into our physical realm. On the other hand, as we conjure new ideas into place, the old reflections are swept aside, and these new thoughts begin to evolve into our living reality. If we withdraw older impressions only partially, and mingle them with new thinking, we begin to generate composites. In other words, our experience will share the nature of both kinds of thought. We may conclude then, that our happiness resides within us, and that each of us will experience happiness only to the level our thinking permits.

> **Our happiness resides within us. Each of us will experience happiness only to the level that our thinking permits.**

It is valuable to remember that all of us come with some form of internal thermostat that regulates the amount of joy and love we allow ourselves. It takes conscious participation to reset this internal control. So once again it is important that we recognize that our happiness is all about the choices we are making. It is continually an effect of how we habitually think and how we re-act to all external and internal stimuli. The longer we dwell on specific thoughts, the stronger they become. Our intention and attention invites manifestation.

So, what does this all mean? It means that in the most fun-damental way, our thoughts invite to ourselves the reality we subconsciously expect. In due course, we may come to realize that everything we truly desire will appear on our life's stage. The underlying essential truth is that we attract unto ourselves that which we think about.

**The underlying essential
truth is that we attract
unto ourselves that
which we think about.**

Happiness or misery, joy or discontent, love or loneliness, they are all simply choices. They are our choices. These states of mind and their resultant emotions are contained within us. Happiness does not arrive from the outside world, instead it comes as we understand who we are, why we're here, what our purpose is, and perhaps most importantly, as we learn to suspend self-judgment. We must unlearn our misconceptions, our false beliefs of negativity, and be willing to improve our internal paradigms. Happiness exists. It exists for each one of us. It exists in our hearts and minds, and nowhere else. The outside world does not hold our happiness; we have it. It's here for us to discover. Let's find it now.

> The time to be happy is now,
> The place to be happy is here,
> The way to be happy is to make
> others so.
>
> Robert Ingersoll (1842-1910)

It's All *Thought!*

Chapter 16

WHO AM I?

"You, like all others, are seeking the joy of living. You wish to be needed, to be loved, to be included in the great drama of life. This urge is in every individual. It is in everything."

Ernest Holmes

Spiritual, philosophical, and scientific inquiry, are humanity's great, and sometimes heroic, attempts at knowing who we are. These different approaches to understanding seem poised at a place of convergence. It appears that society is on the verge of a massive paradigm shift that will rock the intellectual world. Spiritual wisdom, philosophical argument, and scientific investigation, have each revealed fascinating insights to the underlying interconnectedness of our existence.

What Are We?

Who am I is a vastly different question than what am I? Nevertheless, it is valuable to begin our search for who we are with an improved understanding of what we are. This is a question science can respond to, whereas the question "Who Am I?"

is usually considered to be the province of philosophers, ministers, rabbis, gurus, and priests.

There are many religions around the world. Almost all of them take the position that humankind exists as a duality. This can be summed up as: We are physical beings made of atoms and cells, yet we are also spiritual beings.

We are physical beings made of atoms and cells, yet we are also spiritual beings.

The universe is incomprehensively huge, but everywhere we look, we see the same physical laws in operation. For billions of years gravity has been pulling the gas and dust that swirls throughout the universe into massive clouds, that grow more and more dense, until their very concentration generates sufficient heat to ignite nuclear fusion and become stars.

As stars begin to shine, the nuclear fusion in their cores begins to cook the hydrogen and helium gas into heavier atoms. As stars die, they spread these atoms and molecules back into the interstellar medium, where they become part of the clouds that condense to form new stars and planets. All of the atoms in our bodies, except hydrogen, were made inside stars. Dr. Michael Seeds, author of *Horizons, Exploring the Universe*, a current university text on Astronomy, put it this way:

> "If your atoms could talk, they could tell you some wild stories. Some of your atoms, such as carbon, were cooked up in the cores of medium mass stars like the sun, and were puffed out into space when those stars died and produced planetary nebulae. Some of your atoms, such as the calcium in your bones, could tell you how they were made inside massive stars, and were blown out into space during Type II Supernova

> explosions. Ask the iron atoms
> in your blood, and most would
> tell you how they were made
> by the sudden fusing of carbon
> when white dwarfs collapsed in
> Type Ia Supernova explosions."

In short, as we discussed in Chapter 1, we are made of star stuff. We are literally star children, made from ancient atoms constantly recycled through our bodies, the earth, and other living things. All of our food, and the air we breathe, originate in sunlight. Photosynthesis in plants and algae convert sunlight into chemical energy and oxygen. We survive, and thrive, by eating the chemical energy stored in plants and in the animals that feed on plants. We breathe the oxygen made in stars, released by plants interacting with sunlight. We come from stars, our food comes from stars, and the very air we breathe, comes from stars.

We are living, thinking, beings that dwell at the medium between the microscopic and the telescopic universe. We are earthlings, living on the outer crust of the land masses of our planet. Each of us is the composite of approximately 100 trillion human cells working together to keep us alive at the biological level.

> **Each of us is the composite
> of approximately 100
> trillion human cells working
> together to keep us alive
> at the biological level.**

Evolution and Creation

Our cells are mostly water therefore, we are mostly water. Our cells operate collectively, and in concert with one another, based on a set of internal plans. Switched on DNA forms our basic structural plan; it constitutes the recipe for each one of us. It is not the DNA of our genome that is so critically important, only the genes that have been activated. There is now significant research to support the belief that it is our very thoughts and feelings that determine which genes are turned on and which are not. Dr. Bruce Lipton suggests that approximately 95 percent of our gene activation is determined by us.

Our cells are made of molecules, the smallest particle into which an element or compound can be divided without changing its chemical and physical properties. Our molecules are assembled from the immortal atoms, which have temporarily come together, to comprise our bodies. In the words of my Zen teacher, Dr. Neale Povey (a scientist, with deep spiritual roots in both Christianity and Buddhism):

> "Nature wants to create life.
> There is a natural tendency
> for life to be *produced*. There
> is intentionality out there.
> Intentionality is a fundamental
> quality of God. Evolution and
> life is one consequence."

The above concept was also eloquently expressed by Willigis Jager, a Catholic scholar, monk, and Zen master:

> "Life is actually the principle of
> evolution. It is the readiness of an
> atom to bind itself with another
> atom to form a molecule. It is the
> readiness of molecules to jointly
> create a cell, the readiness of cells
> to become a greater organism. This
> readiness for self-transcendence
> can be recognized throughout the
> cosmos. It is none other than the
> driving force of life and evolution."

David R. Hawkins, M.D., PhD adds further light to the Creation-Evolution discussion with these thoughtful considerations:

> "An innate quality of creation is
> evolutionary progress. Whether
> the source of life is considered to

be a random chemical accident
(bottom-up theory), or Divinity
(top-down theory), the fact that
it is evolutionary is certainly
documentable and strikingly
obvious…With a little reflection,
it would appear that there really is
no conflict between Evolution and
Creation for they are intrinsically
one and the same process
(e.g., Creation is progressive,
ongoing, continuous, unfolding,
and emerging as Evolution.)"

So, again …What are we? We are a special breed of think-ing, living beings, conscious of ourselves, aware that we stand at the very threshold of knowledge because we know that we don't know. This conundrum is the beginning of all knowledge. We are free to ask questions, if we dare. It is only by daring to seek that we are able to learn. It is the courage to pursue fresh understand-ing that allows us access to the fount of knowledge. Clearly the source of our creation has provided us with both the desire and the capacity to learn and evolve. Curiously, curiosity itself may be the best indicator of our intelligence and capacity. We are born curious. We are compelled by our very nature to wonder and learn. Without curiosity we become uninterested, uninteresting, stunted, dull, and unhappy.

Without curiosity we become uninterested, uninteresting, stunted, dull, and unhappy.

Why would we ever allow our curiosity to become stunted? Why allow unhappiness to become our condition? Before con-ditioning, as young children, we are most happy when exploring, discovering and experiencing new things. What does that tell us? Why have we turned our backs on the wonder of life and all that is around it? In truth, we are children of a wonderfully complex, fascinating, and elegant universe. There is much to learn, much to explore, much to be thrilled by. Allowing our curiosity to re-exert itself elevates our paradigms and we become more inter-ested in living, and more interesting to others.

The Field

What was controversial in the early 1900's has been sup-ported by thousands of scientific experiments today. At the base-ment level of creation, all living things, in fact everything we can touch, smell, taste, or observe, with or without instrumentation, is simply energy vibrating. In the words of the indomitable Max Planck:

> "Matter itself doesn't exist.
> There exists only the invigorating
> invisible and immortal spirit as
> the source of all material."

We can say with great certainty that each of us, along with the entire physical universe, is a construct of vibrating energy oscillating at different frequencies. Many philosophers, scientists, spiritual giants, and investigative authors, call our creative source God - by many different names. The pulsing energy field from whence everything appears to emanate is sometimes referred to as the power of God, Spirit, the Life-force, or more recently, as the energy of the Zero Point Field, or Source Energy.

Dozens of historical names for the "source of all that is" are culturally specific, yet they usually mean approximately the same thing, and fold into the basic concept of a creator. Other names for the concept of God are used as people struggle with language endeavoring to explain that which none of us are quite capable of completely understanding. Some now refer to the source of our origin, the spring of all creation, as the potentiality at the Planck scale, Scaler waves, universal consciousness, the Field, the Force, and a host of other terms of similar meaning.

It cannot be over emphasized, what a surprise it has been to traditional science to discover that the physical universe is inher-ently nonphysical. Many scientists still ignore the implications of this repeatedly proven assertion, no matter how many times it is demonstrated through scientific rigor. The material universe, which includes everything we can observe through whatever means available, be it telescope, microscope, or collider; as revealed through radio wave, microwave, x-ray, gamma-ray, and everything in between, arises from a field more subtle than any energy source we can yet understand. The field is there. It is more amazing than anything we could have envisioned, or than any science fiction writer dared to propose. Ultimately, our physicality comes from this place of unlimited energy. We are of this source.

When we suspend what we're doing for any length of time, and consider the implications of what science is now telling us, the underlying essential questions present themselves once more: Who am I? Why am I here? Where am I going? What's it all about? "Alfie?" (You either got that little age-revealing ditty, or you're too young!)

Research now points to the conclusion that what we previously thought of as the empty space, between and within atoms, is not empty at all. This universal field of the sub-microscopic is so abundant with potentiality that one cubic centimeter is now thought to contain a trillion times more $E=mc^2$ energy, than all the solid matter in the universe. This cosmic ocean of ultra high frequency energy vibration, the source of everything we know, looks more like intelligence or perhaps consciousness, than any other metaphor we can use to describe it. This has led some to refer to God as Universal Consciousness, a term they deem to be more politically correct.

We have learned that energy, and some form of consciousness, are the building blocks of all things. And, what we might surmise is that these may be the same thing. The energy field that many are now calling Universal Consciousness emanates from the quantum plane. Science has demonstrated that this is a place beyond time and space, or at least as we understand these terms. Everything we know of appears to radiate forth from the nonmaterial (the cosmic ocean of all potentiality), into the material. Things emanate from the most subtle submicroscopic energy state into matter. The process whereby the immaterial becomes material, or the un-manifest becomes manifested, is the mechanism we call creation. Creation appears to be the constant evolution of energy into atoms, atoms into molecules, molecules into inanimate mass or living cells, cells into complex life forms.

Everything material is in movement. All things are either evolving or breaking down. Everything is growing or shrinking; becoming something of greater complexity, or degenerating back into its most basic components. The growth side of this process is called evolution, which merely means slow change. The dissolution side of creation is described in physics, as the Second Law of Thermodynamics.

Participation in this shared reality of earth life provides us a space where there is a time and place for us to evolve. This infers that our evolution of character, personality, and emotional make-up, has purpose. Evolution with purpose is what the religious generally are speaking to when they refer to spiritual growth.

Will

For an individual to choose to become something other than what he or she has already become, means to accept the premise that there is such a thing as free will. Most people, without ever thinking about it, believe in free will. It is a natural conclusion. After all, each one of us ponders and decides many things each day, and we are quite sure that the decision to do or not do is ours. However, up until recently much scientific theory has been based on the belief that there is no such thing as free will. That perspective was based on the inaccurate belief that the universe and everything in it is simply the equivalent of a complex machine, governed by external impersonal forces, or what science would call universal laws.

Before quantum studies, the essential belief system of the pragmatic scientist was that we do what we do because of the sum total of the rules of law, or those operating programs resident within and without us. And, that the appearance of free will within an individual was only that...the *appearance* of free will. This particular scientific belief has collapsed under the greater understanding of quantum physics. For example, in the recent book, entitled "The Mind & the Brain, Neuroplasticity and the

Power of Mental Force," scientist and medical doctor, Jeffrey Schwartz says:

> "Quantum theory elegantly explains
> how our actions are shaped by our
> will and our will by our attention,
> which is not strictly controlled
> by any known law of nature."

Each of us has free will, which means we have the ability to choose. Sure, that's rather intuitive, but science has also confirmed that the power of our mind gives our thoughts its ability to *literally create the new realities we shall be experiencing.* As Dr. Schwartz puts it:

> "Intention governs attention, and
> attention exerts real physical effects
> on the dynamics of the brain."

We do make our own choices, no matter the influences of things outside of us, nor of our prior programming. And yes, those influences matter, and sometimes they matter a lot, but we are still free to change our minds, and focus our attention upon different outcomes. Therefore, each of us chooses our own personal evolutionary course whether we admit it, care to take responsibility for it, or whether we even consciously know it, or not. Thus, it follows that there IS purpose in existence and that each of us decides what that is for us individually. We may be able to rise in resonance with loftier planes of consciousness, but whether we do so or not is our choice. We can decide to think better thoughts, or not. We can decide to live by higher law, or not. We can decide to grow, develop, and transcend our current level of being, or not.

The experiences we encounter are largely determined by the attitudes we hold. As we've discussed, attitudes are habits of thinking. Habits of thought precede and form the basis of all the choices we will ever make, both consciously and subconsciously. All of our emotional reactions are the result of thoughts we've thought before. The thoughts we think underlie the feelings we experience. Our reality, or in other words, the life we live and are immersed within, is the result of our subliminal thought patterns, and/or conditioning, triggering our reactions and emotional experience. This critical understanding leads to the conclusion that each of us has been granted sufficient independence from our source, as to manifest in our reality whatever we are subliminally seeking.

This gives rise to another question. Do we know what it is we are subliminally seeking? Seeking we are. Consciously knowing that which we seek, we usually are not.

Very few of us really know what we are subconsciously directed towards. We say one thing but all too frequently are subconsciously focused on something else entirely. In other words, our auto-pilot is already programmed by our belief system, to seek something other than what we consciously believe we want. The bottom line is that we get what we give the most attention too. Period! We do not experience what we consciously say we want. We manifest only that which we subconsciously believe, that which we've given the most energy to thinking. Our energy is our power. Where we focus our power, knowingly or not, is the point of our creation. We are the creator of our own experience. So what does that tell us about who we are?

If we were NOT free to make choices, to imagine various philosophical, emotional, and physical outcomes, then we would be strictly animals responding to instinctual programming. Biologically-speaking, humans are indeed animals in every sense of the physical, but humans are more than that…we are free to imagine, to choose, to create, to design new experiences for ourselves and for others. And, these choices, based as they are upon our various desires, may be as grand, exalted and noble, or as base, negative, and ignoble, as we will.

Our individual desires are made known to the universe, as a consequence of the vibrational harmonics we project. Again, we do not bring forth what we say we want; we manifest only that with which we are in vibrational resonance. Our vibrational transmission draws to us its harmonic equivalent. We literally create our reality through the thoughts we think, powered by intention, attention, and the emotions we feel. The thoughts we think equal our point of attraction. Thus, we get what we think about, whether we want it or not.

We get what we think about,
whether we want it or not.

Whenever we are focused on our past, the present, or considering the future, we are resonating at the vibrational frequency that represents our emotional set point. This frequency oscillation is the magnet, the point of our attraction. Ergo, what we think, believe, and feel, we summon into our world-reality. They are vibrationally synchronistic.

As we look about, it is not the energetic vibrating fields of force patterns we observe, it is the world our mind and human-sensory apparatus put together for us to see. What we actually view comes to us via our mind's eye. But first, everything is filtered through the lens of our belief, then the reality model of our prior experience, and finally through the active pattern of our emotions. Each of these processes tint and shade, color and determine, what we believe we are seeing. The movie playing in our brain is what we have vibrationally drawn unto ourselves, coupled with what we have the physical ability to see, and what our belief system will allow us to see.

The movie playing in our
brain is what we have
vibrationally drawn unto
ourselves, coupled with what
we have the physical ability
to see, and what our belief
system will allow us to see.

Levels of Truth

Every choice we make is based upon some construct of what is real for us. To evolve, it is important that we recognize that reality is comprised of a hierarchy of truths. You are real, but in this physical life you are also a large and vibrant community of cells. And, as we've reviewed, about a hundred trillion cells, are working together to keep you functioning at the biological level. So, then, you are your cells. But, you are also your molecules. Both of these statements are true. You are your atoms. You are also your subatomic particles. These statements are true. Your subatomic particles emerge from source energy. At this substratum, we are connected to every other thing, inasmuch as at the atomic and subatomic plane we are in a constant state of exchanging electrons and information. At this level of our existence we are all united. We are one with the cosmic ocean of evolutionary potentiality. So, what is the truth of all this? It is all true. These are just different levels to the truth of our reality.

As we ascend up the hierarchy of our physicalness, and look more closely at the macroscopic us, questions arise. For example, most people identify strongly with their bodies. But, are you your body? Or, would you prefer to say you *have a* body? Who looks out through your eyes and sees your body in the mirror? Was it you who looked at your body and saw it five years ago? After all, since then all of your cells have been replaced - most of them many times, considering that they are constantly dying off and being replaced. At least from a physical perspective you are a different body than you were before. So, are you the same you? Are you the same person, but one who has evolved? If you are the same person, but one who has evolved, then who is it that evolved? In other words, are you the same you, with changes of appearance, and understanding?

Who dreams when you go to sleep? Who sees? Who hears? Who thinks? Who considers, and reflects? If you were struck blind and could no longer see the outside world or view your body, would you still be you? Why?

Are you your feelings? Or, do you *have* feelings? Are you the same person who lives in the outside "real" world, but experiences the inside world of your thoughts and feelings? Are you the same person, regardless of whether you're exploring and feeling inside emotions or exploring and observing the outside world? Yes? Then, where are you? That is to say, where is the YOU that is YOU? Are you in your head? How about your heart? Are you confused yet?

The Ego

When your internal voice will not shut up and leave you in peace, who is it that's doing the talking? You do hear your thoughts, don't you? I mean, sorta, kinda, hear your thoughts? Why can't you shut those thoughts off when they're spinning around in your head, hitchhiking off one another? Perhaps if you are skilled at meditation you can, but most people can't. That internal voice is the source of all our mental and emotional stress. You know the sensation; it's when you are experiencing runaway thoughts, and you can't shut off the worrisome voice in your head.

Would you say that you are your thoughts? Or that your thoughts express who you are? If either is true, then who is it that's listening to the thoughts you can't shut off? The question was posed in Chapter 10 as to whether or not there are two of you inside your head. Is one of you constantly talking and the other listening? Is your head spinning about now? Why are we exploring all this nonsense? Hmmm, just stick with it for a while longer.

Who's observing when your internal voice isn't making commentary? Who's observing, when somehow or another, you've turned off "the voice" and you're at peace? If you're not the voice, perhaps you are the one who experiences the peace? Maybe this deep peace thing happens when you are walking on a quiet beach or on a hiking trail somewhere. This is that time and place, or that space, when you are feeling serene and calm. Maybe it's just after you've made love and nothing in the world seems important enough to interrupt your peace. But, isn't it still YOU that's doing the walking, or lying comfortably in bed, or quietly drifting in hypnotic distraction? Isn't this the real you? Aren't you the one then at peace, the one who has suspended judgment, the one observing quietly, the one simply being? The difference now is that the "voice" has stopped yammering.

Interesting that the only time we can feel truly tranquil and at peace is when our internal voice is silent. So, who is the "voice" if it's not you? Who is the "me" of you?

Have you ever had a deeply moving experience? Dig that up, and think about it for a moment. Our deepest most profound experiences are usually thought of in terms of the spiritual.

Now, who was it that had the experience? Was it your body? Was it your emotions? Was it your brain? Maybe it was your ego.

Do you believe that you have a higher SELF? This is what most of us in the West will instinctively think of as our spirit. If this is who you are, then who is the voice that seems to specialize in driving you nuts at times? Psychology tells us that is our ego. The ego sometimes comes across as an internal voice. The ego is the program running in your brain that insists on endless analysis. The ego identifies with the body, mind, and emotions. It is concerned with physical survival, emotional pleasure, and personal gain. The ego is focused almost entirely on self-interest.

Can you identify with the ego's desire to be right? As we've reviewed, the ego invariably insists on being right. It is so focused on being right, it will do most anything rather than admit to being wrong. Scientists tell us that the ego's evolutionary purpose was to ensure survival in the animal world. It is easy enough to believe that the ego is an important mental program. Its job is to rapidly determine friend from foe. It controls the flight or fight response. It is our primary physical protection device. But, as we've learned, ego is also hyper sensitive to both real and imagined slights. To our ego, there is no difference between physical vulnerability, and imagined emotional vulnerability. For those not strongly committed to transcending their ego-self, their animalistic self-interest will control all thought, emotion, and automatic reflex mechanisms.

Most thinking is of egocentric origin. The ego functions like one of those talking heads on cable news programs; it is a continuous stream of constant commentary. Why the review of ego? It's because the ego is a real obstacle to our happiness. Unless we develop the skills to quiet the monster within, we'll be subject to the constant mental chatter that our ego produces.

It is also important that we remember it is the ego that gets our attention with every kind of fearful scenario. Ego is an alarmist, it motivates through fear. True, we can allow ourselves to feel pretty darn good when bathed in other people's compliments, but permitting ourselves to be manipulated by praise, just sets us up for the alternative.

Do you remember how to recognize where your vibratory level of thinking is predominately resonating? Listen to how your closest friends are speaking. Then if you're really brave, listen to the words you are using in routine conversations, especially those conversations where feelings are attached.

Finally, can you recall what the antidote to an over-controlling ego is? Yes? No? The answer is honest humility, but of course the ego abhors true humility. Ego will allow feigned humility at times, but the real thing is threatening to the whole self-sustaining program because that means it must admit it doesn't know everything. And remember, the ego demands to be right. Like a spoiled child, it stamps its foot and refuses to apologize.

Once more let's recall, that when we learn to view our ego from a more enlightened place, we begin to recognize it is a useful tool for protection, but that we are perfectly capable of transcending its selfish games. To ascend beyond the ego's grasp, we must live in a place of gratitude, forgiveness, kindness, compassion, love, and HUMILITY.

So in asking the question, "Who am I," would you say that your ego is a proper reflection of who you really are? That of course, is what the ego believes, but it is only a complex program of the subconscious, a tool to be used. Unfortunately, most of us allow our ego programming to run our lives by default, often at our peril. The ego cannot fathom lasting happiness. It manipulates, based on threat and fear. Yes, your ego will permit temporary pleasure, but will not engender feelings of humility, deep heartfelt gratitude, unselfish love, and true bliss. Ego-living is not the source of happiness, and never can be.

Ego-living is not the source of happiness, and never can be.

Are we then cursed to never be really happy? What do you think? Or, perhaps more correctly, what do you want? You are the creator of your experience. The problem is that most of us allow our ego programming to be the default creator.

The undisciplined mind generates thoughts nonstop. Is it not both comforting and restorative to quiet the chatterbox within?

Isn't it wonderful to just let go, to become silent, and just exist in our surround? In order to be happy, we must learn to give our mind permission to be quiet. In so doing we can discover the joy of inner solitude.

The egos constant tirade can be silenced. To curb the unruly internal voice, it may be valuable to repeat written affirmations like a mantra. It takes practice to form a new habit, and especially one that requires you assert control where in the past you've just let things develop in a way you think of as natural. You need to take the time to establish a new natural.

An effective way to quiet the fear machine within is to focus on the creative visualization of preset, desirable goals. Positive thoughts must be held in mind, and carefully focused upon, or within moments the ego will have wormed its way back into control, warning us of all the things that can go wrong. Remember: Intention, attention, and feelings. Observe your thoughts. You know, it's pretty crazy when you really get it, yet it is unnerving at how quickly we default back to ego thinking. When you learn to quiet your mind, and watch thoughts arise, to let them flow in and out, and to not attach power to them, you're moving in the right direction. This process is widely known as meditation.

The Higher Self

For those of us with a spiritual bent, we usually think of "me" as an immortal spirit, wearing a physical body. With a mortal body we are able to experience this space-time reality. Here it is that our spirit has been joined with a magnificent biological structure that comes with an incredible brain capable of doing the most remarkable things. We are infused with five primary energy-vibration translators, in order to provide us with some degree of vision, hearing, taste, touch, and smell. In this physical state, we are blessed with an emotional control center and a number of emotional sensing facilities. All these sensory mechanisms work in concert with, and through, feelings, memory, and intellect, in order that we may experience the world around us. Dr. William A. Tiller, Professor Emeritus, Stanford University, explains us this way:

"The outermost zone consists of the two-layered physical bio-bodysuit that we put on when we are born into this space-time reality of experience and shuck off when we die, passing from this domain of experience. I label this our "Personality Self" with the outermost layer being made of particulate, electric atom/molecule stuff and the inner layer being made of our magnetic, information-wave stuff."

The SELF who observes incoming sensory data, who observes the ego's emotional responses, who observes and computes input with archived memory, is the "higher self," what a lot of us think of as our spirit self. Science sometimes refers to this higher self as consciousness, although in spite of the hundreds of draft proposals to define it, it has no real working definition. Still, we all experience consciousness, and we are indeed conscious, living beings.

Consciousness is more than mere brain activity; it is the life-force that permeates every aspect of us. It is who we are, that highly refined energy-spirit self, the higher SELF, the immortal self. A physical body, impugned with the spiritual life force, combines to be what we think of as the "soul." Body and spirit together constitute a living soul. At death, our spirit form, our consciousness, the life-force-energy, leaves the body. The body belongs strictly to this biological plane of existence. The body is mortal and temporary. (At least at this particular point in our developmental progress) It seems reasonable that our spirit SELF is comprised of a finer, higher, vibrating energy, aka: intelligence, which has been allotted individual identity.

As we learn from physics, energy has always existed, and everything is made of it. Energy is infinite and cannot be harmed or destroyed, and while it may change form, it will not cease to exist. This indestructibility of energy is well established. The fundamental law of physics guarantees the continuation of existence. Life-energy, or spirit, is continuously moving into form, through form, and out of form.

Science has discovered that the higher the frequency (the tighter and shorter the wave function), the more powerful - yet subtle - the energy. Humans are one form of energy condensate. We are conscious and fused with intelligence, and the life-force that emanates from Divinity. God, by whatever name you use to mean our source, is therefore the provider, giver, or father, of our spirit, our higher SELF, our conscious self. In death we are not dissolved, nor can we be.

We are as immortal as the energy of which we are comprised. Physical life is simply a phase of our existence. Consciousness continues. Of this I have received a powerful witness. Not empirical, in the sense of a scientist's laboratory experience. A much more potent witness than our physical reality can provide. I was blessed with a witness so encompassing, so penetrating, and so ultra real, that all physical sources of confirmation seem faint and feeble by comparison. So, rather than say I believe, it is much more accurate for me to say that I *know* that there is life beyond the grave, I *know* that we are immortal, I *know* that there is purpose to each one of our individual lives, and the experiences that we are having within them. And, I am absolutely certain there is great meaning to it all.

The infinite, timeless field of consciousness is all pervasive. Through it and from it, all matter unfolds. Mass emerges into the physical universe, evolving in accordance with the laws irrevocably declared to govern this material kingdom. There is mind behind the matrix. This explanation is consistent with the observed universe, and with the scriptural purity of most of the world's great religions. Life emanates by degree of God. Spirit, or life-force, is the source of life. When the life-force leaves, the body remains to return to the biological matrix from which it sprang.

Once again let us consider the greatest question of all: *Who Am I?* This calls for profound contemplation. It requires that we think deeply about our physical and spiritual source. What is our purpose for existence? Is there meaning to life? Where did I come from? Why am I here? Where am I going? These questions are all a part of the essential life-transforming question of Who am I? In the final analysis you are the one that must answer these questions. Yes, there are many who will provide you with their answers to the Great Questions, and to some limited extent I am one of those, but unless you have explored these questions deeply within your very soul, any answer you receive from another is strictly an intellectual one. Intellect cannot provide spiritual confirmation. Remember, Intellectual thinkingness is akin to studying the map. It is not experiencing the territory. It is learning about, not experiencing.

Studying the great wisdom literature is good. In many ways it is the equivalent of studying a map left by those who've gone before. On the other hand, immersing oneself in spiritual devotion is dramatically more beneficial than the academic approach. Immerse yourself in the greatest experiences of life. Look within. The map is simply a guide. Doing it, living it, being it, is hugely different than learning about it.

East Verses West

The western world of religious practice tends to emphasize prayer, and the doing of things. The more ancient world of religious understanding as reflected in many eastern traditions, evolved with an emphasis on meditation and peaceful being. Prayer is the act of thanking and asking the Divine. Meditation is the process of quiet observation. Meditation is either centered upon keenly focused contemplation or the suspension of thought. The essence of western religion is in the thanking, asking, and doing. The essence of eastern spiritual practice is in observing and listening.

> **The essence of western religious practice is in thanking, asking, and doing. The essence of eastern spiritual practice is in observing and listening.**

Perhaps, it would not be an inappropriate simplification to summarize, by saying that the west is focused on talking to God, the east on listening for God's inspiration. Is a bridge connecting these two great traditions in order here?

We see from history and observation that both eastern and western forms of spirituality provide great benefits to those disciplined and devoted to them. So why not incorporate the best of both worlds? One might consider developing a spiritual practice that actively embraces earnest prayer and service to others, coupled with the turning down of the volume on daily distractions, looking inward and becoming quiet and reflective through meditative practice. Logic and personal experience suggests that honoring both of these time-tested modes of spirituality provides greater dividends than focusing on one practice to the exclusion of the other.

Who Am I?

Most of the world's great spiritual leaders have encouraged their disciples to discover who they were. They've taught that we are well advised to invest time in prayerful consideration, to look within, to conjure a powerful belief unto the obtaining of a faith so pure that we may move the mountains of our life. This is a confidence born of internal examination, of seeking the Kingdom of God within us. In the Biblical Old Testament, God asks a series of questions of Job that together point him towards answering the great pivotal question, which is the title of this Chapter.

> THEN the LORD answered Job out
> of the whirlwind, and said, Who
> *is* this that darkeneth counsel by
> words without knowledge? Gird
> up now thy loins like a man; for I
> will demand of thee, and answer
> thou me. Where wast thou when
> I laid the foundations of the earth?
> declare, if thou hast understanding.
> Who hath laid the measures
> thereof, if thou knowest? or who
> hath stretched the line upon it?

Whereupon are the foundations
thereof fastened? or who laid the
corner stone thereof; When the
morning stars sang together, and all
the sons of God shouted for joy?

In Proverbs (8:22-31) David speaks of man's pre-existent state
with God. He records that we were with God from everlasting.
He tells us that we were present when the world was designed
and organized. What does this say about who we are?

The LORD possessed me in the
beginning of his way, before his
works of old. I was set up from
everlasting, from the beginning, or
ever the earth was. When *there
were* no depths, I was brought
forth; when *there were* no fountains
abounding with water. Before the
mountains were settled, before
the hills was I brought forth: While
as yet he had not made the earth,
nor the fields, nor the highest part
of the dust of the world. When
he prepared the heavens, I *was*
there: when he set a compass upon
the face of the depth: When he
established the clouds above: when
he strengthened the fountains of
the deep: When he gave to the sea
his decree that the waters should
not pass his commandment: when
he appointed the foundations of
the earth: Then I was by him,
as one brought up *with him:* and
I was daily *his* delight, rejoicing
always before him; Rejoicing in the
habitable part of his earth; and my
delights *were* with the sons of men.

Consider a few verses from the traditional King James version of the Bible in light of the all-important question, Who Am I?

Num. 16: 22: And they fell upon their faces, and said, O God, the God of the spirits of all flesh... Num. 27: 16: Let the LORD, the God of the spirits of all flesh... Job 38: 7: When ...all the sons of God shouted for joy? Eccl. 12: 7: Then shall the dust return to the earth as it was: and the spirit shall return unto God who gave it. Jer. 1: 5: Before I formed thee in the belly I knew thee; and before thou camest forth out of the womb I sanctified thee...Zech. 12:1: THE burden of the word of the LORD for Israel, saith the LORD, which stretcheth forth the heavens, and layeth the foundation of the earth, and formeth the spirit of man within him. John 8: 58: Jesus said unto them, Verily, verily, I say unto you, Before Abraham was, I am. John 16: 28: I came forth from the Father, and am come into the world: again, I leave the world, and go to the Father. Acts 17: 28: For in him we live, and move, and have our being; as certain also of your own poets have said, for we are also his offspring. Rom. 8: 29: For whom he did foreknow, he also did predestinate to be conformed to the image of his Son, that he might be the firstborn among many brethren. Eph. 1: 4: According as he hath chosen us before the

foundation of the world <u>2 Tim. 1: 9</u>:
Who hath saved us, and called us ...
according to his own purpose ...
before the world began, <u>Titus 1: 2</u>:
In hope of eternal life, which God,
that cannot lie, promised before
the world began; <u>Heb. 12: 9</u>:
Furthermore we have had fathers of
our flesh which corrected us, and
we gave them reverence, shall we
not much rather be in subjection
unto the Father of spirits, and live?

There are hundreds of biblical verses that give insight to who we are, and thousands more if one considers some of the more significant of the extra biblical works by inspired men and women. The religious writings of many of the more ancient spiritual disciplines are collectively referred to as the great wisdom literature. Writings from India, Tibet, and China, writings from throughout the Middle East, around the Mediterranean, even from the Americas; they all tell similar stories. Deep spiritual insight garnered by widely separated sages affirms our royal heritage. The great religious institutions, those that have stood the test of time, all speak to mankind's intimate relationship with divinity.

Those who have had experiences with unembodied spirits all agree that they look similar to our physical bodies. There have been tens of thousands, perhaps millions of people who have had experiences of a mystical nature, wherein they observed and spoke with those that have gone on before. If you've had the experience there is no need for proof, if you have not, and you are skeptical of such things (as I was at an earlier time), there is hardly any body of evidence that is completely convincing. Still, there are innumerable witnesses that testify that our mortal bodies are organized in the exact image of our spiritual selves. It's simply an historical fact that, in almost every case, where one speaks of having seen or spoken with a spirit, they are in the form of a person.

The life-force of God apparently combines our energy-constructed spirit body with intelligence to become consciousness. We are conscious, intelligent, infinite, magnificent, children of God. The life-force that permeates all living things is pure spirit. Physical life emerges when matter is infused with spirit. It seems likely then that the power of God, or perhaps the spirit of God, is the infinite field of consciousness, that vibrating field of pure energy that science is just now beginning to explore. This is the zero-point field, the source of everything we know of, that energy which comprises universal consciousness.

The earth and everything upon it has been formed of the elements produced in the nuclear furnace of stars. The biological bodies of modern man provide the physical vehicle through which we function in this world. Our world may well have been organized with the express purpose to function as a learning environment for the spiritual children of God.

The physical universe emerges as matter from the "super position" or unlimited potential, of universal consciousness, when observed with clear intention. Creation can only be known by life that has received an inheritance of consciousness. So, we are spirit children of God, and although our access to super consciousness may yet be in embryo, we are here learning to be co-creators with our Creator.

> **We are spirit children of God, and although our access to super consciousness may yet be in embryo, we are here learning to be co-creators with our Creator.**

We can see by both scientific study and direct observation, that we are the literal creators of our own reality. So once again it begs the question, "Who Am I?" The biblical Psalmist said it this way:

> "I have said, ye are gods; and all of you are children of the most High."
> Psalms 82:6 KJV

Hundreds of years later, Jesus, "walked in the temple in Solomon's porch" responding to inquiring Jews that were asking him to "tell us plainly" as to whether or not he was the Christ (meaning the anointed one who had been prophesied to come). Jesus responded in the affirmative, and then referring to the above quotation from the Psalms, said:

> "...Is it not written in your
> law, I said, Ye are gods?"
> John 10:34 KJV

Who are we? The scriptures and much of the world's wisdom literature tells us that we are the children of God. If we are truly God's children, then we are each of us gods in embryo. So, here we are experiencing what we think of as earth life, and we are just now beginning to contemplate our unlimited potential. Here we are learning to create. Here we are learning the consequences of our creations.

Three remarkable eastern sages of the past century, Nisargadatta Maharaj, Ramana Maharshi, and Paramahansa Yogananada, counseled all people everywhere that the shortest way to a happier, meaningful, blissful life, is to focus one's attention on the essential question, "Who Am I?" Why? Because when you really get it, when you really feel as though you know who you are, when you sense the essence of your divinity, it changes everything. Ponder it. Meditate on it. Pray about it. Seek your own personal confirmation of the spirit.

May we be wise. May each of us transcend our perceived obstacles in life. May we recognize our struggles, burdens, and difficulties, as our treasured teachers, our opportunities to evolve. May we become ever more conscious of our eternal opportunities. The matrix that intersects all our interactions is the vehicle and the opportunity for our becoming.

> "Walk straight ahead, no matter
> what - all fear is illusion." (Thought)
> Tenet of Zen Buddhism

It's All *Thought!*

Emotional Index

Feelings in Play	Emotional Level
Serene Happiness, Transcendence, Pure Love	Enlightenment
Harmony, Tranquility, Serenity	Peace
Deep Gratitude, Unconditional Love, Pure Kindness	Compassion
Worship, Reverence, Beauty all around, Love	Love
Elation, Ecstasy, Profound Pleasure	Joy
Forgiving, Merciful, Caring, Absolving	Forgiveness
Cheerful, Hopeful, Confident, Buoyant	Optimism
Believing, Reliant, Faith, Confident Dependence	Trust
Excitement, Enthusiastic, Infatuation, Obsession	Passion
Satisfied, Gratified, Ease, Pleasured	Content
Affirmed, Audacious, Validated, Daring	Courage
Self-important, Impatient, Arrogant, Scornful	Pride
Weary, Dull, Tedious, Monotony	Boredom
Distrustful, Doubting, Negative, Cynicism	Pessimism
Aggressive, Irritated, Frustrated, Hateful	Anger
Besieged, Inundated, Weighed down, Beleaguered	Overwhelmed
Fearful, Withdrawing, Jealous, Worry, Nervous, Angst	Anxiety
Depression, Misery, Gloom, Anguish	Despair
Shame, Blaming, Remorse, Humiliation	Guilt
Hopelessness, Weak, Wretched, Useless, Helpless	Powerless

Beginning at the bottom of the column "Feelings in Play," work your way up and consider what tier best describes the thoughts that tend to predominate in your life. Look across the chart horizontally to discover the descriptive level of your present vibration. The Emotional Level reveals your vibrational set-point.

Reference the Emotional Index often, this gradient understanding allows you to more easily recognize the way your subconscious mind is coloring new incoming data. The emotional tier you are now experiencing reflects your subconscious self-view. These are the lens through which you view the world and the lens through which you view yourself.

When one devotes themselves to the process of thinking higher vibrational thoughts, each upward shift is accompanied by a significant increase in personal power and a corresponding rise in happiness.

It's All *Thought!*

"As a being of power, intelligence, and love, and the lord of your own thoughts, you hold the key to every situation, and contain within yourself that transforming and regenerative agency by which you may make yourself what you will."

James Allen